THE
PRONUNCIATION OF
ENGLISH

THE
PRONUNCIATION OF
ENGLISH

BY

DANIEL JONES

M.A. (Cantab.), Dr Phil. (Zürich), Hon. LL.D. (Edinb.)

Professor Emeritus of Phonetics in the University of London
Corresponding Member of the German Academy of Sciences, Berlin
Honorary Member of the Royal Irish Academy

WITH 43 ILLUSTRATIONS

FOURTH EDITION
REVISED AND ENLARGED

CAMBRIDGE
AT THE UNIVERSITY PRESS
1969

Published by the Syndics of the Cambridge University Press
Bentley House, 200 Euston Road, London N.W.1
American Branch: 32 East 57th Street, New York, N.Y.10022

Standard Book Numbers:
521 05448 6 clothbound
521 09369 4 paperback

First edition 1909
Second edition 1914
Third edition, rewritten 1950
Reprinted 1955
Fourth edition, revised and enlarged 1956
Reprinted with minor corrections 1958
Reprinted with corrections 1963
Reprinted with corrections 1966
First paperback edition 1966
Reprinted 1967, 1969

Printed in Great Britain
at the University Printing House, Cambridge
(Brooke Crutchley, University Printer)

PREFACE
TO THE FOURTH EDITION

This book was completely rewritten in 1950 in the light of my 42 years' experience in teaching phonetics at University College, London. That (3rd) edition differed in numerous respects from the original edition of 1909 and its reprints. However, the work remained, as originally planned, an account of the phonetics of English presented from the point of view of the English learner, though it was much altered in details and was considerably enlarged. Improved methods of description and explanation were introduced, new facts were collected, the forms of transcription were adjusted on lines suggested by the theory of phonemes, many new diagrams were added and some of the old ones were improved upon. And finally a new attitude was adopted in regard to the much-discussed subject of standard pronunciation. This was because I found, as I still find, that it can no longer be said that any standard exists, nor do I think it desirable to attempt to establish one. It is useful that descriptions of existing pronunciation should be recorded, but I no longer feel disposed to recommend any particular forms of pronunciation for use by English people or to condemn others. It must, in my view, be left to individual English-speaking people to decide whether they should speak in the manner that comes to them naturally or whether they should alter their speech in any way. Anyone desiring to modify his pronunciation will find in this book suggestions as to how changes may be effected, but I feel that the responsibility for putting any such suggestions into effect should rest with him.

Since the appearance of the 3rd edition some new facts have come to light which have necessitated making a number of further additions and improvements in the present (4th) edition. The most important of these follow below.

The paragraphs relating to the use of the diphthongs ae, ʌi, and ʌu in Scottish English (§§ 179, 180, 190, 191 of the 1950 edition) have been rewritten, and are now numbered 180, 180 a, 181, 191. Most of the rectifications needed here were first pointed out to me by Mr J. Braidwood of Queen's University, Belfast, who most kindly put at my disposal the results of his own investigations into this somewhat involved subject. The new paragraphs are in the main a summary of the information he supplied to me, and the illustrative examples are taken from a list of some 300 which accompanied it. I am greatly indebted too to Prof. David Abercrombie, Professor of Phonetics in the University of Edinburgh, for drawing my attention to a number of noteworthy facts that he has discovered relating to these and other sounds of Scottish English. He has convinced me that the above diphthongs are best rendered by the notation ae, ʌi, ʌu. Fig. 18, illustrating the nature of ae and ʌi, has been redrawn on lines suggested by him. He has further pointed out to me a number of errors in the specimen of Scottish pronunciation in the 1950 edition, and has supplied me with the authoritative version now appearing on p. 205.

§ 202 (dealing with the use of jəː as an alternative to iə) has been recast. A section on the 'rising diphthongs' ǐə and ǔə has been added (§§ 219 a–219 g) and consequential amendments have been made in the transcriptions of all words containing these sounds (e.g. *serious* in § 202 and *casual* in § 92). Attention has been called to the difference in pronunciation between *nitrate* and *night rate* (an example first noted by M. Swadesh and S. Newman in America about 1936) (footnote 3 to § 270). Important alterations have been made in §§ 358 and 361 (dealing with the disappearance of final r and the origin of 'intrusive r'). § 401 (iii), dealing with the date of the change sj > ʃ, has been modified, and amplified by an explanatory note. The photographs in the 1950 edition illustrating 'lateral spreading' and 'lateral contraction' of the tongue (Figs. 42, 43) were unsatisfactory, and have been replaced by better ones.

PREFACE

Section XVII (on phonemes) has been enlarged by a reference to 'allophones' (§ 497) and by the addition of paragraphs on the bearing of the phoneme theory on methods of constructing systems of phonetic transcription (§§ 499–502). A new section (XVIII) has been added on Syllable Separation (§§ 503–510).

I have found it desirable to make considerable alterations in Part 2, some of the older texts in the previous editions having become unsuitable for the teacher and student of today. I have deleted the texts previously numbered 7, 12, 13 and 15, and have introduced seven more modern specimens; I have also taken this opportunity of rearranging the texts, putting them in a more logical order.

The reconstructed pronunciations of Shakespeare and Chaucer illustrated in Texts 20 and 21 have been revised in the light of the latest researches, and particularly those of the late H. Kökeritz and E. J. Dobson set out in their monumental works *Shakespeare's Pronunciation* (Yale, 1953) and *English Pronunciation, 1500–1700* (Oxford, 1957). In this task I have been greatly helped by A. C. Gimson, Professor of Phonetics at University College, London, and Prof. R. Quirk, Professor of English in the University of London, both authorities on the pronunciation of Early English, for whose assistance I am glad to express my sincere thanks. I have made several rectifications in the Shakespeare text in accordance with Kökeritz's findings. In particular I have, with the concurrence of Prof. Gimson and Prof. Quirk, accepted his view that the older diphthongs ɛi and ɔu (as in *day, know*) had by the late sixteenth century fallen together with the monophthongal ɛː and oː (as in *make, bone*), and have accordingly altered the ɛi's and ɔu's of the 1950 edition to ɛː and oː—though I feel that the alternative possibility that the coalescence might have been in favour of the diphthongs (a development which would have accounted for the emergence of the modern diphthongs ei and ou) should not be lost sight of. I have also followed Kökeritz, again with the concurrence of Prof. Gimson and Prof. Quirk, in writing juː

in place of iu in *you, funeral, Lupercal, refuse*. In the words where r precedes (*Brutus, brutish*) I have likewise written juː, though I feel that the older 'falling' diphthong iu may well have been preserved in these words (at least as an alternative).

In one respect I find myself unable to follow Kökeritz's lead, namely in the matter of his theory that the words of the *speak, meat* class were said at that period with the same vowel-sound as the words of the *take, make* class. I am therefore adhering to my previous mode of rendering such words: with eː in *speak*, etc. and ɛː in *make*, etc.

I have to thank the following authors, publishers and agents for kindly allowing me to reproduce copyright matter: Messrs Sampson Low, Marston and Co. for the illustrations of the larynx (Fig. 3) which are taken from Browne and Behnke's *Voice, Song and Speech*, Mrs E. O. Lorimer and her publisher Messrs George Allen and Unwin for the passage from *Language Hunting in the Karakoram* (Text No. 1), Sir Osbert Sitwell and Messrs Pearn, Pollinger and Higham and Messrs Little, Brown and Company (Boston) and the original publisher Messrs Macmillan and Co. for the passage from *Left Hand, Right Hand* (Text No. 2), the late Miss Josephine Tey and her publisher Peter Davies Ltd. for the passage from *The Daughter of Time* (Text No. 3), Mr E. F. Benson and his publisher Messrs Methuen for the passage from *Dodo* (Text No. 8), Messrs George Bell and Sons for the poem *Contentment* by C. S. Calverley (Text No. 9), Messrs Sidgwick and Jackson for the poem *The Blackbird* by John Drinkwater (Text No. 10), the Society of Authors as the literary representative of the trustees of the estate of the late A. E. Housman and Messrs Jonathan Cape Ltd., publisher of A. E. Housman's *Collected Poems*, for *The Cherry Tree* (Text No. 11), the trustees of the Hardy estate and Messrs Macmillan and Co. for the extract from the Introduction to *A Few Crusted Characters* in Thomas Hardy's *Life's Little Ironies* (Text No. 16), Mr Sinclair Lewis and his publisher Messrs Jonathan Cape Ltd. and Messrs Harcourt, Brace and Co. Inc. (New York) for the extract from *Babbitt* (Text No. 18), and Mr Pett Ridge for the passage from *London Only* (Text No. 19).

I also desire to renew my thanks to Miss B. Honikman who was of much assistance to me in connexion with the preparation of the 1950 edition, and to whom I am indebted for a number of valuable suggestions.

DANIEL JONES

GERRARDS CROSS
19 February 1958

NOTE ON THE THIRD IMPRESSION OF THE FOURTH EDITION

A few corrections and improvements have been made in this reprint. The most important are the following:

The expression 'push from the chest wall' has been substituted for 'push from the diaphragm' wherever it occurs (e.g. in § 438).

A reference to the pronunciation of *allowance* has been added in § 194.

A new paragraph (153 *a*) has been added after § 153.

The correct reference to the article on *Syllabic* l and n has been given at the end of § 422.

A stress-mark has been added to 'tɛtsi in the footnote to § 269.

'denotes' replaces 'notes' in the last line of § 301.

['θʊʧte] replaces ['θʊʧtɪ] in § 321.

A sentence has been added at the end of § 353.

§ 394 has been re-written.

A further example has been added at the end of § 447.

The intonation mark on 'kan, at the bottom of p. 163, has been rectified.

The words 'and a longer n' have been added at the end of footnote 1 on p. 175.

Several additions have been made to the lists of books on pp. 161, 222, 223.

D. J.

GERRARDS CROSS
August 1962

CONTENTS

CONTENTS

PART 2: PHONETIC TEXTS

CONTENTS

LIST OF ILLUSTRATIONS

Frontispiece. X-ray photographs of the tongue positions of the cardinal vowels i, a, ɑ, u.

LIST OF ILLUSTRATIONS

LIST OF PHONETIC SYMBOLS

(i) Symbols used in transcribing Southern 'received' pronunciation

ɑː	as in	'fɑːðə (*father*)
ɑ	,,	nɑu (*now*), flɑi (*fly*) (§§ 175, 187)
a	,,	pak (*pack*)
ʌ	,,	mʌtʃ (*much*)
b	,,	bout (*boat*)
d	,,	dei (*day*)
dʒ	,,	dʒʌdʒ (*judge*)
ð	,,	ðɛn (*then*)
ei	,,	plei (*play*)
ɛ	,,	rɛd (*red*)
ɛə	,,	skɛəs (*scarce*)
əː	,,	bəːd (*bird*)
ə	,,	ə'bʌv (*above*), 'soufə (*sofa*)
f	,,	fut (*foot*)
g	,,	giv (*give*)
h	,,	həːt (*hurt*)
iː	,,	siː (*see, sea*)
i	,,	lip (*lip*)
iə	,,	piəs (*pierce*)
ĭə	,,	'hapĭə (*happier*) (§ 219d)
j	,,	jɑːd (*yard*)
k	,,	kould (*cold*)
l	,,	liːv (*leave*), fiːl (*feel*) (§ 291 ff.)
m	,,	mɑːk (*mark*)
n	,,	nɛt (*net*)
ŋ	,,	sɔŋ (*song*)
o	,,	no'vɛmbə (*November*) (§ 173)
ou	,,	lou (*low*)

ɔː	,,	sɔː (*saw*)
ɔ	,,	lɔŋ (*long*)
ɔə	,,	mɔə (*more*) (one pronunciation, §§ 210, 211)
ɔi	,,	bɔi (*boy*)
p	,,	pei (*pay*)
r	,,	rait (*right*) (§ 352)
s	,,	sʌn (*sun*)
ʃ	,,	ʃou (*show*)
t	,,	tuː (*too*)
tʃ	,,	tʃəːtʃ (*church*)
θ	,,	θin (*thin*)
uː	,,	fuːd (*food*)
u	,,	gud (*good*)
uə	,,	tuə (*tour*)
ŭə	,,	'inflŭəns (*influence*) (§ 219e)
v	,,	vein (*vain*)
w	,,	wain (*wine*)
z	,,	ziːl (*zeal*)
ʒ	,,	'meʒə (*measure*)

ˈ means that the following syllable has strong stress, e.g.
  əˈbʌv (*above*), ˈmeʒə (*measure*)

ˈˈ means that the following syllable has extra strong stress

ˌ preceding a syllable means that that syllable is pronounced
  with secondary stress

ˌ placed under a consonant symbol, as in ṇ, ḷ, means that
  the consonant is syllabic. It is not usually necessary to
  insert this mark; see § 420.

ã ⎫
ã ⎪
ẽ ⎬ nasalized vowels (§ 389)
ɛ̃ ⎪
ĩ ⎪
ũ ⎭

(ii) Other symbols

$\left.\begin{matrix}\tilde{v}\\ \tilde{l}\end{matrix}\right\}$ nasalized consonants (§ 389)

ë   a centralized e (§ 171)

ï   a high central vowel (§ 123)

ö   an advanced o (§ 171, 300)

ü   an advanced u (§§ 123, 300)

ɨ = ï

ʉ = ü

ɐ   a retracted ɛ, or a sound intermediate between ɛ and ʌ (§ 163)

ɩ   special letter for denoting the quality of 'short i' (§§ 75, 429)

ɷ   special letter for denoting the quality of 'short u' (§ 429)

ɒ   special letter for denoting the quality of 'short ɔ' (§ 429)

ɯ   unrounded u (§§ 119, 483)

ɤ   unrounded o (§§ 120, 133)

ị   lowered i (§ 76)

ɛ̣   lowered ɛ (§§ 204, 299)

ạ   a raised variety of a (= a̟ or æ) (§ 299)

ọ   a very 'close' variety of o (§§ 299, 300)

ʌ̠   a retracted variety of ʌ (§ 399)

ɔ̆, ŏ   non-syllabic ɔ, o

y   rounded i (§ 481)

ø   rounded e (§ 481)

œ   rounded ɛ (§ 481)

$\left.\begin{matrix}ɑ\\ ʕ\\ əι\end{matrix}\right\}$ r-coloured vowels (§§ 99, 355, 356)

$\left.\begin{matrix}b̥\\ d̥\\ g̥\\ d̥ʒ̥\end{matrix}\right\}$ weak voiceless consonants (§§ 385, 386)

m̥   voiceless m (§§ 274, 275)

n̥   voiceless n (§§ 281, 282)

ŋ̊   voiceless ŋ (§ 290)

LIST OF PHONETIC SYMBOLS

l̥   voiceless l (§ 306)

r̥   voiceless r (§§ 310, 352)

v̥   voiceless v (§ 326)

z̥   voiceless z (§ 339)

ȝ̊   voiceless ȝ (§ 345)

t̪   dental t (§ 231)

c   breathed palatal plosive (§§ 484, 485)

ɟ   voiced palatal plosive (§ 484, 485)

ʈ   retroflex t (§§ 484, 485)

ḍ   retroflex d (§§ 484, 485)

q   breathed uvular plosive (§§ 484, 485)

ɢ   voiced uvular plosive (§ 484)

ʔ   glottal stop (§§ 25, 233, 254)

ɱ   labio-dental nasal (§ 398)

ɬ   strong voiceless l (a variety of l̥, § 306)

ł   'dark' l (§§ 293–304)

ɾ   flapped r (§ 317)

ɹ   fricative r or frictionless continuant r (§§ 351, 352, 356)

R   rolled uvular r (§ 313)

ʁ   voiced uvular fricative (§ 316)

x   breathed velar fricative (§§ 314, 484)

ɣ   voiced velar fricative (§ 314, 484)

ç   breathed palatal fricative (§ 376)

ʍ   breathed w (§ 380)

ɦ   voiced h (§ 373)

+   advancement

⊢ (or -)   retraction

ˌ   raising

ˍ   lowering

ˬ   voicing (§ 232)

ʻ   aspiration (§§ 221, 227, 245, 382)

*   prefixed to a phonetically transcribed word means that it
is a proper name

CURSIVE FORMS OF PHONETIC SYMBOLS

ɑ	*ɑ*		ʃ	*ʃ*
a	*a*		θ	*θ*
ʌ	*ʌ or Ω*		z	*z*
ɛ	*ɛ*		ʒ	*ʒ*
ə	*ə*		ʝ	*ʝ*
ɔ	*ɔ*		t	*t or ʈ*
ɫ	*ɫ or ʮ or ɤ*		ɖ	*ɖ or ɟ*
ɷ	*ɷ*		ʔ	*ʔ*
ð	*ð*		ʄ	*ʄ*
ŋ	*ŋ*		ʀ	*ʀ*
r	*r (or ɼ when no confusion can arise)*		ʁ	*ʁ*
ɹ	*ɹ or ɻ*		ɣ	*ɣ*

SPECIMENS OF PHONETIC WRITING

ðə fə:st rekwizit əv ə gud alfəbit iz ðət
it ʃud bi keipəbl əv bi:iŋ ritn ənd red
wið i:z ənd ritn wið mɔdərit kwiknis.

(Henry Sweet.)

i:z ənd kwiknis əv raitiŋ rikwair
ðət ðə letəz ʃud bi: i:zili dʒɔind təgeðə.

(Henry Sweet.)

xxiii

The length mark : also has a cursive form *⌣* , as shown in the following example.

it iz indid rimakəbl hau ʌnkɔnʃəs ðə
greitə nʌmbər əv pərsənz əpiə tə bi ðət
eniwʌn in ədnri səsaiəti prəmaunsiz
difrəntli frəm ðəmselvz.

(A. J. Ellis.)

PART I
PHONETIC THEORY

I. TYPES OF PRONUNCIATION

§ **1.** No two people pronounce exactly alike. The differences arise from a variety of causes, such as locality, early influences and social surroundings; there are also individual peculiarities for which it is difficult or impossible to account.

§ **2.** It is thought by many that there ought to exist a standard, and one can see from several points of view that a standard speech would have its uses. Ability to speak in a standard way might be considered advantageous by some of those whose home language is a distinctly local form of speech; if their vocations require them to work in districts remote from their home locality, they would not be hampered by speaking in a manner differing considerably from the speech of those around them. A standard pronunciation would also be useful to the foreign learner of English.

§ **3.** But though attempts have been made to devise and recommend standards, it cannot be said that any standard exists. Londoners speak in one way, Bristolians in another, Scotsmen in several other ways, and so on. American speech too (of which there are many varieties) is very different.

§ **4.** There are also styles of speech for each individual. There is rapid colloquial style and slow formal style, and there are various shades between the two extremes.

§ **5.** The science dealing with such matters is called Phonetics. This book is an elementary manual of phonetics dealing particularly with the pronunciation of the English language, and the subject is treated from the view-point of the English student. In it is given a fairly detailed description of one form of English pronunciation which, though not a standard, can at least be said to be easily understood throughout the English-speaking world, and attention is called to some of the more outstanding divergences commonly heard in various localities and to differences of style employed by individual speakers. The 'widely understood pronunciation' here described may be termed 'Received Pronunciation' (abbreviation RP). This is not a particularly good term, but it is doubtful whether a better one can be found.

§ **6.** Nearly every reader is likely to find points in which his pronunciation differs from the RP here described. It is to be hoped that users of this book will take note of the discrepancies. It will probably be found in the majority of cases that the differences are not such as would cause them to be unintelligible in any part of the English-speaking world.

'Good' speech and 'bad' speech

§ **7.** 'Good' speech may be defined as a way of speaking which is clearly intelligible to all ordinary people. 'Bad' speech is a way of talking which is difficult for most people to understand. It is caused by mumbling or lack of definiteness of utterance.

§ **8.** A person may speak with sounds very different from those of his hearers and yet be clearly intelligible to all of them, as for instance when a Scotsman or an American addresses an English audience with clear articulation. Their speech cannot be described as other than 'good'. But if a speaker with an accent similar to that of his hearers articulates in a muffled way so that they cannot readily catch what he says, his way of speaking must be considered 'bad'.

§ **9.** A dialect speaker may speak 'well' or 'badly'. The sounds of his dialect are, it is suggested, neither good nor bad intrinsically. They are adequate for communicating with others speaking the same dialect, unless he mumbles his words.

4

§ **10.** The sounds of London dialect (Cockney), for instance, are not in themselves bad. Words pronounced in Cockney fashion are perfectly intelligible to others who speak with local London pronunciation. Users of RP often find London dialect pronunciation difficult to understand, but their difficulty is to be attributed to unfamiliarity with that manner of speech and not to any inherent 'badness' in the sounds.

§ **11.** The view has sometimes been expressed that for speech to be 'good' it must not only be clearly intelligible but also 'pleasing' to the hearer. It is suggested that this condition is not one that can be applied in practice. For what is 'pleasing' to one person is not necessarily pleasing to another. People's ideas as to what is pleasing or displeasing are often determined by associations with circumstances under which certain kinds of pronunciation are used, and not by any inherent goodness or badness of the sounds uttered.

II. ORGANS OF SPEECH

§ **12.** To get an understanding of the nature of speech and the means by which it is produced, it is necessary in the first place to have a rough idea of the structure and the functions of the various parts of the 'organs of speech'. A detailed study of the anatomy and physiology of these organs is not needed.

§ **13.** The following diagrams show most of what is required for the purposes of this book. A study of these diagrams should be supplemented by an examination of the inside of the mouth by means of a hand-mirror. The best way of doing this is to stand with one's back to the light and to hold the mirror in such a position that it reflects the light into the mouth, and at the same time enables the observer to see the interior thus illuminated. It is not difficult to find the right position for the mirror. It is also useful to feel the roof of the mouth with the tip of the tongue, beginning at the edge of the upper front teeth and sliding the tongue-tip backwards until it is curled up as far as it will go.

§ 14. It will be observed in particular that the main part of the roof of the mouth is divided into two parts, the front part constituting the *hard palate* and the back part the *soft palate*. The foremost part of the roof of the mouth which is convex to

B. Back of Tongue.
Bl. Blade of Tongue.
E. Epiglottis.
F. Front of Tongue.
FP. Food Passage.
H. Hard Palate.
LL. Lips.
P. Pharyngeal cavity
    (Pharynx).
R. Root of Tongue.
S. Soft Palate.
TR. Teeth-Ridge.
TT. Teeth.
U. Uvula.
V. Position of Vocal
    Cords.
W. Wind-pipe.

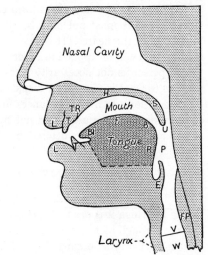

Fig. 1. The organs of speech.

the tongue is called the *teeth-ridge* (or *gum*). It extends from the back of the upper front teeth to the point where the roof of the mouth ceases to be convex to the tongue and begins to be concave.

§ 15. *AA* in Fig. 2 is the *pharyngeal arch*. The sides of it are generally held wide apart as shown in the illustration. It is, however, possible to draw the sides towards each other so as to leave only a narrow aperture between them. It is a good

...ced. Examples of breathed sounds are **p, f, h**; examples of *...iced* sounds are **b, v, ɑ:**.[1]

§ 23. When we speak in a whisper, voice is replaced throughout *...y* whisper (§§ 19, 20), the breathed sounds remaining un*...altered.* It will not be necessary to deal further with whisper.

§ 24. It does not require much practice to be able to recognize by the ear the difference between breathed and voiced sounds. The following well-known tests may, however, sometimes be found useful. (*a*) If breathed and voiced sounds are pronounced while the ears are stopped, a loud buzzing sound is heard in the latter case but not in the former. (*b*) If the throat is touched by the fingers, a distinct vibration is felt when voiced sounds are pronounced, but not otherwise. (*c*) It is possible to sing tunes on voiced sounds but not on breathed ones. Compare in these ways **f** with **v**, **p** with **ɑ:**.

§ 25. The 'glottal stop' (§ 254) is an exceptional sound in which there is neither breath nor voice during its articulation. A 'click', such as the sound we use to urge on horses, has no voice and does not necessarily have any breath either. It is possible to pronounce a click with simultaneous voice, and sounds of this description actually occur in the Zulu and Kaffir languages. It is good practice for students of speech to exercise themselves by making such sounds.

§ 26. When one listens to connected speech, it is generally *...easy* to tell which of the sounds are breathed and which are

[1] Letters in black type are phonetic symbols. In naming the *...phonetic* symbols, many teachers consider it expedient to *...designate* them by their sounds and not by the ordinary names *...f* the letters: **p** and not **piː**, **f** and not **ɛf**. It may be said on *...he* other hand that it is convenient that easily recognizable *...ames* should exist for the graphic designs which we call th*... ...tters* of the alphabet, as also for the special additional lett*... ...eded* in books on phonetics.

exercise for students of speech to practise widening and narrowing this aperture, while looking at the throat in a mirror. The width of this opening has an effect on voice quality.

§ 16. The *soft palate* is movable upwards and downwards with a sort of hinge where the hard palate begins. When lowered,

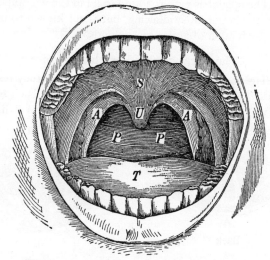

Fig. 2. The mouth seen from the front.

AA. Pharyngeal arch.   *PP*. Pharyngeal cavity (pharynx).
S. Soft palate (velum).   *T*. Tongue.   *U*. Uvula.

it takes up the position shown in Fig. 1. When raised to its fullest extent it touches the back wall of the pharynx as shown approximately in Fig. 5 (p. 13).

§ 17. The tongue has no physical divisions like the palate. It is, however, convenient for the purposes of phonetics to imagine the surface of the tongue to be divided into parts corresponding to the parts of the roof of the mouth. The part normally lying opposite the soft palate is called the *back*. The part normally lying opposite the hard palate (excluding the teeth-ridge) is called the *front*. The part lying opposite the teeth-ridge when the tongue is in the position of rest is called the *blade* (see Fig. 1). Particular note should be taken of the technical meaning in phonetics of the terms *back* and *front*.

§ **18.** The epiglottis acts as a kind of lid to the windpipe. It is used in the action of swallowing, but is not known to be used in the production of any speech sounds.

The vocal cords. Breath and voice

§ **19.** The vocal cords are situated in the larynx; they resemble two lips. They run in a horizontal direction from back to front (see Figs. 1 and 3). The space between them is called the

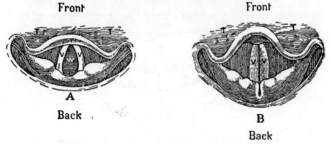

Fig. 3. The larynx as seen through a laryngoscope.
A. Position for breath.   B. Position for voice.
TT. Tongue.   VV. Vocal cords.   W. Windpipe.

glottis. The cords may be kept apart, or they may be brought together so as to close the air passage completely. When they are brought close together and air is forced between them, they vibrate, producing the sound known as *voice*. When they are wide apart and air passes between them, the sound produced is called *breath*. Certain intermediate states of the glottis give rise to *whisper*. The sound h (§ 369) is pure breath; voice is heard in many sounds and particularly in the vowels.

§ **20.** Just above the vocal cords there is and called the *false vocal cords*. They are generally h apart than the true vocal cords; they are not sh It is possible to constrict them, but it is doubtfu be brought into complete contact along their w There is constriction of the false cords in the pro loud whisper.

§ **21.** *Breath* and *voice* may be illustrated artificially following simple experiment. Take a short tube of w glass T, say $1\frac{1}{2}$ in. long and $\frac{1}{4}$ in. in diameter, and tie on to one end of it a piece of thin rubber tubing, of a rather larger diameter, say $\frac{3}{4}$ in., as shown in the accompanying diagram. The tube of wood or glass represents the windpipe, and the rubber part the larynx. The space enclosed by the edge of the rubber *EE*, represents the glottis. If we leave the rubber in its natural position and blow through the tube, air passes out, making a slight hissing sound. This corresponds to breath. If we take hold of two opposite points of the edge of the rubber *E, E*, and draw them apart so that two edges of the rubber come into contact along a straight line, we have sentation of the glottis in the position for voice, the t which are in contact representing the two vocal cor if we blow down the tube, the air in passing out edges to vibrate and a kind of musical sound is This corresponds to voice.

Fig. 4. illustrati working vocal c

§ **22.** Most ordinary speech sounds require eithe voice in their articulation. Those which contain called *breathed*,[1] and those which contain voic

---

[1] Recommended pronunciation: brεθ

voiced. One can usually hear quite easily that such sounds as p, k, f, s, h are breathed and that ɑ:, u:, b, g, v, z are voiced. There are, however, a few sequences of three consonants in which the breathed or voiced character of the middle one is not very definite. Examples are the sound of *s* in *obstacle* or of the *d* in *looked like*. It is probable that a majority use breathed s and t ('ɔbstəkl, 'luktlɑik).

§ **27.** It has to be noticed too that in some situations the sounds represented by the letters b, d, g, v, ð, z, ʒ are not voiced. (See §§ 225, 240, 252, 326, 332, 339 and 345.)

§ **28.** General quality of voice varies from one individual to another. When someone says 'I like that man's voice', it often means that he likes the quality (*timbre* or *tamber*)[1] of the sounds uttered when the speaker's vocal cords vibrate. The expression is also used loosely meaning that he likes the general effect of the speech, including the particular shades of vowel used and the intonation.

§ **29.** Some particular voice qualities appear to be connected with locality. A husky voice quality, for instance, seems rather prevalent in parts of the North of England, and a more strident voice quality may be heard in London.

III. SOUNDS AND LETTERS

§ **30.** Sounds are heard. Letters are seen. Letters provide a means of symbolizing sounds. If they do so in a logical manner —in other words, if the essential sounds of any particular language or dialect are represented consistently—the writing is said to be *phonetic*.

---

[1] *Tamber* is an anglicized form of the French *timbre*. The term was invented by Robert Bridges, the late Poet Laureate.

IV. CLASSIFICATION OF SOUNDS

§ 31. The sounds which the organs of speech are capable of uttering are of many different kinds. Some of the continuous voiced sounds produced without obstruction in the mouth are what may be called 'pure musical sounds' unaccompanied by any frictional noise. They are called *vowels*. All other articulated sounds are called *consonants*. Consonants include: (i) all breathed sounds, (ii) all voiced sounds formed by means of an obstruction in the mouth, (iii) all those in which there is a narrowing of the air passage giving rise to a frictional noise, and (iv) certain sounds which are 'gliding'.

Vowels

§ 32. If the tongue is held very close to the roof of the mouth and a voiced air-stream of ordinary force is emitted, a frictional noise is heard in addition to the voice. The sound is a consonant. In the production of vowels the tongue is held at such a distance from the roof of the mouth that there is no perceptible frictional noise. Fig. 5 illustrates the 'vowel limit'. The tongue positions for vowels are below the dotted line. Tongue positions which extend above the dotted line but yet do not touch the central line of the palate give rise to fricative consonants (§ 56, vii), when air is expelled with strong or moderate force of exhalation.

§ 33. When the tongue takes up a vowel position, a resonance chamber is formed which modifies the quality of tone produced by the voice, and gives rise to a distinct quality or tamber which we call a vowel. The number of possible vowels is very large, but the number actually used in any particular language is small. In some languages, e.g. Spanish, there are only five essential vowels. In English there are more; see Table of Vowels on pp. 23, 24.

exercise for students of speech to practise widening and narrowing this aperture, while looking at the throat in a mirror. The width of this opening has an effect on voice quality.

§ **16.** The *soft palate* is movable upwards and downwards with a sort of hinge where the hard palate begins. When lowered,

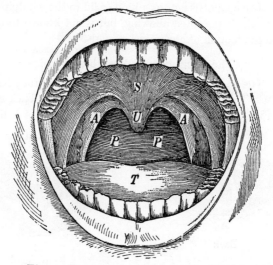

Fig. 2. The mouth seen from the front.

AA. Pharyngeal arch. *PP.* Pharyngeal cavity (pharynx).
S. Soft palate (velum). *T.* Tongue. *U.* Uvula.

it takes up the position shown in Fig. 1. When raised to its fullest extent it touches the back wall of the pharynx as shown approximately in Fig. 5 (p. 13).

§ **17.** The tongue has no physical divisions like the palate. It is, however, convenient for the purposes of phonetics to imagine the surface of the tongue to be divided into parts corresponding to the parts of the roof of the mouth. The part normally lying opposite the soft palate is called the *back*. The

7

part normally lying opposite the hard palate (excluding the teeth-ridge) is called the *front*. The part lying opposite the teeth-ridge when the tongue is in the position of rest is called the *blade* (see Fig. 1). Particular note should be taken of the technical meaning in phonetics of the terms *back* and *front*.

§ **18.** The epiglottis acts as a kind of lid to the windpipe. It is used in the action of swallowing, but is not known to be used in the production of any speech sounds.

The vocal cords. Breath and voice

§ **19.** The vocal cords are situated in the larynx; they resemble two lips. They run in a horizontal direction from back to front (see Figs. 1 and 3). The space between them is called the

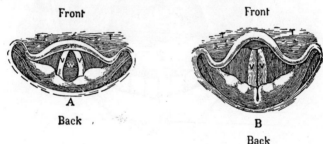

Fig. 3. The larynx as seen through a laryngoscope.
A. Position for breath.   B. Position for voice.
TT. Tongue.   VV. Vocal cords.   W. Windpipe.

glottis. The cords may be kept apart, or they may be brought together so as to close the air passage completely. When they are brought close together and air is forced between them, they vibrate, producing the sound known as *voice*. When they are wide apart and air passes between them, the sound produced is called *breath*. Certain intermediate states of the glottis give rise to *whisper*. The sound h (§ 369) is pure breath; voice is heard in many sounds and particularly in the vowels.

8

§ 20. Just above the vocal cords there is another pair of lips called the *false vocal cords*. They are generally held much wider apart than the true vocal cords; they are not shown in Fig. 3. It is possible to constrict them, but it is doubtful if they can be brought into complete contact along their whole length. There is constriction of the false cords in the production of loud whisper.

§ 21. *Breath* and *voice* may be illustrated artificially by the following simple experiment. Take a short tube of wood or glass T, say 1½ in. long and ¼ in. in diameter, and tie on to one end of it a piece of thin rubber tubing, of a rather larger diameter, say ¾ in., as shown in the accompanying diagram. The tube of wood or glass represents the windpipe, and the rubber part the larynx. The space enclosed by the edge of the rubber *EE*, represents the glottis. If we leave the rubber in its natural position and blow through the tube, air passes out, making a slight hissing sound. This corresponds to breath. If we take hold of two opposite points of the edge of the rubber *E, E*, and draw them apart so that two edges of the rubber come into contact along a straight line, we have a representation of the glottis in the position for voice, the two edges which are in contact representing the two vocal cords. Now, if we blow down the tube, the air in passing out causes the edges to vibrate and a kind of musical sound is produced. This corresponds to voice.

Fig. 4. Tube illustrating the working of the vocal cords.

§ 22. Most ordinary speech sounds require either breath or voice in their articulation. Those which contain breath are called *breathed*,[1] and those which contain voice are called

---

[1] Recommended pronunciation: brɛθt.

voiced. Examples of breathed sounds are **p**, **f**, **h**; examples of voiced sounds are **b**, **v**, **ɑ:**.[1]

§ 23. When we speak in a whisper, voice is replaced throughout by whisper (§§ 19, 20), the breathed sounds remaining unaltered. It will not be necessary to deal further with whisper.

§ 24. It does not require much practice to be able to recognize by the ear the difference between breathed and voiced sounds. The following well-known tests may, however, sometimes be found useful. (*a*) If breathed and voiced sounds are pronounced while the ears are stopped, a loud buzzing sound is heard in the latter case but not in the former. (*b*) If the throat is touched by the fingers, a distinct vibration is felt when voiced sounds are pronounced, but not otherwise. (*c*) It is possible to sing tunes on voiced sounds but not on breathed ones. Compare in these ways **f** with **v**, **p** with **ɑ:**.

§ 25. The 'glottal stop' (§ 254) is an exceptional sound in which there is neither breath nor voice during its articulation. A 'click', such as the sound we use to urge on horses, has no voice and does not necessarily have any breath either. It is possible to pronounce a click with simultaneous voice, and sounds of this description actually occur in the Zulu and Kaffir languages. It is good practice for students of speech to exercise themselves by making such sounds.

§ 26. When one listens to connected speech, it is generally easy to tell which of the sounds are breathed and which are

---

[1] Letters in black type are phonetic symbols. In naming the phonetic symbols, many teachers consider it expedient to designate them by their sounds and not by the ordinary names of the letters: **p** and not **pi:**, **f** and not **ɛf**. It may be said on the other hand that it is convenient that easily recognizable names should exist for the graphic designs which we call the letters of the alphabet, as also for the special additional letters needed in books on phonetics.

voiced. One can usually hear quite easily that such sounds as p, k, f, s, h are breathed and that ɑː, uː, b, g, v, z are voiced. There are, however, a few sequences of three consonants in which the breathed or voiced character of the middle one is not very definite. Examples are the sound of s in *obstacle* or of the d in *looked like*. It is probable that a majority use breathed s and t (ˈɔbstəkl, ˈluktlɑik).

§ 27. It has to be noticed too that in some situations the sounds represented by the letters b, d, g, v, ð, z, ʒ are not voiced. (See §§ 225, 240, 252, 326, 332, 339 and 345.)

§ 28. General quality of voice varies from one individual to another. When someone says 'I like that man's voice', it often means that he likes the quality (*timbre* or *tamber*)[1] of the sounds uttered when the speaker's vocal cords vibrate. The expression is also used loosely meaning that he likes the general effect of the speech, including the particular shades of vowel used and the intonation.

§ 29. Some particular voice qualities appear to be connected with locality. A husky voice quality, for instance, seems rather prevalent in parts of the North of England, and a more strident voice quality may be heard in London.

III. SOUNDS AND LETTERS

§ 30. Sounds are heard. Letters are seen. Letters provide a means of symbolizing sounds. If they do so in a logical manner —in other words, if the essential sounds of any particular language or dialect are represented consistently—the writing is said to be *phonetic*.

---

[1] *Tamber* is an anglicized form of the French *timbre*. The term was invented by Robert Bridges, the late Poet Laureate.

IV. CLASSIFICATION OF SOUNDS

§ 31. The sounds which the organs of speech are capable of uttering are of many different kinds. Some of the continuous voiced sounds produced without obstruction in the mouth are what may be called 'pure musical sounds' unaccompanied by any frictional noise. They are called *vowels*. All other articulated sounds are called *consonants*. Consonants include: (i) all breathed sounds, (ii) all voiced sounds formed by means of an obstruction in the mouth, (iii) all those in which there is a narrowing of the air passage giving rise to a frictional noise, and (iv) certain sounds which are 'gliding'.

Vowels

§ 32. If the tongue is held very close to the roof of the mouth and a voiced air-stream of ordinary force is emitted, a frictional noise is heard in addition to the voice. The sound is a consonant. In the production of vowels the tongue is held at such a distance from the roof of the mouth that there is no perceptible frictional noise. Fig. 5 illustrates the 'vowel limit'. The tongue positions for vowels are below the dotted line. Tongue positions which extend above the dotted line but yet do not touch the central line of the palate give rise to fricative consonants (§ 56, vii), when air is expelled with strong or moderate force of exhalation.

§ 33. When the tongue takes up a vowel position, a resonance chamber is formed which modifies the quality of tone produced by the voice, and gives rise to a distinct quality or tamber which we call a vowel. The number of possible vowels is very large, but the number actually used in any particular language is small. In some languages, e.g. Spanish, there are only five essential vowels. In English there are more; see Table of Vowels on pp. 23, 24.

Consonants

§ 34. Some consonants are breathed and others are voiced, as has already been mentioned in § 22. To every breathed consonant (other than the 'glottal stop', § 254) there corresponds a voiced consonant, i.e. one produced with the same

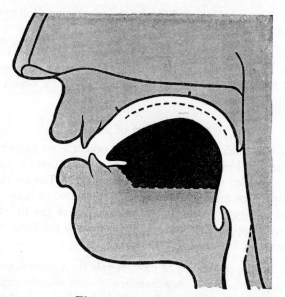

Fig. 5. The vowel limit.

position or movement of the articulating organs, but with voice substituted for breath or vice versa. Thus **v** corresponds to **f**, and **b** to **p**. The breathed consonants corresponding to several of the English voiced consonants do not occur regularly in English. For instance the breathed consonants corresponding to **m** and **l** (phonetic symbols m̥, l̥) only occur 'accidentally'; see §§ 275, 306. Most people find them difficult to produce intentionally. It is a good exercise to practise making such sounds. They may be acquired by practising continuous sequences like vfvf..., zszs..., until the method of passing from voice to breath is clearly perceived, and then applying the same method to m, l, etc., thus obtaining mm̥mm̥..., l̥ll̥..., etc.

§ 35. Some people have difficulty in pronouncing a fully voiced v or z in isolation. For this see § 488.

§ 36. It is possible to voice an h, and a voiced h does in fact occur 'accidentally' in the speech of many English people; see § 374. It is a useful exercise to try to sound a voiced h by itself.

Classification of vowels

§ 37. The qualities of vowels depend upon the positions of the tongue and lips. It is convenient to classify them according to the position of the main part of the tongue. The position of the tip has no great effect on vowel quality, except in the cases noted in § 355. In the following explanation the tip of the tongue is supposed to be touching or near to the lower teeth, as shown in Figs. 5, 8 and 9.

§ 38. In the production of most vowels the tongue is convex to the palate. Vowels may therefore be conveniently arranged *according to the position of the highest point of the tongue.*[1] Fig. 6 is a conventionalized diagram showing how the classification may be made. There are *front vowels*, in the production of which the 'front' of the tongue is raised in the direction of the hard palate (see Fig. 8, p. 19). Example iː in fiːd (*feed*).

---

[1] The movements of the tongue in passing from one vowel position to another (e.g. as in pronouncing ɑɛɑɛ..., iːəːiːəː..., əːɑəːɑ...) should be examined with a looking-glass or felt with the finger.

There are *back vowels*, in the production of which the 'back' of the tongue is raised in the direction of the soft palate (see Fig. 9, p. 20). Example uː in fuːd (*food*). Then in the middle and upper part of the figure (shown by the interior triangle) there are vowels intermediate between front and back; we call them *central vowels*. Example əː in bəːd (*bird*).

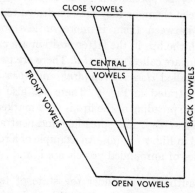

Fig. 6. Conventionalized diagram of vowel positions.

§ **39.** One essential element in the classification of vowel sounds is thus *the part of the tongue which is raised*. A second is *the height to which it is raised*. Those in which the tongue is held as high as possible consistently with not producing a frictional noise are called *close* vowels. Examples are iː in fiːd (*feed*), uː in fuːd (*food*). Those in which the tongue is as low as possible are called *open vowels*. An example is ɑː in 'fɑːðə (*father*).

§ **40.** It is convenient to distinguish two intermediate classes, *half-close* and *half-open*, in the formation of which the tongue occupies positions one-third and two-thirds of the distance from 'close' to 'open'. Key words illustrating half-close and half-open vowels depend upon the pronunciation of different speakers. Scotsmen ordinarily use half-close e and o sounds in words like *day* and *go* (Scottish pronunciation **de, go**). Many English people, especially in the North, use a half-open vowel in words like **pɛn** (*pen*), **lɛft** (*left*).

§ **41.** Vowel quality is also largely dependent on the position of the lips. The lips may be held in a natural or neutral position; they may be spread out so as to leave a long narrow opening between them, or they may be drawn together so that the opening between them is more or less round. Vowels produced with the lips in the latter position are called *rounded* vowels. Others are called *unrounded*. There are two main types of rounding, called *close lip-rounding* and *open lip-rounding*. These are illustrated in Fig. 7. There are also intermediate degrees. If the spreading of the lips is very marked, the vowels may be termed *spread*. Lip-spreading and neutral lip-position are illustrated in Fig. 7 (*a*), (*b*). An example of a rounded vowel is **uː**; examples of unrounded vowels are **i, ɑː**.

§ **42.** Some authorities consider the state of tension of the tongue to be an important factor in the production of various vowel qualities, and they distinguish *tense vowels* from *lax vowels*. Some vowels certainly do require in their formation a greater degree of tongue tension than others. Most people can easily feel, for instance, that the **iː** of **liːp** (*leap*) has a tenser articulation than the **i** of **lip**, and that the **uː** of **buːt** (*boot*) as pronounced in Southern England has a tenser articulation than the **u** of **fut** (*foot*). This can be tested by placing the finger against the outside of the throat about half-way between the chin and the larynx. When pronouncing the vowel of **lip** this part feels loose, but when pronouncing the vowel of **liːp**, it becomes tenser and is pushed forward.

§ **43.** It is doubtful if a whole series of corresponding tense and lax vowels can be established. Differences of tension can be noticed in vowels of 'closer' types, but it is difficult, and perhaps impossible, to form an idea of the degrees of tenseness of the tongue in the production of 'opener' vowels.

§ 44. The position of the soft palate may affect vowel quality. In the articulation of normal vowels the soft palate is raised

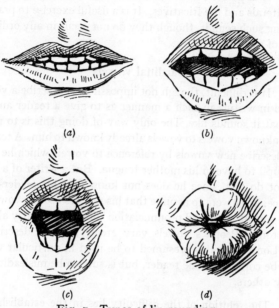

(a)   (b)

(c)   (d)

Fig. 7. Types of lip-rounding.

  (a) Close lip-spreading.   (b) Neutral lip position.
  (c) Open lip-rounding.   (d) Close lip-rounding.

so that it touches the back wall of the pharynx as shown in Figs. 5, 8 and 9. The result is that no air can pass through the nose. It is, however, possible to lower the soft palate so that it takes up the position shown in Fig. 1 (p. 6) and the air can then pass out through the nose as well as through the mouth. When vowels are pronounced with the soft palate lowered in

17

this way, they are said to be *nasalized*. Nasalized vowels are heard in the speech of those who have 'nasal pronunciation'. They are common in various forms of English, and notably in London dialectal speech and in American English (see §§ 389–393). It is possible to nasalize some consonants, and notably the laterals and the fricatives. It is a useful exercise to practise making such sounds, though they do not occur in any ordinary type of speech.

Cardinal vowels

§ **45.** It is difficult, though not impossible to describe a vowel-sound in writing in such a manner as to give a reader an idea of what it sounds like. The only way of doing this is to relate the unknown vowels to vowels already known to him. A teacher can describe new vowels by reference to vowels which he finds his pupil to have in his mother tongue. But a writer of a book cannot do this, since he does not know how his readers pronounce. If he were to assume that his readers use the vowels of some sort of 'standard pronunciation', he would nearly always be wrong. People's vowels vary greatly, and a description based on the vowels presumed to be used in particular words may be correct for one reader, but is sure to be misleading for many others.

§ **46.** The solution of the difficulty lies in the establishment of a set of what may be called *cardinal vowels*, i.e. specially selected vowel-sounds which can conveniently be used as points of reference from which other vowels can be measured. If a reader knows the sounds of, say, cardinal vowels 2 and 3, he can form a very good idea of what is meant when an author speaks of a sound half-way between these two or even of a vowel a third of the distance from No. 2 to No. 3. And so on.

§ **47.** Various systems of cardinal vowels have been invented. The one which up to now appears to have given the best results is a system of eight. They have been selected in the following way. No. 1 is the vowel which combines the greatest degree of 'closeness' with the greatest degree of 'frontness'. It is not possible to make a 'fronter' vowel; and if the tongue were raised any higher, normal breath pressure would give rise

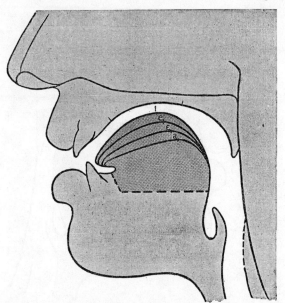

Fig. 8. Approximate tongue positions of the front cardinal vowels, i, e, ɛ, a.

to a frictional noise and the sound uttered would not be a vowel at all. No. 5 combines the greatest degree of 'openness' with the greatest degree of 'backness'. The tongue is incapable of being lower, and if it were retracted further a frictional noise would be produced by the air issuing through the narrow space between the back of the tongue and the back part of the roof of the mouth: it would be a consonant, namely the sound represented phonetically by ʁ (§ 316). Cardinal vowels Nos. 2, 3 and 4 are vowels of the 'front' series selected so as to form (as nearly as can be judged by ear) equal degrees of acoustic separation between Nos. 1 and 5. Nos. 6, 7 and 8 are selected so as to continue these equal degrees of acoustic separation in

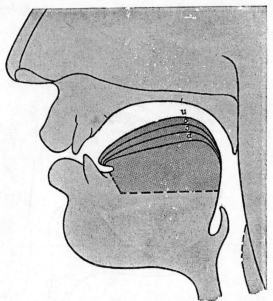

Fig. 9. Approximate tongue positions of the back cardinal vowels, ɑ, ɔ, o, u.

the back series of vowels (as nearly as can be judged by ear). These eight vowels are represented phonetically by the letters i, e, ɛ, a, ɑ, ɔ, o, u.

§ 48. The approximate tongue positions of these cardinal vowels are shown in Figs. 8 and 9 and by the dots on the conventionalized diagram (Fig. 10). The positions of Nos. 1, 4, 5 and 8 have been ascertained by X-ray photography (see

Frontispiece). Their true positions relative to each other have been found to be as shown in Fig. 11. A diagram of this shape is, however, not very convenient to work with in practical teaching, being difficult to draw. The conventionalized shape

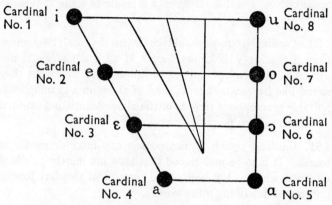

Cardinal i
No. 1

Cardinal u
No. 8

Cardinal e
No. 2

Cardinal o
No. 7

Cardinal ɛ
No. 3

Cardinal ɔ
No. 6

Cardinal a
No. 4

Cardinal ɑ
No. 5

Fig. 10. Conventionalized diagram illustrating the tongue positions of the cardinal vowels.

shown in Fig. 10 is easy to draw and at the same time sufficiently accurate for ordinary practical purposes.

§ 49. Cardinal vowels Nos. 1–5 have spread or neutral lips. No. 6 has open lip-rounding (Fig. 7 (c)), No. 8 has close lip-rounding (Fig. 7 (d)). No. 7 has an intermediate degree of lip-rounding.

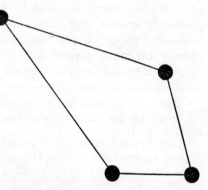

Fig. 11. Relative tongue positions of cardinal vowels Nos. 1, 4, 5, 8 (ascertained by X-ray photography).

§ 49a. There are ten 'secondary' cardinal vowels derived from the above eight primary cardinal vowels. Nos. 9–16 have the same tongue positions as Nos. 1–8 but different lip positions. Nos. 17 and 18 have tongue positions intermediate between those of Nos. 1 and 8. Reference is made to some of these in §§ 481–483.[1]

§ 50. Cardinal sounds should be learnt by oral instruction from a teacher who knows them. If such a teacher is not available, the student can get to know fairly well what they sound like by constant repetitions of them on a gramophone. Suitable gramophone records of the above-mentioned cardinal vowels have been prepared.[2]

§ 51. Cardinal vowels do not possess any intrinsic merits as sounds. It is to be understood that they are merely points of reference which it has been found convenient to select for the purpose of describing other vowels.

Diphthongs

§ 52. When a sound is made by gliding from one vowel position to another, it is called a *diphthong*. Diphthongs are represented phonetically by sequences of two letters, the first showing the starting point and the second indicating the direction of movement. ei and ɑu are examples of diphthongs.

---

[1] For fuller information see the pamphlet 'Cardinal Vowels' published by the Linguaphone Institute, 207 Regent St., London, W. 1.

[2] Linguaphone double-sided records Nos. ENG 252–3 and 254A–5, spoken by D. Jones. The matrices of another double-sided record of the primary cardinal vowels, also spoken by D. Jones, are in existence. They are in the possession of the H.M.V. Gramophone Co., and it is understood that the Company is prepared to make records from them if a sufficient number are ordered. This record is numbered B 804.

English vowel diagrams

§ **53.** The following are diagrams showing approximately the mode of formation of the vowels and diphthongs used in one type of Received English. The positions of the dots show

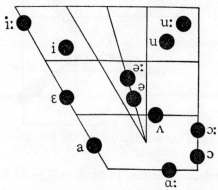

Fig. 12. Diagram illustrating the formation of the pure vowels of RP.

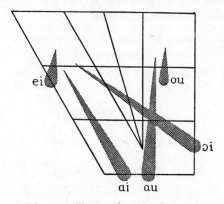

Fig. 13. Diagram illustrating the formation of the 'closing' diphthongs of RP.

approximately the relationships of their tongue positions to those of the above-mentioned cardinal vowels (Figs. 8, 9, 10).

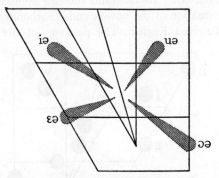

Fig. 14. Diagram illustrating the formation of the 'centring' diphthongs of RP.

These vowels are examined in detail in §§ 70 ff.

§ 54. It is convenient in practical teaching to give numbers to the vowels and diphthongs of RP for purposes of reference. The following system is suggested:

					Pure Vowels						
iː	i	ɛ	a	ɑː	ɔ	ɔː	u	uː	ʌ	əː	ə
1	2	3	4	5	6	7	8	9	10	11	12

	Closing Diphthongs			
ei	ou	ai	au	ɔi
13	14	15	16	17

	Centring Diphthongs		
iə	ɛə	ɔə	uə
18	19	20	21

Classification of consonants

§ 55. Consonants may be classified: (i) according to the organs which articulate them, (ii) according to the manner in which the organs articulate them. If we classify them according to the organs which articulate them, we distinguish seven main classes:

(i) *Labial* or lip sounds, which may be subdivided into
  Bi-labial, namely sounds articulated by the two lips. Examples p, m.
  Labio-dental, namely sounds articulated by the lower lip against the upper teeth. Example f.

(ii) *Dental*, namely sounds articulated by the tip of the tongue against the upper teeth. Example ð.

(iii) *Alveolar*, namely sounds articulated by the tip or blade of the tongue against the teeth-ridge. Example normal English t.

(iv) *Palato-alveolar*, namely sounds which have alveolar articulation together with a simultaneous raising of the main body of the tongue towards the roof of the mouth. Example ʃ.

(v) *Palatal*, namely sounds articulated by the front of the tongue against the hard palate. Example j.

(vi) *Velar*, namely sounds articulated by the back of the tongue against the soft palate.[1] Example k.

(vii) *Glottal*, namely sounds articulated in the glottis. Example h.

§ 56. If we classify consonants according to the manner in which the organs articulate them, we distinguish eight main classes:

(i) *Plosive*, formed by completely closing the air passage and suddenly removing the obstacle (or one of the obstacles), so that the air escapes making an explosive sound. Examples p, d.

---

[1] The *velum* is the technical name for the soft palate.

(ii) *Affricate*, resembling a plosive but with separation of the articulating organs performed less quickly, with the result that a fricative sound is perceived during the process of separation. Example tʃ.

(iii) *Nasal*, formed by completely closing the mouth at some point, the soft palate remaining lowered so that the air is free to pass out through the nose. Example m.

(iv) *Lateral*, formed by an obstacle placed in the middle of the mouth, the air being free to escape at one or both sides (see § 292). Example l.

(v) *Rolled*, formed by a rapid succession of taps of some elastic part of the speech mechanism. Example rolled r.

(vi) *Flapped*, formed like a rolled consonant but consisting of a single tap only. Example flapped r.

(vii) *Fricative*, formed by a narrowing of the air passage at some point so that the air in escaping makes a kind of hissing sound. Examples f, z, fricative r.

| | Labial | | Dental | Al-veolar | Palato-alveolar | Palatal | Velar | Glottal |
	Bi-labial	Labio-dental						
Plosive	p b			t d			k g	ʔ
Affricate					tʃ dʒ			
Nasal	m			n			ŋ	
Lateral				l			(l)	
Rolled				[r]				
Flapped				[r]				
Fricative		f v	θ ð	s z r	ʃ ʒ			h
Semi-vowel	w					j	(w)	

(Consonants appearing twice on the chart have double articulation, the secondary articulation being shown by the symbol in ( ). Symbols enclosed in [ ] are unusual varieties in English.)

(viii) *Semi-vowel*, a gliding sound in which the speech organs start at or near a 'close' vowel (§39) and immediately move away to some other vowel (or occasionally to some other sound of equal or greater prominence, such as syllabic l). Example **w**.

§ 57. The classification may be conveniently shown by arranging the consonants in a table, horizontal rows containing sounds articulated in the same manner, and vertical columns containing sounds articulated by the same organs. In the table on p. 26 the most important consonants are arranged in this way.

V. PRINCIPLES OF TRANSCRIPTION

§ 58. Phonetic transcription has often been defined as a kind of alphabetic writing in which each letter represents one sound and never any other—'one sound one symbol'. This description is not strictly accurate. For in phonetic transcription we write **k** at the beginning of **kiːp** (*keep*) and also at the beginning and end of **kuk** (*cook*), but a little experimenting easily shows us that these **k**'s differ from each other. Similarly it is easy to perceive that the **t** of the word **at** (*at*) said by itself is not the same as the **t** used in such an expression as **ət ði ˈɛnd** (*at the end*), nor is it the same as the **t** of **truː** (*true*). The use of these different sounds is determined by the other sounds adjacent to them in the word or sentence.

§ 59. Besides this, when we compare one language with another or one dialect with another, we find that symbols often have to be used with somewhat different values in each language or dialect. For instance, we may transcribe the word *back* phonetically as **bak**, but the value of the **a** is generally different in the North of England from what it is in the South.[1]

---

[1] The cardinal vowel letters often have to be used with values differing to some extent from the cardinal values.

§ **60.** Each letter of a phonetic notation therefore really represents a small family of sounds. The values to be attached to the letters vary to some extent, and depend upon (i) the phonetic context, and (ii) the language or dialect which is being written. We have to give this elasticity to the letters of phonetic transcription, since strict adherence to the principle 'one sound one symbol' would involve the introduction of a very large number of symbols and marks. This would render phonetic transcriptions cumbrous and difficult to read.

§ **61.** Transcriptions may be 'broad' or may have various degrees of 'narrowness'. A *broad transcription* is a form of phonetic writing which uses the smallest number of letters and marks which will represent a given form of a language without ambiguity, and uses for this purpose familiar letter shapes as far as possible. It differentiates in writing all the words of a given language or dialect which are different in sound. The reduction of the number of symbols to a minimum is effected by applying certain conventions which have to be stated once for all. One such convention is, for instance, that the long iː and the short i of ordinary Southern English differ in quality as well as in quantity; the short sound is at the same time an 'opener' one (see positions shown in Fig. 12). This convention relieves us from the necessity of introducing a special letter to denote the quality of the short i.

§ **62.** One may devise a more precise kind of transcription by introducing extra symbols to denote some of the sound-qualities that are implied by the conventions in broad transcriptions. Such transcriptions are said to be *narrow*. There are two kinds of 'narrowness': *linguistic* narrowness and *typographical* narrowness. For these see §§ 500, 502.

§ **63.** For most linguistic purposes broad transcriptions are the most practical, since they combine accuracy with the greatest measure of simplicity. In teaching the pronunciation of a foreign language, for instance, a broad transcription is generally to be recommended.

§ **64.** Narrower forms of transcription are serviceable in comparative work, and particularly when it is desired to make comparisons between the pronunciations of different people speaking the same language. For this reason the transcription of RP in this book is narrowed to the extent of introducing three special letters, ɛ, ɑ and ɔ, which are not needed in a broad transcription of the same style of speech. In a broad transcription, intended for use in teaching English pronunciation to foreign learners who do not aspire to become specialists in phonetics, the common letters e, a and o may be used in their stead.[1]

§ **65.** A transcription of a language—or rather of a given form of a language—is only intelligible if the transcriber explains: (i) what sounds are meant by his symbols, and (ii) what conventions are to be understood when he uses symbols in different phonetic contexts. As has already been pointed out, there must necessarily be quite a number of such conventions, since it is not practicable to denote by separate letters and marks all the distinguishable shades of sound occurring in a language. The values of the letters used in transcribing RP in this book and the chief conventions concerning their use are stated in the paragraphs relating to each sound.

§ **66.** In transcribing other types of English, letters often have to be used with values differing to some extent from those they have in RP. Besides this, other types of English often need

---

[1] As is done for instance in MacCarthy's *English Pronunciation*, Scott's *English Conversations*, Tibbitts's *Phonetic Reader* (all published by Heffer, Cambridge), MacCarthy's *English Conversation Reader* (Longmans) and Hornby and Parnwell's *English Reader's Dictionary* (Oxford University Press).

additional symbols and conventions differing from those followed in the case of RP.

§ 67. Transcriptions of words in which the values of the letters or the conventions with which they are used differ from those in transcriptions of RP are enclosed in square brackets [ ] throughout Part 1 of this book.

For fuller particulars of the principles of phonetic transcription, and their application to many languages, readers are referred to *The Principles of the International Phonetic Association* (1949),[1] and to the Appendix on *Types of Phonetic Transcription* in the 1956 edition of the author's *Outline of English Phonetics*.[2]

VI. ENGLISH SPEECH SOUNDS IN DETAIL

§ 68. In the following descriptions the technical terms defined above (and particularly in §§ 38–41, 55 and 56) will be used without further explanation. Raising of the soft palate, as shown in Figs. 8, 9, etc., is to be implied in the case of all sounds except the nasal consonants, unless the contrary is stated.

§ 69. Thus when we say that k is a *breathed velar plosive*, no further description is necessary. Reference to §§ 19, 22, 55 and 56 will show that the term 'breathed velar plosive' means that the sound is a consonant articulated by raising the back of the tongue so that it touches the soft palate; the soft palate is raised so that no air can pass through the nose; air is forced upwards from the lungs without causing the vocal cords to vibrate, and the tongue is suddenly removed from the soft palate, the result being an explosive sound. Similarly, *voiced*

---

[1] Obtainable from the Secretary of the Association, Dept. of Phonetics, University College, London, W.C. 1 (3s. 6d.).

[2] Published by Heffer, Cambridge.

labio-dental fricative is a sufficient description of the sound **v**. It means that **v** is a consonant articulated by placing the lower lip against the upper teeth so as to leave only a very narrow space for the air to escape; the soft palate is raised so that no air can pass through the nose; air is forced upwards from the lungs, and the vocal cords are so placed that the air passing between them causes them to vibrate, producing voice; the air in passing between the lower lip and upper teeth escapes continuously, making a fricative noise. So also the description of **n** as a *voiced alveolar nasal* consonant will be seen from §§ 19, 22, 55 and 56 to mean that in forming it the tip and blade of the tongue touch the teeth-ridge making complete closure; the soft palate is lowered, so that the air is free to pass out through the nose; air is forced upwards by pressure from the lungs, and the vocal cords are placed so as to produce voice. Again, a description of a particular kind of **ɛ** as *between half-close* and *half-open* means that it is formed by raising the 'front' of the tongue in the direction of the hard palate to about half the distance from the lower vowel limit to the upper vowel limit, the soft palate being raised and there being no lip-rounding.

Pure vowels

§ **70.** **iː**, No. 1 of RP. Close front unrounded. Tongue position approximately as shown in Fig. 12. Example: **miːt** (*meet, meat*), **tʃiːf** (*chief*).

§ **71.** Many people use a somewhat diphthongal (§ 52) variety of this, especially in final position. The diphthong may be symbolized by **ij**. They pronounce *see* as **sij** rather than **siː**.

§ **72.** In the local dialect of London a wide diphthong of the type **əi** (Fig. 15) is used in such words: [səi] (*see*), [ə ˈkap ə ˈtˢəi] (*a cup of tea*). When followed by 'dark' **l** (§§ 292, 293 and 296), the vowel is reduced to simple **i**, e.g. [fiɫd] or [fiɤd] (identical with *filled*) for RP **fiːld** (*field*).

§ 73. Some use iː as the first element of the diphthong in *hear*, thus hiːə for the more usual hiə.[1]

§ 74. i, No. 2 of RP. Front unrounded vowel between close and half-close and somewhat retracted. Tongue position approximately as shown in Fig. 12. Examples: **bit** (*bit*), **fil** (*fill*), also such words as **ˈbɑːskit** (*basket*), **ˈlaŋgwidʒ** (*language*), **ˈakjurit** (*accurate*).

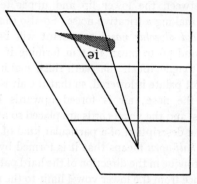

Fig. 15. Diagram illustrating the formation of the diphthong əi of London dialect.

§ 75. In varieties of Scottish and American English in which there are no consistent relationships between length and quality, a lower and still more retracted variety of vowel is generally used. The sound has to be represented by a special symbol (ɩ); see §§ 429, 431. In Scottish English the words *feet* and *fit* are distinguished as [fit], [fɩt], both vowels being short. In the type of Scottish English illustrated on p. 205 the ɩ is a somewhat ə-like sound.

§ 76. In final position, as in **ˈsiti** (*city*), **ˈhɛvi** (*heavy*), **ˈtwɛnti** (*twenty*), an opener variety of i is commonly used in RP. This

---

[1] The term 'more usual' is to be taken here and elsewhere to mean 'more usual in Southern English'.

sound may if desired be shown by adding the mark of openness ('sitĮ, 'hɛvĮ).

§ 77. In many forms of English the final short i of RP in such words as *city*, *heavy*, *twenty* is replaced by the long and closer iː, thus 'sitiː, 'hɛviː, 'twɛntiː. This pronunciation may be heard in London, in the South-West, and in many other parts of the country; also in Australia and New Zealand. In London the sound is often replaced by the dialectal variant [əi], thus ['sitəi], ['hɛvəi], ['twɛntəi]; it would seem, however, that this pronunciation is not used in all words; *really* and *generally*, for instance, appear to be said with short i by many who use əi in other words ('riːli, 'dʒɛnrəli). Londoners who use final iː or əi sometimes change the sound to the short 'open' i when another word immediately follows; *twenty-five*, for instance, is pronounced dialectically ['twɛni'faiv] as well as ['twɛnəi'faiv]. The long, or diphthongal, sound is retained in the inflected forms of words, e.g. 'sitiːz (or in London dialect ['sitəiz]) (*cities*).

§ 78. Another not uncommon pronunciation of words like *heavy* is with a close i but short. This is found in various parts of England and Scotland, in South Africa and in the speech of many Americans. With most of those who pronounce thus (except the Americans) a distinction of length is observed between the short final sound of *city*, *heavy*, etc., and a long one in *coatee*, *pedigree*, etc. To transcribe this pronunciation it is therefore necessary to introduce a special symbol (ι) to represent the opener i-sound, and write for instance bιt (*bit*), 'fιl (*fill*), 'sιti (*city*), 'hɛvi (*heavy*), but 'koutiː (*coatee*), 'pɛdιgriː (*pedigree*).

§ 79. The South African ι of most words[1] is a low and retracted variety which may well be transcribed by ə. The South African

---

[1] Except before and after k, g, after h and before ŋ, when a sound of the ordinary open i type is used: e.g. kιt (*kit*), gιv (*give*), hιl (*hill*), pιk (*pick*), dιg (*dig*), sιŋ (*sing*).

pronunciation of the above words may be written bət, fəl, 'səti, 'pɛdəgriː, etc.

§ 80. The weak prefixes *be-*, *de-*, *pre-* and *re-* are usually said in RP with i. Examples : bi'fɔː (*before*), di'livə (*deliver*), pri'vɛnt (*prevent*), ri'zʌlt (*result*). It is, however, not uncommon to hear these prefixes pronounced with ə, thus bə'fɔː, prə'vɛnt, etc. In Southern and South-Western dialectal speech they often have iː or its dialectal equivalent: biː'foːə (South Western biː'foːɹ), diː'livə (S.W. diː'livɹ), riː'zʌlt.[1] The same may often be heard in *eleven* (RP i'lɛvn, S.W. iː'lɛvn).

§ 81. The suffixes *-less*, *-ness*, *-est* are treated similarly. The usual forms of *careless*, *goodness*, *greatest* in RP are 'kɛəlis, 'gudnis, 'greitist, but 'kɛələs, 'gudnəs, 'greitəst may also be heard. The same applies to some of the words ending in *-ace*, *-ate*, *-ain*, *-et*. For instance, *furnace*, *private*, *fountain*, *basket* are generally pronounced 'fəːnis, 'praivit, 'fauntin, 'bɑːskit, but occasionally 'fəːnəs, 'praivət, 'fauntən, 'bɑːskət. It would seem that the termination *-age* in older words is nearly always pronounced with i except in dialect: 'kabidʒ (*cabbage*).[2] The feminine suffix *-ess* is generally -is, as for instance in 'houstis (*hostess*); but is strongly stressed and has the vowel ɛ in prin'sɛs (*princess*).[3] *Manageress* is usually 'manidʒə'rɛs, but 'manidʒəris may also be heard.[4]

---

[1] The strong prefixes *de-* (meaning undoing), *pre-* (before), *re-* (again) are pronounced with iː in RP: 'diːkəm'pouz (*decompose*), 'priː'neitl (*prenatal*), 'riː'rait (*rewrite*).

[2] In various newer words of French origin the sound is -ɑːʒ, e.g. 'bɑrɑːʒ (*barrage*).

[3] Attributively 'prinsɛs, as in 'prinsɛs vik'tɔːrïə (*Princess Victoria*).

[4] Further information on this subject will be found in Section XXII of the Explanations in the author's *English Pronouncing Dictionary*, 1956 and subsequent editions.

§ 82. ə is an alternative to i in words like *ability* (ə'biliti or ə'biləti), *policy* ('pɔlisi or 'pɔləsi).

§ 83. The weak prefix *ex-* is generally pronounced with i in the South but with ɛ in the North. For instance, *expect*, *example* are pronounced iks'pɛkt, ig'zɑːmpl in the South but ɛks'pɛkt, ɛg'zampl in the North. The same applies to the endings of *subject* and *object* which are commonly pronounced 'sʌbdʒikt, 'ɔbdʒikt in the South[1] but 'sʌbdʒɛkt, 'ɔbdʒɛkt in the North.

§ 84. Some words are said with i by some, but with ɑi by others. Such are *composite* ('kɔmpəzit or 'kɔmpəzait) and the proper name *Caroline* (more commonly 'karəlain but also 'karəlin). Sometimes one or the other definitely does not belong to RP. For instance 'rɛptil (for 'rɛptail, *reptile*) is Northern and American, but on the other hand 'ɔpəzait and 'ɔpəsait (for 'ɔpəzit or 'ɔpəsit, *opposite*) belong to London dialect.

§ 85. The penultimate *i* of *-sity* and *-city* is often not sounded. People often say for instance ilas'tisti for ilas'tisiti (*elasticity*). This reduced pronunciation is particularly common in the word juːni'vəːsti (*university*). The full pronunciation -siti, with a variant -səti, is usual in the rarer words.

§ 86. Some people slightly diphthongize the short i by adding a trace of ə in certain final syllables, and particularly before a final t, d, n, s or z. E.g. hiᵊt, diᵊd, tiᵊn, miᵊs, hiᵊz, for hit, did, tin, mis, hiz (*hit, did, tin, miss, his*). This may be because they make these final consonants rather 'dark' (like final l, see § 296).

§ 87. i occurs in RP as the initial part of the diphthong iə. Example hiə (*here, hear*). See § 198.

---

[1] Compare 'insɛkt (*insect*), 'aspɛkt (*aspect*).

§ 88. ɛ, No. 3 of RP. Between half-close and half-open, front, unrounded (see Fig. 12). Examples: pɛn (*pen*), hɛd (*head*).

§ 89. The vowel in such words varies considerably with individuals. Some use an almost half-close e (pen, hed); this often gives the effect of a very precise pronunciation. Others use a much opener sound. In the North it is usual to say these words with cardinal ɛ or even an opener sound than this. In London dialectal speech a variety of close e is used in many words; *get*, for instance, is geʔ.

§ 90. In the South slight diphthongization towards ə may often be observed in certain positions, and especially before final t, d, n, s. This is particularly common in the word *again* which is often pronounced ə'gɛᵊn (for ə'gɛn or ə'gein). It may also be heard in such words as *set*, *head*, *desk* (sɛᵊt for sɛt, etc.). This slightly diphthongized sound is kept apart from the full diphthong ɛə (§ 203).

§ 91. a, No. 4 of RP. Intermediate between half-open and open, front, unrounded (see Fig. 12). Examples: man (*man*), pak (*pack*).

§ 92. Here again different people use different shades of vowel. Many in the South use a sound just about half-way between cardinal ɛ and a. (This sound is often denoted phonetically by the symbol æ.) With others the sound is between this and cardinal a. In the North, cardinal a is very commonly heard. In Scottish speech many varieties are used, the most frequent being round about cardinal a. The difference between the Scottish and Southern English a is particularly noticeable in some words, for instance ['gaðɪr] (*gather*), [sʌb'stanʃl] (*substantial*), ['kaʒjuɪl] (*casual*), ['famɪle] (*family*), [naʃn̩'alɪte] (*nationality*), [ɪ'taljɪn] (*Italian*). In Scottish dialectal speech a definitely back ɑ appears to be in common use (mɑn, pɑk, 'gɑðɪr, etc.).

§ 92 a. In RP when **a** precedes a 'dark' l, a lowered and retracted variety of the vowel is used. Compare for instance the **a** of 'kalkjuleit (*calculate*) with that of kat (*cat*).

§ 93. In the South it is not uncommon to hear a slight diphthongization towards ə similar to that of i and ɛ (§§ 86, 90) in syllables ending in t, d, n, s, z: kaᵊt for kat (*cat*), glaᵊd for glad (*glad*), maᵊn for man (*man*), gaᵊs for gas (*gas*), haᵊz for haz (*has*),[1] etc.

§ 94. ɑ (written ɑː when long, as is generally the case), No. 5 of RP. Open, nearer to back than front, lips neutral (see Fig. 12). Examples: 'fɑːðə (*father, farther*), stɑː (*star*).

§ 95. Here again different shades of sound are used by different speakers. In the genuine London dialects the sound used in such words is a fully back ɑː. Some Londoners, however, go to the other extreme and use a fairly front variety (aː). In New Zealand too a rather front aː is commonly used.

§ 96. In the North no difference is, as a rule, made corresponding to that between the Southern ɑː and a. *Psalm* and *Sam* are pronounced alike, with a vowel near to cardinal a.

§ 97. Those in the North who make a difference generally use a short sound approximating to the Southern a in many words spelt with *a* followed by *nt, nd, nce, f, th, s*. They say plant, kə'mand, dans, 'aftə(r), paθ, gras where most users of RP would say plɑːnt, kə'mɑːnd, dɑːns, 'ɑːftə, pɑːθ, grɑːs (*plant, command, dance, after, path, grass*).

§ 98. Some Southern people use a diphthong ɑə in place of ɑː, especially when final, e.g. fɑə for the more usual fɑː (*far*).

§ 99. In the West and North-West it is usual to make a distinction between words which are and are not spelt with the

---

[1] Strong form. (See §§ 154-6.)

letter *r* (finally or before a consonant) by giving 'r-colouring' (§ 355) to the vowel in the former case. This is effected either by curling the tip of the tongue backwards while the vowel is being pronounced, or by retracting the whole tongue in such a way as to leave a considerable space between the tip and the lower teeth. (The sounds produced by these two methods are acoustically indistinguishable from each other.) Representing r-colouring by adding ɹ, this way of pronouncing *farther* would be written 'fɑɹðər (compare RP 'fɑːðə). See further §§ 355, 356 and Figs. 34, 35.

§ 100. ɔ, No. 6 of RP. Nearly open, back with slight lip-rounding (see Fig. 12). Examples: hɔt (*hot*), lɔŋ (*long*).

§ 101. Some, especially in the West, use a sound of similar tongue position but without lip-rounding, i.e. a variety of ɑ (short). In American English our short ɔ is represented by a variety of ɑ (generally a middle one, between cardinal ɑ and a) in some words, and by a sound similar in quality to our long ɔː in other words. For instance Americans commonly pronounce *hot, office, operate, Oxford* with ɑ [hɑt, 'ɑfəs, 'ɑpɹet, 'ɑksfɹd], but *long* and *dog* with their variety of ɔ [lɔŋ, dɔg]. In both cases the length of the vowel is variable in American speech.

§ 102. In Scotland the sound commonly used in all such words is about cardinal ɔ.

§ 103. Occasionally RP speakers pronounce words containing weakly stressed ɔ alternatively with the monophthongal o-sound referred to in § 173. For instance *torrential* which is generally tɔ'renʃl or tə'renʃl is sometimes pronounced to'renʃl. This, being an unstable pronunciation (§ 173), cannot be considered as characteristic of RP.

§ 103 a. The word *because* (which is normally bi'kɔz) is sometimes pronounced with an unstressed ə (bikəz) or even with a stressed ə (bi'kəz).

§ 104. ɔː, No. 7 of RP. Intermediate between open and half-open, back, rounded (see Fig. 12). Examples: sɔː (*saw, soar, sore*), θɔːt (*thought*), hɔːs (*horse, hoarse*).

§ 105. Many words spelt with *of, os, oth* are pronounced by some with ɔ and by others with ɔː. Such are ɔf or ɔːf (*off*), ˈɔfn or ˈɔfən or ˈɔftən or ˈɔːfn or ˈɔːfən or ˈɔːftən (*often*), krɔs or krɔːs (*cross*), lɔst or lɔːst (*lost*). Formerly the pronunciation with ɔː was very common; now the pronunciation with ɔ is much the more usual, except possibly in *off, often*. The same applies to words written with *aust-* such as ɔsˈtreiljə or ɔːsˈtreiljə (*Australia*). A few words written with *a* have a similar variation of pronunciation, except that the pronunciation with ɔː is probably more frequent than the pronunciation with ɔ. The chief words in this category are sɔːlt or sɔlt (*salt*) and fɔːls or fɔls (*false*). gɔn (*gone*) is pronounced gɔːn by some, but this pronunciation seems to be becoming old-fashioned or restricted to dialectal speech.

§ 106. Some people substitute ɔə (§ 210) for ɔː in many of the words written with *r*, e.g. sɔə (*sore, soar*) but sɔː (*saw*), flɔə (*floor*) but flɔː (*flaw*), kɔəs (*course, coarse*) but kɔːz (*cause*). Some do this only in final position. Others use ɔə in final position when the spelling has *ore, oar, our, oor* but ɔː when the spelling has *or*; they distinguish between fɔə (*four, fore*) and fɔː (*for*), tɔə (*tore*) and tɔː (*tor*). ɔə may also sometimes be heard in words spelt with *au* and *aw*, but this pronunciation must probably be regarded as dialectal.

§ 107. Some words containing weakly stressed ɔː have an alternative pronunciation with the monophthongal o-sound referred to in § 173. *Information*, for instance, is generally pronounced infəˈmeiʃn, but has alternative forms infɔːˈmeiʃn and (occasionally) infoˈmeiʃn. This latter pronunciation is unstable (§ 173) and cannot be considered as characteristic of RP. So also with *auricula* (əˈrikjulə, ɔːˈrikjulə, also -kjələ, and occasionally oˈrik-).

§ **108.** In London dialect ɔː is replaced by a closer and more rounded sound which may be written [oː] or by a diphthong [oːə]. *Saw* is pronounced [soː] or sometimes [soːə], *four* is pronounced [foːə]. Some Londoners use a disyllabic sound resembling owə, e.g. 'fowə (for *four*).

§ **109.** In the West and North-West it is usual to make a distinction between words which are and are not spelt with the letter *r* by giving 'r-colouring' to the vowel in the former case. This is effected by the means described in §§ 99, 355.

§ **110.** In Scotland the RP ɔː is generally replaced by the Scottish [o] (§ 169) in the words spelt with *ore, oar, our, oor* and in the following words spelt with *or*: *afford, ford, horde, sword, fort, port* (and the compounds *export, important, proportion,* etc.), *sport, forth, divorce, force, borne, sworn, torn, worn, forge, pork.* Examples of this Scottish use of close o are [mor] (*more*), [bord] (*board*), [kors] (*course*), [flor] (*floor*), [port] (*port*), [fors] (*force*). ɔ is always used in Scottish speech in the words written with *au, aw, ou,* such as *caught, saw, Lawrence, thought,* in *warn* and *quartz,* and in the following words written with *or*: *cord* (and compounds *record,* etc.), *chord, lord, order, form* (and *reform,* etc.), *border, storm, adorn, born, corn, horn, morn(ing), scorn, shorn, cork, fork, stork, York, sort* (and compounds *resort,* etc.), *short, snort, north, George, gorge, horse, gorse, remorse, corpse, forty, fortify.* Examples of this Scottish use of open ɔ are [fɔr] (*for*),[1] [bɔrn] (*born*), [kɔrd] (*cord*).

§ **111.** In the speech of many from the West of England and in Ireland, where *r* final or before a consonant is pronounced ɹ, o and ɔ are used in precisely the same words.[2] Thus moːɹ, boɹd, etc., and poɹt, foɹs, etc., but fɔɹ (*for*),[3] bɔɹn (*born*), kɔɹd, etc.

---

[1] Strong form. [2] With occasional individual exceptions.
[3] Strong form.

§ 112. It will be noticed that Scottish and Western speech distinguishes some words which are not distinguished in RP. Examples: Scottish ['bordɪr] (*boarder*), ['bɔrdɪr] (*border*), ['mornɪŋ] (*mourning*), ['mɔrnɪŋ] (*morning*), [worn] (*worn*), [wɔrn] (*warn*). In RP the words are pronounced 'bɔːdə, 'mɔːnɪŋ, wɔːn.

§ 113. In the North-East, too, o is used in some words written with *or* and ɔ is used in others. The distribution of the two sounds differs, however, to some extent from that of Scotland and the West, and there are many variations of usage between individual speakers.

§ 114. People may occasionally be met with who do not sound *r*'s finally or before consonants but who make vowel differences corresponding to those mentioned in the preceding paragraphs. They have two kinds of ɔː, a closer one which may be represented by [oː] as well as the ordinary ɔː. They distinguish for instance soːd (*sword*) from sɔːd (*sawed*).

§ 115. In words where the vowel is not followed by r Scottish people whose pronunciation has not been influenced by Southern speech make no difference corresponding to the Southern difference ɔ ɔː. They use in all cases the Scottish [ɔ] which is about cardinal No. 6. For instance, they make *knotty* and *naughty* identical in sound ['nɔte], also *cot* and *caught* [kɔt]; *want* is made to rhyme with *haunt* [wɔnt, hɔnt] and *clock* with *talk* [klɔk, tɔk], and so on.

§ 116. In the North of England ɔ replaces RP ʌ in a few words, and notably in wɔn for RP wʌn (*one*), 'nɔθɪŋ (*nothing*) for RP 'nʌθɪŋ.

§ 117. Some Americans use ʌ in some words where British English has ɔ. Such are *what*, *of* (American hwʌt, ʌv,[1] British

---

[1] Strong form.

(h)wɔt, ɔv[1]). Other American forms of these words are hwɑt, əv,[1] hwat, av.

§ 118. u, No. 8 of RP. Between close and half-close, back, with medium lip-rounding; see Fig. 12. Examples: gud (*good*), put (*put*), wul (*wool*). Also used by some in words like pru'siːd (*proceed*), hu'raizn (*horizon*), for the more usual prə'siːd, hə'raizn.

§ 119. Some Southern people use an unrounded u (phonetically ɯ) in a few words, e.g. gɯd for gud (*good*), lɯk for luk (*look*), especially when they are used interjectionally. The conditions under which this variant is employed have not yet been ascertained.

§ 120. In parts of the North short u is replaced by a partially unrounded o (phonetic symbol ɤ). In Scotland both short u and long uː are commonly replaced by a short 'advanced' u (ü). For these see § 124.

§ 121. uː, No. 9 of RP. Nearly close, back, rounded (see Fig. 12). Examples: muːn (*moon*), tʃuːz (*choose*), ruːd (*rude*).

§ 122. Many RP speakers use in place of uː a diphthongal sound which may be represented by uw, thus muwn, tʃuwz, ruwd. This diphthongal pronunciation is particularly noticeable in final position, as in tuw (*too, two*).

§ 123. In London dialectal speech a much 'wider' diphthong is used. It starts with a central sound, a variety of ə or ï,[2] and moves towards u or, more often, towards an advanced ü (Figs. 16, 17). Thus: məün, tʃəüz, rəüd, tˢəu, 'əü ə 'jəü (*who are you?*), or mïün, tʃïüz, etc.

---

[1] Strong form.
[2] ï (also written phonetically ɨ) denotes a sound intermediate between ɯ (§ 119) and i. It has the same tongue position as ü, but the lips are spread.

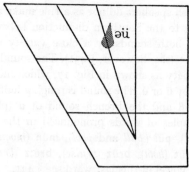

Fig. 16. Diagram illustrating the formation of the diphthong əü of London dialect.

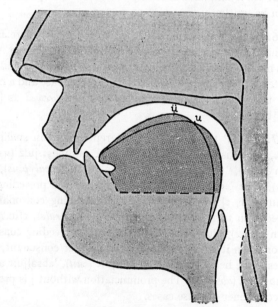

Fig. 17. Tongue position of ü compared with that of cardinal u.

§ **124.** Scottish speakers do not as a rule make any difference corresponding to the Southern distinction between u and uː. They replace both sounds by a close variety of u which is generally short (see, however, § 431). The sound is usually an advanced variety as shown in Fig. 17, which may be denoted phonetically by ü or ʉ. The sound is roughly half-way between cardinal No. 8 and the French sound of *u* (phonetically y, § 482). Examples of words pronounced in the Scottish way are güd (*good*), pül (*pull* and *pool*), mün (*moon*), rüd (*rude*), bük (*book*), büt (*boot*), brüz (*bruise*), brüːz (*brews*). For the length of the vowel in this last word see § 431.

§ **125.** In a simplified transcription of Scottish pronunciation ü can be written u. See text on p. 205.

§ **126.** Some Americans use an advanced u (ü) where British RP has uː. Crooners adopt this pronunciation. Some Americans make a distinction between words spelt with *oo* and those written with *ew*, using a back u in the former case and a central ü in the latter; they distinguish *brood* and *brewed* as [brud] and [brüd].

§ **127.** In RP the sound uː when represented in spelling by *u, eu, ew, ui* is often preceded by j. Examples: juːz (*use*, v.), tjuːn (*tune*), 'mjuːzik (*music*), juːkə'liptəs (*eucalyptus*),[1] njuː (*new*), sjuːt (*suit*). j is not inserted when the preceding consonant is r, tʃ, or dʒ, or when the preceding consonant is l preceded in turn by a consonant, e.g. ruːl (*rule*), tʃuː (*chew*), dʒuːn (*June*), bluː (*blue, blew*). When the preceding consonant is s or when it is l not preceded by another consonant, usage varies. One hears suːt as well as sjuːt (*suit*), 'absəljuːt as well as 'absəluːt (*absolute*). The pronunciation without j is probably the commoner in these cases.

---

[1] Also pronounced juːkə'liptəs (with short u).

§ 128. Welsh people use juː or iu after r, tʃ, dʒ or consonant +l, e.g. tʃjuː or tʃiu for RP tʃuː, bljuː or bliu for RP bluː.

§ 129. Some Londoners use a diphthong iu in place of juː in some of the words mentioned in § 127, e.g. 'miuzik for 'mjuːzik.

§ 130. Some of the words spelt with *oo* are pronounced with uː by some Southern speakers and with u by others. Notable among them are *room*, *broom* and *groom*. These words are pronounced rum, brum, grum by many and especially by older people; but ruːm, bruːm, gruːm appear to be the commoner forms now. sun is a not uncommon variant of suːn (*soon*), and ruf, huf and tuθ may occasionally be heard for ruːf (*roof*), huːf (*hoof*), tuːθ (*tooth*). In the North, too, there are variations in pronunciation of the *oo* words; kuːk may be heard for kuk (*cook*) in Lancashire, while those with a Yorkshire accent commonly use ɤ (§§ 120 and 133) in the words which have u in the South, such as hɤd for hud (*hood*), fɤl for ful (*full*).

§ 131. ʌ, No. 10 of RP. Half-open, central, unrounded (see Fig. 12). Examples: kʌp (*cup*), dʌl (*dull*), 'mʌðə (*mother*).

§ 132. The vowel in such words varies both locally and with individuals. In London dialectal speech the sound used is near to cardinal No. 4 [a], i.e. an open front vowel, thus [kap], [dal], ['maðə or 'mavə], ['batəkap] (*buttercup*); and in the South generally there is a tendency among many to use a rather forward variety of ʌ.

§ 133. In the North a 'backer' variety is generally heard. So also in America. Sometimes, especially in Yorkshire, the sound used is so 'back' as to be reminiscent of u from which it is believed to have been derived.[1] This Yorkshire sound is a nearly unrounded o (phonetically ɤ).

---

[1] See article on Shakespeare's pronunciation in *English Pronunciation through the Centuries*, p. 39 (published by the Linguaphone Institute).

§ 134. People with a pronounced Yorkshire accent use ɤ not only in place of RP ʌ but also in place of RP u. Examples: kɤp, dɤl, 'fɤni (*funny*), gɤd (*good*), fɤl (*full*). See § 130.

§ 135. In Lancashire both ʌ and u are heard, but the distribution of these sounds is not always the same as in RP. For instance the pronunciation 'bʌtʃə(r) for RP 'butʃə (*butcher*) is common there.

§ 136. Many Southern speakers use ə for ʌ in *such* and in the adverb *just*, even when they are strongly stressed: thus sətʃ, dʒəst for the normal sʌtʃ, dʒʌst. The adjective *just* is not altered in this way; it is always dʒʌst in the South. *Such, just* and *because* (§ 103 a) are probably the only words in which a stressed short ə is at all common.

§ 137. With very many Midland and Northern speakers there is no ʌ distinct from ə. *Come up at once* is pronounced 'kəm 'əp ət 'wəns. Those who speak in this way do not make the distinction generally heard in the South between 'hʌri (*hurry*) and 'fəːri (*furry*),[1] 'tʌrit (*turret*) and 'əːriŋ (*erring*); they say 'həri, 'fəri, 'tərit, 'əriŋ. Many Americans pronounce similarly.

§ 138. In a number of words written with *o* some RP speakers use ʌ and others ɔ. Examples: 'drʌmədəri or 'drɔmədəri (*dromedary*), ə'kʌmpliʃ or ə'kɔmpliʃ (*accomplish*), 'brʌm(p)tən or 'brɔm(p)tən (*Brompton*). The forms with ʌ are probably older, and the forms with ɔ modern 'spelling pronunciations'. The latter are becoming increasingly common and are likely eventually to supersede the pronunciation with ʌ in many of the words. *Wont* is now generally pronounced wount, like *won't*, but wɔnt may occasionally be heard. A pronunciation wʌnt is still to be found in dictionaries, though it does not appear to be used any longer, at any rate in the South.

---

[1] Some Southerners pronounce *furry* as 'fʌri.

§ **139.** əː, RP No. 11. Between half-close and half-open, central, unrounded (see Fig. 12). Examples: fəː (*fir, fur*), bəːd (*bird*), ˈkəːnl (*kernel, colonel*).

§ **140.** Various shades of this sound may be heard from different RP speakers, closer and opener varieties being quite common and not restricted to any particular districts. A closer variety may be represented phonetically thus əⱥː (fəⱥː, bəⱥːd, etc.), and an opener one thus əᴛː (fəᴛː, bəᴛːd, etc.). A particularly open variety resembling a lengthened ʌ may often be heard in London (fʌː, bʌːd, etc.). At the other extreme is an almost close sound, not far from ɯː (unrounded uː), thus fɯː, bɯːd, etc. The use of this last sound appears to be confined to people with experience of public speaking; its existence is difficult to account for.

§ **141.** In the West and North-West the RP əː is generally represented by a central vowel with 'r-colouring' or 'retroflexion', which may be denoted phonetically by the letter ɹ, thus fɹː, bɹːd, and so on. Words like *furry, stirring* (RP ˈfəːri, ˈstəːriŋ) are pronounced in these parts ˈfɹːi, ˈstɹːiŋ.[1]

§ **142.** A similar pronunciation is usual in America, except that the American retroflexed vowel is a distinctly closer variety than that heard in England.

§ **143.** In Scotland the əː of RP is variously represented. In words written with *ir* its place is commonly taken by ɪr (i.e. an ə-like ɪ followed by a flapped or slightly rolled r, or, with some Scottish speakers, a fricative r). Examples: fɪr (*fir*), bɪrd (*bird*), θɪrst (*thirst*). ɛr is generally used in words written with *er* and *ear*, and ʌr in words written with *ur*. Examples: fɛrn (*fern*), ˈɛrle (*early*) and fʌr (*fur*), tʌrn (*turn*). There are, however, Scottish speakers, especially in Edinburgh, who

---

[1] Compare *string*, the pronunciation of which would be transcribed striŋ.

47

do not make these distinctions, but use ər in all cases, i.e. in fərn, 'ərle, fər (*fur*), tərn (*turn*), fər (*fir*), bərd, θərst, tərn (*tern*).

§ **144.** ə, RP No. 12. RP speakers make use of several distinguishable varieties of this sound, their use depending upon the phonetic context. The quality of the commonest one is practically indistinguishable from that of əː (RP No. 11), but it is very short and consequently difficult to analyse with precision. We may say that it is, like əː, between half-close and half-open, central and unrounded (see Fig. 12). Examples of this variety: ə'lɔŋ (*along*), ə'tak (*attack*), sə'praiz (*surprise*), 'moumənt (*moment*), 'mɛθəd (*method*), 'greiʃəs (*gracious*).

§ **145.** An opener variety is generally used in final positions, as when the following words are said by themselves: 'ouvə (*over*), 'mʌðə (*mother*), 'soufə (*sofa*), 'tʃainə (*China*). With many Southern speakers ʌ is substituted in such words, thus 'ouvʌ, 'mʌðʌ, 'soufʌ, 'tʃainʌ. A less open variety appears to be usual finally when ʃ, ʒ, tʃ or dʒ precedes, as in 'eiʃə (*Asia*), 'plɛʒə (*pleasure*), 'fəːnitʃə (*furniture*), 'laːdʒə (*larger*).

§ **146.** In some non-final positions, and especially when next to k or g, a very close variety of ə is fairly commonly used. This sound approximates to the close central vowel which we represent by i̇ or ï (see footnote 2 to § 123). Examples: kəm'pɛl (*compel*), 'bak əgein (*back again*), tə 'gou (*to go*). The precise shade of ə used in such cases is not of much consequence, as long as the sound is a fairly close variety. The words would, however, not sound right if a much opener sound like that mentioned in § 145 were employed.

§ **147.** In many regions, especially in the West and North-West of England and in America, ə is replaced by an 'r-coloured' ə when the spelling has *r* finally or followed by a consonant. The 'r-colouring' is effected either by 'retroflexion' (also called 'inversion') which means curling backwards the tip of the tongue, or by contracting the tongue laterally (§ 489) and retracting the whole body of the tongue in such a way as to leave a considerable gap between the tip of the tongue and the lower teeth (Fig. 35). This retroflexion takes place simultaneously with the vowel articulation. Retroflexed ə may be represented by the digraph əɹ or more simply by ɹ alone. Examples: tə'gɛðɹ (*together*), 'ouvɹ[1] (*over*), 'standɹd (*standard*), 'hɹːbɹt[2] (*Herbert*).

§ **148.** It can be said as a general rule[3] that ə occurs only in syllables with weak stress. It is often used in syllables where ordinary spelling and the pronunciation of cognate words would suggest some other vowel. Compare

'moumənt (*moment*)	mou'mɛntəs or mə'mɛntəs (*momentous*)
'mirəkl (*miracle*)	mi'rakjuləs (*miraculous*)
'vinjəd (*vineyard*)	jaːd (*yard*)
'foutəgraːf or 'foutəgraf (*photograph*)	fə'tɔgrəfi (*photography*)
'kʌbəd (*cupboard*)	bɔːd (*board*)
'gladstən (*Gladstone*)	stoun (*stone*)
'prɔvəb[4] (*proverb*)	prə'vəːbjəl (*proverbial*)
'sʌbstəns (*substance*)	səb'stanʃ(ə)l (*substantial*)

§ **149.** Written *i* is not often pronounced ə, but it has this value in the commoner words written with *-ible*, such as 'pɔsəbl (*possible*), 'hɔrəbl (*horrible*), əd'misəbl (*admissible*), 'fiːzəbl (*feasible*). Some pronounce these words with -ibl.[5] The

---

[1] American ['ovɹ].   [2] American ['hɹbɹt].
[3] Subject to the exceptional cases mentioned in §§ 103*a*, 136.
[4] Also 'prɔvəːb.
[5] Including the words *feasible* and *responsible* in which from the point of view of derivation (from French *faisable*, *responsable*) -əbl would be more appropriate.

termination -*ity* is pronounced -iti by some and -əti by others:
e.g. ə'biliti or ə'biləti (*ability*).

§ **150.** As already mentioned in §§ 80, 81, ə is used by many in
prefixes and suffixes like *be-, re-, pre-, -less, -ness, -est*, where the
more usual Southern pronunciation has i. Examples: bi'fɔː or
bə'fɔː (*before*), ri'mein or rə'mein (*remain*), pri'vɛnt or prə'vɛnt
(*prevent*), 'waiəlis or 'waiələs (*wireless*), 'gudnis or 'gudnəs
(*goodness*), 'bigist or 'bigəst (*biggest*). Also in words like
'ɔːkistrə or 'ɔːkəstrə (*orchestra*), 'kariktə or 'karəktə (*character*).
The forms with i are probably the more usual in the South,
but the pronunciation with ə seems to be gaining ground.

§ **151.** Words with the prefixes *con-* and *ob-* are pronounced in
the South with ə when the following syllable has strong stress.
Examples: kən'tein (*contain*), kən'vɛnʃ(ə)n (*convention*), əb'zəːv
(*observe*). In the North it is usual to pronounce these words with
ɔ (kɔn'tein, ɔb'zəːv or ɔb'zɛɹv, etc.). This pronunciation may
also sometimes be heard in the South in very formal speech, but
it is doubtful if it really makes for clearness; it is true that the
prefix sounds clearer, but at the same time this pronunciation
detracts from the more important syllable that follows.

§ **152.** Words like ək'nɔlidʒ (*acknowledge*), səb'stanʃ(ə)l (*substantial*), sək'sɛs (*success*) are treated similarly. Forms such as
ak'nɔlɛdʒ, sʌb'stanʃ(ə)l, sʌk'sɛs are used in the North. In the
South they are only heard in very formal speech; they are apt
to sound artificial, as giving undue prominence to the less
important syllables.

§ **153.** Characteristic Scottish speech as exemplified in Text
No. 17 (p. 205) differs from Southern English in having no ə.
In positions where ə would be employed in Southern English
a Scotsman will use one of his normal vowels, generally ʌ or ɪ.
Thus *in a minute* may be heard as [ɪn ʌ 'mɪnɪt], *take it away* as
['tek ɪt ʌ'we], *rather* as ['raðɪr], *the book* as [ðɪ 'buk], *there is* as

[ðɪr 'ɪz]. (Southern English in ə 'minit, 'teik it ə'wei, 'rɑːðə, ðə buk, ðər 'iz.) Note also the Scottish expression 'amɪnt ae (=Southern 'ɑːnt ai, *an't I?*)

§ 153 a. Being unable to pronounce əː, most Scotsmen when they hesitate utter the sound eː.

Strong and weak Forms

§ 154. Many words have two pronunciations which are called 'strong' and 'weak' forms. In most of these cases the weak form contains ə, while the strong form contains some other vowel. Whether a word is pronounced in the strong way or in the weak way depends on the kind of sentence in which it occurs.

§ 155. The chief words which have a weak form containing ə are *a, am, an, and, are, as, at, can, could, do, does, for, from, had, has, have, must, of, or, Saint, shall, should, some, than, that, the, there, to, us, was, were, would.*

§ 156. Examples of the use of strong and weak forms:

	Strong form	Weak form
at	'wɔt ə juː 'lukiŋ at?	ai m 'lukiŋ ət ðat 'triː
	What are you looking at?	*I'm looking at that tree*
of	'wɔt 'ɔv it?	'wɔt əv 'ðat?
	What of it?	*What of that?*
have	hiː l 'hav tə 'finiʃ it tə'mɔrou	hiː l əv 'finiʃt bai 'nau
	He'll have to finish it to-morrow	*He'll have finished by now*
for	'wɔt did juː 'duː it fɔː?	ai 'did it fə 'fʌn
	What did you do it for?	*I did it for fun*
	'fɔː(r) ənd ə'gɛnst[1]	'wʌns fər 'ɔːl
	For and against	*Once for all*

---

[1] Also ə'geinst.

Strong form	Weak form
would 'jɛs, ai 'wud	it əd bi ə 'vɛri gud 'θiŋ
Yes, I would	*It would be a very good thing*
Saint ə 'seint	sənt[1] 'pɔːlz
A saint	*St Paul's*

§ 157. *A, an* and the relative pronoun *that* are almost always said with weak forms (ə, ən, ðət). Examples: ə 'man (*a man*), ən 'ɑːm (*an arm*), ðə 'buk ðət wəz ɔn ðə 'teibl (*the book that was on the table*). Strong forms ei, an, ðat exist, but are hardly ever used except when speaking about these words, as in 'ei iz 'wʌn fɔːm əv ði 'in'dɛfinit 'ɑːtikl (*A is one form of the indefinite article*). The conjunction *that* is almost always pronounced ðət, except in very formal speech; example: 'nɔt ðət ai 'nou ɔv (*not that I know of*).

§ 158. *The* is pronounced ðiː by itself, ði before vowels, as in ði 'apl (*the apple*), ði 'ɔːdə (*the order*),[2] but ðə before consonants, as in ðə 'taim (*the time*), ðə 'buk (*the book*).

§ 159. Among small words which only have strong forms may be specially mentioned *on* and *then* (ɔn, ðɛn). There are other small words having weak forms which are used only rarely or in special expressions. For instance, *by* is generally said in its strong form bai, but many use a weak form bə in a few special expressions such as 'sɛliŋ ðəm bə ðə 'paund (*selling them by the pound*).

Diphthongs

CLOSING DIPHTHONGS

§ 160. ei, RP No. 13. Examples: dei (*day*), meik (*make*). Several varieties of this diphthong can be regarded as belonging to RP. A very common one begins at about half-way between

---

[1] Or sn 'pɔːlz, or snt 'pɔːlz, or sin(t) 'pɔːlz, also sm 'pɔːlz.

[2] Also ðiː, especially when the following vowel is iː or i, e.g. ði 'iːst or ðiː 'iːst (*the east*), ði 'iŋk or ðiː 'iŋk (*the ink*).

the half-close and half-open positions (that is, between cardinal vowels Nos. 2 and 3) and moves upwards in the direction of i (see Fig. 13). The starting-point is a little higher than that of the ε described in § 88 (Fig. 12). The lips are spread. The movement of the tongue is easily felt if one repeats the diphthong ei a number of times in succession.

§ **161.** Other 'received' (i.e. non-dialectal) varieties start somewhat higher and somewhat lower than this common sound. A variety which may be written εi belongs therefore to RP, provided that the ε is not a very low variety.

§ **162.** Another variety which has in recent years become very frequent among RP speakers is a 'narrow' kind of diphthong (i.e. one in which there is not much movement) starting with a vowel nearer to cardinal No. 3 than to cardinal No. 2. It might be represented by the notation εe. With some it is almost a monophthongal ε:. This variety may often be observed in the speech of B.B.C. announcers, and is particularly noticeable in the frequently recurring word tə'dεe or tə'dε: (alternatives for tə'dei, *today*).

§ **163.** Yet another sound which may be heard from RP speakers is a diphthong beginning with a retracted variety of ε, i.e. one tending to central articulation. This may be represented phonetically by ε₋i or ɐi.

§ **164.** In dialectal speech the sound corresponding to RP ei varies within very wide limits. In Scotland and often in the North of England the sound is replaced by a monophthongal e:.[1] In the North, too, one often hears a diphthong of the ei type beginning with a 'tense' e, i.e. cardinal No. 2 or a sound near to this. In Southern dialectal speech on the other hand the tendency is to use 'wide' diphthongs (i.e. diphthongs

---

[1] Not necessarily long in Scotland, see § 431.

showing considerable movement) beginning with cardinal No. 3 or vowels opener than this. In London dialectal speech, for instance, the sound is often aᴧi (æi) or even ai, thus daᴧi or dai for *day*, maᴧi? or mai? for *make*. In New Zealand English there is a diphthong of the ɛi-type ending with a close i.

§ **165.** In RP when ei is followed by ə, as in 'pleiə (*player*), the diphthong is 'narrower' than usual. The whole sequence may even be levelled to a centring diphthong eə, thus pleə for 'pleiə. It is distinct from the diphthong ɛə described in § 203.

§ **166.** ou, RP No. 14. Examples gou (*go*), roud (*road*). Here, too, several varieties may be regarded as belonging to RP. One of the most frequent starts at a point in advance of the back position and about half-way between the half-close and half-open positions, as shown in Fig. 13; at the beginning of the sound the lips are slightly rounded. As the sound proceeds the organs move in the direction of u, that is to say the back of the tongue rises slightly and the lips become more rounded. These movements can be observed by repeating the diphthong ou a number of times in succession.

§ **167.** Various divergences from this may be heard from RP speakers. The starting-point of the tongue is with some a little higher, with others somewhat lower, with others more advanced (central); there are also differences in the degree of lip-rounding with which the sound begins. There are thus RP variants tending towards ɔu and əu. Pronunciations such as gəu, rəud can hardly be regarded as outside the range of RP.

§ **168.** The use of an ɔu beginning with cardinal No. 6 or any opener sound (gɔu, rɔud) must probably be considered dialectal, though sounds of this type may sometimes be heard from distinguished public speakers.

§ **169.** In dialectal speech many other divergences are found. In Scotland the sound used is not a diphthong but a pure [o], about cardinal No. 7; *go* and *road* are pronounced [go], [rod], and *rowed* is [ro:d]. A similar sound is also common in the North of England; it may be represented by o:, since it is definitely long and its length does not vary like that of the Scottish o (§ 431). In the North, too, one may often hear a diphthong of the ou type beginning at about cardinal No. 7.

§ **170.** In dialectal speech of the London region the ou sounds of RP are replaced by diphthongs starting with lower tongue positions and without lip-rounding, i.e. sounds of the type ʌu and au, e.g. gʌu, rʌud or gau, raud.

§ **171.** Some Southern speakers use a more 'central' diphthong than that described in § 166. It may be denoted phonetically by öü. A variant of this starts without lip-rounding, phonetically ëü, and yet another is an almost front sound, phonetically øy. Sounds of these types are said, probably incorrectly, to belong to the 'Oxford accent', or are considered to be 'affected'.[1]

§ **172.** It is a useful exercise for students of speech to practise saying such a sentence as *Oh no, I don't know* with the various sounds described above: 'ou 'nou ai 'dount 'nou, 'əu 'nəu ai 'dəunt 'nəu, 'o: 'no: ai 'do:nt 'no:, 'ʌu 'nʌu ai 'dʌunt 'nʌu, 'öü 'nöü ai 'döünt 'nöü, etc.

§ **173.** Sometimes in RP, when ou is weakly stressed, its diphthongal character is hardly perceptible. It may then be denoted phonetically simply by o. This pronunciation may be noticed in such words as *November, molest* which are pronounced

---

[1] Whether they are affections or not depends on the meaning attached to this term. It is suggested that only those pronunciations should be considered as 'affectations' which have been purposely acquired, and which are therefore in some degree unnatural. If this definition is accepted, then the above-mentioned diphthongs may be affected in the speech of some and not in the speech of others.

sometimes nou'vɛmbə, mou'lɛst, sometimes nə'vɛmbə, mə'lɛst, and sometimes in an intermediate manner no'vɛmbə, mo'lɛst. This barely diphthongal o may be called an unstable sound. It is difficult to say it in isolation or indeed to make it with precision at all. The words in which it may be heard all have alternative pronunciations with ə and generally also with fully diphthongal ou. See also §§ 103, 107.

§ 174. In the above examples the syllable concerned immediately precedes a strong stress. Barely diphthongal o with a variant ə also occurs sometimes in syllables immediately following a strong stress, but this pronunciation can hardly be regarded as belonging to RP. Examples are 'windo or 'wində for the usual 'windou (*window*), 'fɛlo or 'fɛlə for 'fɛlou (*fellow*). The forms with ə are probably confined to negligent or dialectal speech. So also are cases where intrusive r (§ 361) is added, such as 'swɔlərin for 'swɔlouiŋ (*swallowing*), ðei 'kɛpt ðə 'windər oupən for ðei 'kɛpt ðə 'windou oupən (*they kept the window open*).

§ 175. ai, No. 15 of RP. Examples: taim (*time*), trai (*try*), ai 'faind it s 'kwait 'rait (*I find it's quite right*). Several easily distinguishable varieties of the diphthong here written ai must be regarded as belonging to RP. The beginning of the diphthong ranges with different RP speakers from a 'middle' a to about a cardinal a. In ordinary pronunciation the speaker immediately leaves the starting-point and proceeds in the direction of i. The formation of the variety starting with middle a is shown in Fig. 13. In phonetic terminology the diphthong begins with an open unrounded vowel varying between front and midway between front and back; it proceeds in the direction of a close unrounded front position.

§ 176. Although the diphthong 'proceeds in the direction of i', it rarely reaches there. The movement ae or even aɛ is sufficient to give the acoustic effect of the sound. (See also § 184.)

§ **177.** In dialectal speech the limits of the beginning of the diphthong are extended in both directions. In London one commonly hears a variety of ɑi starting with a fully back ɑ (ɑ˗): tɑ˗im, kwɑ˗it, trɑ˗i. Sometimes a variety of ɔi is used: tɔim, kwɔit, trɔi (*time, quite, try*). At the other extreme there is a diphthong beginning with a raised front a (a˖): ta˖im, kwa˖it, tra˖i. Though this sound is not unfrequently heard, it seems difficult to ascertain who uses it; it does not appear to belong to any particular locality. Some would call it an 'affected' pronunciation (see footnote to § 171).

§ **178.** Another fairly common type of diphthong used in such words may be written ʌi. It begins with a rather open central vowel: tʌim, kwʌit, trʌi. The opinion has been expressed that this is commoner than any other in the South, but it is doubtful if this contention can be maintained.

§ **179.** A variety of ʌi beginning with a rather low and retracted kind of ʌ replaces RP ɑi or ai in some types of dialectal English, e.g. in the speech of Buckinghamshire.

§ **180.** Some Scottish people use a variety of ɑi in the same way as Southern English people do. It is, however, much more usual in Scotland to pronounce a diphthong of the type ʌi as shown in Fig. 18, in many words. The following distribution of ɑi (which is better written ae for Scottish speech) and ʌi appears to be a very usual one in Scottish English:

ae is used (1) finally, as in trae (*try*), bae (*buy, by*), hae (*high*),

(2) when inflexional endings such as -d, -z, -ɪr, -le, -nɪs (-*ness*) are added to these words, e.g. traed (*tried*), traez (*tries*), ˈflaeɪr (*flyer*), ˈhaeɪr (*higher*), ˈlaeɪr (*liar*), ˈʃaele (*shyly*), ˈʃaenɪs (*shyness*),

(3) in other words where a vowel sound follows, e.g. ˈdaeɪt (*diet*), ˈfraeɪr (*friar*), ˈfaeɪr (*fire*),

(4) whenever v or θ or ð or z follows in the same syllable, e.g. ʌ'laev (*alive*), saeθ or saeð (*scythe*), praez (*prize*),

(5) before other consonants when the consonant may be considered to begin a following syllable, e.g. 'taegɪr (*tiger*), 'maetɪr (*mitre*), 'paelɪt (*pilot*), 'paeθn̩ (*python*), 'aern̩ (*iron*).

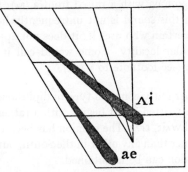

Fig. 18. Diagram illustrating the formation of the Scottish diphthongs ae and ʌi.

ʌi is used in most other situations, and in particular when one of the consonants p, b, t, d, k, g, m, n, l, f or s follows in the same syllable, e.g. wʌip (*wipe*), trʌib (*tribe*), lʌit (*light*), wʌid (*wide*), lʌik (*like*), tʌim (*time*), kʌind (*kind*), mʌil (*mile*), lʌif (*life*), ʌis (*ice*).

§ **180a.** In some words there is variation, e.g. ʌ'blaedʒ or ʌ'blʌidʒ (*oblige*), and there are some exceptions, e.g. kʌn'saes (*concise*). Some of the latter are due to analogy. Such are the plurals wʌivz (*wives*), nʌivz (*knives*), lʌivz (*lives*, plur. of *life*).

§ **181.** It will be observed that in Scottish English ae and ʌi sometimes distinguish one word from another, e.g. taed (*tied*) but tʌid (*tide*), praed (*pried*) but prʌid (*pride*). Compare also 'ʃaenɪs (*shyness*) with 'ʃʌinɪŋ (*shining*), 'haele (*highly*), with 'wʌile (*wily*), 'vaepɪr (*viper*) with 'wʌipɪr (*wiper*).

§ **182.** Some Southern people use əi rather than ɑi in weakly stressed positions. They will say, for instance, əi 'θiŋk sou for the more usual ɑi 'θiŋk sou (*I think so*).

§ **183.** ɑi alternates with i in many words written with *-ile*, e.g. *reptile, hostile, fertile.* In the South of England most of these words are said with ɑil: 'hɔstɑil, 'fəːtɑil, etc. In Scotland the pronunciation with [ɩl] is usual: ['hɔstɩl], ['fɛrtɩl]. The pronunciation with [-ɩl] is also usual in America in some of these words. In *profile* and *imbecile* ɑi alternates with iː; some people pronounce 'proufiːl, 'imbisiːl and others 'proufɑil, 'imbisɑil. The termination *-ine* also has different vowels in different words, e.g. ɑi in 'kɔləmbɑin (*columbine*), 'səːpəntɑin (*serpentine*), 'kɑːmɑin (*carmine*); i in 'fɛminin (*feminine*), 'dɔktrin (*doctrine*), 'ɛndʒin (*engine*), 'disiplin (*discipline*); iː in dʒɛlə'tiːn[1] (*gelatine*), 'klɔːriːn (*chlorine*), magə'ziːn[2] (*magazine*).

§ **184.** When ɑi is followed by ə, the diphthongization of the ɑi is very slight. It is convenient to write the sequence with ɑiə, but a more minutely accurate transcription of it would be ɑeə or ɑɛə.[3] Examples: 'fɑiə (*fire*), 'tɑiəd (*tired*), 'ʌmpɑiə (*umpire*), 'ɑiərəni (*irony*). The sequence is generally treated as if it formed a single syllable—a triphthong—though strictly speaking it is not quite a triphthong.[4] Very often the sequence is reduced to a diphthong of the type ɑə (or aə), or to a monophthong which may be written ɑ+ː or ɑ̟ː. This vowel is generally distinct from the ɑː of such words as fɑː (*far*), tɑːd (*tarred*).

---

[1] Also 'dʒɛlətiːn.

[2] In the North 'magəziːn (§ 442).

[3] Or aeə or aɛə according to the pronunciation of the speaker.

[4] A true triphthong is a vocalic sequence in which the centre part has greater prominence than the two ends. Such a sequence is ŏaĕ, a careless way of pronouncing *why*.

§ **185.** When ə following ɑi is a suffix, some people pronounce the ɑi with fairly full diphthongization; they make a distinction between the ɑiə arising in this way and the ɑiə described in § 184, and do not reduce it to anything resembling ɑə or ɑ:. This distinction may be shown by writing a hyphen in the inflected words, thus ɑi-ə. Examples: 'bɑi-ə (*buyer*), 'hɑi-ə (*higher*), 'ʃɑi-ə (*shyer*), which may be compared with fɑiə (*fire*), hɑiə (*hire*), ʃɑiə (*shire*). Words like 'bɑi-ə have two syllables, but fɑiə, etc., generally count as if they were single syllables.

§ **186.** In Western and North-Western speech, where *r* is sounded before consonants, words like *fire* are commonly pronounced with ɑiəɹ or ɑiɹ. In dialectal speech, variants like ʌiɹ, əiɹ are also met with. (For ɹ see §§ 351, 355, 356.)

§ **187.** ɑu, No. 16 of RP. Examples: hɑu (*how*), tɑun (*town*), ɑut (*out*). Several easily distinguishable varieties of the sound here written ɑu must be regarded as belonging to RP. The beginning of the diphthong has a range with RP speakers rather similar to that of ɑi, namely from a middle ɑ to about a cardinal a. In ordinary pronunciation the speaker immediately leaves the starting-point and proceeds in the direction of u. The formation of the variety starting with middle ɑ is shown in Fig. 13. In phonetic terminology the diphthong begins with an open vowel varying between front and midway between front and back; it proceeds in the direction of a close back rounded position.

§ **188.** Although the diphthong 'proceeds in the direction of u', it nearly always stops short of that point. The movement ɑo or even a lesser degree of movement suffices to give the necessary auditory impression. (See also § 193.)

§ **189.** As with ɑi, the beginnings of the variants of ɑu are extended both in the front and back directions in dialectal speech. Some people use a variety of ɑu beginning with a fully back ɑ; this may be symbolized by ɑ‑u or ɡu. This kind of ɑu is apt to sound foreign; it is not certain whether it is an individual peculiarity or whether it belongs to a definite form of dialectal speech. In London dialect, on the other hand, the corresponding diphthong begins with a very front sound, generally lying between au (with cardinal a) and ɛu; *how, town, out* are pronounced haɪu, tˢaɪun, aɪuʔ or hɛu, tˢɛun, ɛuʔ. With some Londoners the diphthong is replaced by one of the type aɪə or ɛə, or occasionally by a monophthong aɪ: or ɛ:, thus tˢaɪən or tˢɛən for *town*, aɪəʔ or ɛəʔ for *out*, 'ɛ: jə geʔn 'ɔn for *how are you getting on?* In the local speech of Oxfordshire the diphthong used in these words begins at a still higher point, near to cardinal No. 2: heu, teun, euʔ.

§ **190.** Western dialectal speech has the peculiarity of fronting the final element of the diphthong. One may hear in Devonshire, etc., varieties like aü (ending with a forward u) and ɛy (ending with a completely front sound, § 481).

§ **191.** Other variants are ʌu and əu. They appear to belong chiefly to the North and Scotland. The variant ʌu is very common in Scotland. Those who use it substitute it for all the Southern English au's; pronouncing for instance *how, town, out, proud, allowed* as hʌu, tʌun, ʌut, prʌud, ʌ'lʌud. The use of ʌu in Scottish English does not appear to be confined to particular classes of words in the way that ʌi is (§§ 180, 180a, 181).

§ **192.** Some Southern people use əu rather than au in weakly stressed positions. They will say həu'ɛvə and əut'standiŋ for the more usual hau'ɛvə (*however*), aut'standiŋ (*outstanding*).

§ **193.** When au is followed by ə, the diphthongization of the au is generally very slight. It is convenient to write the sequence by the notation auə, though a more minutely accurate transcription of it would be aoə. The sequence is generally treated as if it formed a single syllable—a triphthong—though strictly speaking it is not quite a triphthong (footnote 4 to § 183).

Examples: flauə (*flower, flour*), auəz (*ours, hours*). Very often the sequence is reduced to a diphthongal sound of the type aə or to a monophthong differing little if at all from the ordinary ɑː of 'fɑːðə (*father*). The precise shade of sound differs with different speakers. Some use a somewhat advanced ɑː which may be symbolized by a+ː or ɑ̈ː. Thus one may hear *power* pronounced as paə or pɑ̈ː or even pɑː (like *par*).

§ **194.** When ə following au is a suffix, the au is as a rule pronounced with fairly full diphthongization, and is not reduced to anything resembling aə or ɑː like the auə described in the preceding paragraph. The distinction may be shown in transcription by inserting a hyphen in the inflected words, thus au-ə. Example: 'plau-ə (*plougher*), which may be compared with flauə, or ə'lau-əns (*allowance*) which is distinguished from ə'lɑːns (*a lance*). Some of the less common words containing auə are often treated similarly by some speakers. For instance *cower* and *coward* are often pronounced 'kau-ə, 'kau-əd; it is unusual to reduce them to forms resembling kɑː (*car*), kɑːd (*card*).

§ **195.** In Western and North-Western speech, where *r* is sounded before consonants, words like *flower* are commonly pronounced with auəɹ or auɹ. In dialectal speech, variants like ʌuɹ and əuɹ are also met with. (For ɹ see §§ 351, 355, 356.)

§ **196.** ɔi, No. 17 of RP. Examples: bɔi (*boy*), vɔis (*voice*). This diphthong begins with a sound near in quality to that of long ɔː (§ 104); it immediately leaves this and proceeds in the direction of i (see Fig. 13). It is convenient to represent this diphthong by the notation ɔi, to show the direction of movement. i is, however, not usually reached; a movement as far as a variety of e suffices to give the necessary acoustic effect. In phonetic terminology the diphthong begins at a position which may be described as back, rounded and slightly below half-open; it proceeds in the direction of a fairly close front unrounded position.

§ 197. ɔi does not seem to vary to the same extent as the other diphthongs. A variant beginning with a closer sound [oi] may, however, be heard in London. There exists also a variant beginning with an advanced ɔ, which may be represented phonetically by ɔ+i or œi. It is not certain whether this belongs to a particular part of the country (Northern) or whether it is an individual peculiarity. It is sometimes used by comedians when playing the role of a pretentious or affected person.

§ 198. iə, No. 18 of RP. Examples: hiə (*here, hear*), ai'diə (*idea*), fiəs (*fierce*), biəd (*beard*). This diphthong begins at RP vowel No. 2 and moves to RP vowel No. 12. In phonetic terminology it begins by being fairly close, front and unrounded, and ends at a central, nearly half-open, unrounded position (see Fig. 14). The beginning of this diphthong has stronger stress than the end part (see §§ 219a, 219b).

§ 199. In many regions, including London, a diphthong beginning with a closer sound is substituted. This may be represented by the notation iːə. In the West and North-West a sequence of the type iːəɹ or iːɹ is used in the words written with *r*. In Scotland there exists a sequence [iʌ] in words like [ae'diʌ] (*idea*), ['rʌʃiʌ] (*Russia*), but it is probably to be considered as disyllabic rather than diphthongal; words like *here*, *fierce*, *beard* are pronounced there with [ir]: [hir], [firs], [bird].

§ 200. The terminal part of RP iə varies in the same way as ə (§§ 144–6). In final positions the sound is opener than in non-final positions; for instance the end of hiə (said by itself) is somewhat opener than the end of the iə of fiəs or of 'hiəz ə'nʌðə (*here's another*), 'hiər i'tiz (*here it is*). In some extreme types of pronunciation final iə is replaced by iʌ or iɑ. This pronunciation is often found in the speech of those who use the forward variety of ou (§ 171); they say 'öü 'diʌ or 'öü 'diɑ for 'ou 'diə (*oh dear!*) a manner of saying the words which many would consider an 'affectation' (see footnote 1 to § 171).

§ **201.** In the West and North-West it is usual to make a distinction between words which are and are not spelt with the letter *r* by ending the diphthong with əɹ or ɹ in the former case. Thus in the West *here* and *fierce* are commonly pronounced hiːəɹ, fiːəɹs or hiːɹ, fiːɹs, but *idea* is pronounced ɑi'diə (much as in RP) or ɑi'diːə.

§ **202.** The sequence jəː occurs as an alternative to iə in a few words, of which *here*, *dear* and *serious* are the most noteworthy, thus hjəː, djəː, 'sjəːrïəs for the more usual hiə, diə, 'siərïəs. (For the ï in this last word see §§ 219*c*, 219*d*.) *Year* is commonly pronounced jəː, but some people say jiə.

§ **203.** ɛə, No. 19 of RP. Examples: ðɛə (*there, their*), bɛə (*bear, bare*), skɛəs (*scarce*), stɛəz (*stairs*). This diphthong begins near cardinal No. 3 and moves in the direction of RP vowel No. 12. In phonetic terminology it begins by being half-open, front, unrounded, and ends at a central, nearly half-open, unrounded sound. (See Fig. 14.)

§ **204.** Some Southern speakers begin the diphthong with a very open variety of ɛ, thus ɛ̞ə. Occasionally one hears a monophthongal long ɛː (ðɛː, bɛː, skɛːs, stɛːz).

§ **205.** In many districts, including London, a diphthong beginning with a close e is substituted. This may be represented by the notation eːə, e.g. ðeːə, beːə. In London dialect the sound becomes monophthongal (eː) in some connexions, e.g. 'weː j 'gʌin (*Where are you going?*).

§ **206.** In Scotland one hears generally er [ðer, ber, skers, sterz], etc., or sometimes, especially in Edinburgh, ɛr [ðɛr, bɛr, skɛrs, stɛrz], etc. Some Welsh people use both eːr and ɛːr, and distinguish ðeːr (*their*) from ðɛːr (*there*).

§ **207.** In the West and North-West the written *r* is generally pronounced (as ɹ). In those regions, therefore, words like *there, scarce* are sounded as ðɛəɹ, skɛəɹs or ðɛːɹ, skɛɹs, etc.

§ **208.** In the Midlands there is often confusion between ɛə and əː. It is quite usual, for instance, to substitute əː for RP ɛə, e.g. to pronounce *there* as ðəː or ðəːɹ and *scarce* as skəːs or skəːɹs.

§ **209.** ɛə alternates with short a in a few words where r follows. For instance *apparent* is pronounced ə'pɛərənt by some and ə'parənt by others. It alternates with əː in *were*, the strong form of which is wəː with some RP speakers and wɛə with others. wəː is probably the commoner.

§ **210.** ɔə, No. 20 of RP. Examples: mɔə (*more*), flɔə (*floor*), sɔəd (*sword, soared*). This diphthong starts with a quality similar to that of RP long ɔː and moves to RP ə. In phonetic terminology it begins near to a half-open, back, rounded vowel and ends at a nearly half-open, central, unrounded sound. (See Fig. 14.)

§ **211.** A great many Southern people do not have this diphthong at all, but use ɔː (§ 104) in its stead: they pronounce *more, floor, sword* as mɔː, flɔː (like *flaw*), sɔːd (like *sawed*).

§ **212.** In London dialectal speech a diphthong of the type oːə is substituted in final positions. This sound starts with much closer lip-rounding than the ɔə described in § 210. *More* and *floor* are pronounced moːə, floːə; they sometimes sound almost like 'moːwə, 'floːwə. In non-final positions the sound used in London dialectal speech is a variety of monophthongal oː, thus [soːd] for RP sɔəd or sɔːd.

§ **213.** In the West and North-West a sequence of the type oːəɹ or oːɹ is commonly used, where RP has the possibility of ɔə, thus moːɹə, soːɹd or moːɹ, soːɹd, etc. This is distinguished from the ɔɹ employed in the words listed in § 110. In Scotland one generally hears or in the words under consideration [mor, flor, sord], etc., but sometimes, especially in Edinburgh, ɔr [mɔr, flɔr, sɔrd], etc.

§ 214. uə, No. 21 of RP. Examples: tuə (*tour*), muəz (*moors*). This diphthong starts with a quality similar to that of RP short u and ends with RP ə. In phonetic terminology it begins at a vowel which may be described as between close and half-close, back and moderately rounded, and moves to a nearly half-open, central, unrounded sound. Its movement is illustrated in Fig. 14.

§ 215. Some Southern speakers use a diphthong beginning with a sound opener than u; it may be denoted by oə. They pronounce the above words as toə, moəz. Very many other Southerners substitute for uə the still opener diphthong ɔə or the pure vowel ɔː, especially in the commoner words. They pronounce, for instance, *sure, poor, pure, curious* as ʃɔə, pɔə, pjɔə, 'kjɔərïəs or as ʃɔː (like *Shaw*), pɔː (like *paw*), pjɔː, 'kjɔːrïəs. In the case of *your* the pronunciation with ɔː (jɔː) is probably much more common in the South than the pronunciation with uə (juə), though the latter does exist. The use of ɔː for uə in the above words is so frequent among non-dialectal speakers that it has to be considered as belonging to RP as a recognized variant of uə.

§ 216. In London dialectal speech the sound [oː] (§ 108) replaces the RP uə of *sure*, etc.

§ 217. In Scotland the words under consideration are pronounced with ur: [tur, murz, ʃur, pur, pjur, 'kjureʌs], etc. In the West and North-West of England a sequence of the type uːɹəɹ or uːɹɹ is commonly used, thus ʃuːəɹ, pjuːɹəɹ or ʃuːɹɹ, pjuːɹɹ, etc.

§ 218. In RP j occurs before uə and its variants in cases similar to those in which it precedes uː (§ 127), e.g. in 'kjuərïəs, 'fjuəri (*fury*), in'djuə (*endure*), but not in such words as 'ruərəl (*rural*), ʃuə, 'dʒuəri (*jury*), 'pluərəl (*plural*).

§ 219. əː is used in place of uə by some in a few words, e.g. ʃəː, 'kjəːrïəs for RP ʃuə (ʃɔː, etc.), 'kjuərïəs ('kjɔːrïəs, etc.) (*sure, curious*).

RISING DIPHTHONGS

§ 219 a. The diphthongs described in the foregoing paragraphs are called 'falling' diphthongs, because the 'prominence' (§§ 415–418) of the sound undergoes a diminution as the articulation proceeds. For instance, the end part of the diphthong ɑi is less prominent than the beginning part. In most of the English diphthongs the diminution of prominence is caused by the fact that the end part is inherently less 'sonorous' (§§ 416, 417) than the beginning. This applies to all the 'closing' diphthongs (namely ei, ou, ɑi, ɑu and ɔi) and to the 'centring' diphthongs ɛə and ɔə. It does not apply to iə and uə, since ə is essentially a more sonorous sound than i or u.

§ 219 b. It will be found that the iə and uə described in §§ 198, 214 are nevertheless 'falling' diphthongs, and that the 'falling' effect is brought about by putting greater *stress* on the beginning part than on the end part. The greater sonority of ə is therefore offset by the greater stress of the i and u elements.

§ 219 c. It is naturally very easy to pronounce diphthongs of the iə and uə types in a 'rising' manner, i.e. in such a way that the end part is more prominent than the beginning. And in fact these rising varieties do actually occur in English. They may be represented by the notation ĭə, ŭə (the mark ᵛ denoting lack of prominence), and they may be referred to as diphthongs Nos. 22 and 23.

§ **219d.** ɪə, RP No. 22, occurs only in weakly stressed positions. It is used in such words as ˈhæpɪə (*happier*), ˈɪdɪəm (*idiom*). The word iksˈpɪərɪəns (*experience*) illustrates both kinds of ɪə.

§ **219e.** ʊə, RP No. 23, likewise occurs only in weakly stressed syllables. Examples: ˈɪnflʊəns (*influence*), ˈvæljʊə (*valuer*).

§ **219f.** Words containing ɪə and ʊə always have possible alternative pronunciations with i-ə and u-ə pronounced as two syllables, e.g. ˈhæpi-ə, ˈɪnflu-əns. Some of the words also have alternatives with jə and wə. For instance *idiom* is often pronounced ˈɪdjəm, and *influence* can be pronounced ˈɪnflwəns. Words containing ʊə never have an alternative with ɔː like words containing uə (No. 21); thus although many people pronounce *poor* as pɔː, no one pronounces *influence* as ˈɪnflɔːns.

§ **219g.** Those interested in the subject of rising diphthongs will find further information about them in the author's article *Falling and Rising Diphthongs in Southern English* in *Miscellanea Phonetica II*, 1954 (published by the International Phonetic Association).

Consonants

PLOSIVES

§ **220.** p. Breathed bilabial plosive. Examples: paip (*pipe*), ˈʌpə (*upper*).

§ **221.** When p commences a strongly stressed syllable, it is somewhat 'aspirated' in Southern speech. This means that there is a little puff of breath, i.e. a slight h-sound, immediately following the plosion and preceding the vowel. In very minute transcription this may be shown by a small ʰ or by the sign ';' thus pei (*pay*) and əˈpɑːt (*apart*) might be transcribed pʰei, əˈpʰɑːt or pˈei, əˈpˈɑːt. The amount of aspiration differs with different people. Northern speakers generally do not aspirate p at all.

§ 222. In Southern speech p has little or no aspiration in weakly stressed syllables, as for instance in ˈhapi (*happy*), ˈwispə (*whisper*). Nor is there much aspiration when s precedes in a strongly stressed syllable, as in ˈspɛndiŋ (*spending*). It is a good exercise for the student of speech to listen for the degrees of aspiration in the pronunciation of different people and in different contexts.

§ 223. An 'intrusive' p is sometimes inserted between m and another consonant, as in ˈsʌm(p)θiŋ (*something*), wɔːm(p)θ (*warmth*), am(p)stəˈdam (*Amsterdam*).

§ 224. b. Voiced or partially voiced bi-labial plosive. It is generally uttered with a weaker degree of force than p. Examples: ˈbeibi (*baby*), wɛb (*web*).

§ 225. b is fully voiced when it occurs between voiced sounds, as in ˈhɑːbə (*harbour*), ˈeibl (*able*). In other situations it is partially voiced or, with many speakers, completely voiceless (ḅ, see § 385); these varieties are found particularly in initial and final positions, as when such words as buːt (*boot*), breik (*break*), wɛb (*web*), bʌlb (*bulb*), are said by themselves. They also occur next to voiceless consonants, as in ˈiːsbɔːn (*Eastbourne*), ˈdʌsbin (*dust-bin*). When such a word as buːt is preceded by a voiced sound in the sentence, it has fully voiced b; for instance the b is fully voiced in mai ˈbuːts (*my boots*), though not in blak ˈbuːts (*black boots*). Similarly the b is fully voiced in ˈɛb ən ˈflou (*ebb and flow*), though not in ˈɛb ˈtaid (*ebb tide*).

§ 226. t. The most usual English variety of t is a breathed alveolar plosive, i.e. a sound articulated by the tip of the tongue against the teeth-ridge (Fig. 19). Examples: tɔːt (*taught*), ˈmatə (*matter*).

§ 227. When **t** commences a strongly stressed syllable it is somewhat 'aspirated' in Southern speech. This means that there is a little puff of breath, i.e. a slight h-sound, immediately following the plosion and preceding the vowel. In very minute transcription this may be indicated by a small ʰ or by the

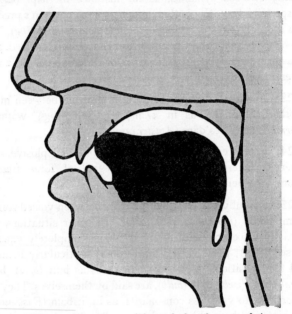

Fig. 19. Tongue position of alveolar **t** and **d**.

sign ', thus tʰiː or t'iː (*tea*), əb'tʰein or əb't'ein (*obtain*). The amount of the aspiration differs with different speakers. In the North **t** is often not aspirated at all.

§ 228. In Southern speech the sound has little or no aspiration in weakly stressed syllables, as for instance in 'lɛtə (*letter*), 'roustiŋ (*roasting*). Nor is there much aspiration when **s** precedes in a strongly stressed syllable, as in 'steibl (*stable*).

§ **229.** t has lateral plosion before l, as in 'litl (*little*). It has nasal plosion before n, as in 'iːtn (*eaten*). A variety with dental articulation is used before θ and ð as in eitθ (*eighth*), ət ði 'ɛnd (*at the end*), and a variety with post-alveolar articulation before r, as in trɛd (*tread*).

§ **230.** In London dialectal speech the aspiration of t is strong and rather s-like. The dialectal pronunciation of *tea* and *two* may be represented phonetically by the notation tˢəi, tˢəu.

§ **231.** In some parts of the North t is pronounced dentally, i.e. articulated against the teeth instead of the teeth-ridge, when r or ər follows. Representing this kind of t by ʈ this Northern pronunciation of *true* and *better* would be written phonetically ʈruː, 'bɛʈər. This pronunciation sounds rather as if θ were inserted after the t; the words sound something like tθruː, 'bɛtθər.

§ **232.** Americans regularly use a kind of single flap r where British speech has weakly stressed t between vowels. It may be denoted phonetically by ʈ or by ɾ. They say ['wɔɾɹ] for 'wɔːtə (*water*), [dɪk'tɛɾɪŋ] for dik'teitiŋ (*dictating*), ['kwɑ̃nəɾi] for 'kwɔntiti or 'kwɔntəti (*quantity*), ['prɑfɪɾəbl] for 'prɔfitəbl (*profitable*). Some English people use a pronunciation resembling this in some words, but the flap is not so distinct. The sound used is more like an ordinary r or sometimes a d. One sometimes hears, for instance, pronunciations like 'sarədi for 'satədi (*Saturday*), 'bjuːdəfl for 'bjuːtəfl (*beautiful*), 'wɔd l juː 'hav (*What'll you have?*); in London one may hear 'wɔd jə gəin ə 'dᶻəü for 'wɔt ə ju gəuiŋ tə 'duː (*What are you going to do?*), 'ger ɛər ə ðə 'wai for 'gɛt aut əv ðə 'wei (*Get out of the way*).[1]

§ **233.** A great many people, apparently in all parts of the country, substitute the 'glottal stop' (ʔ, § 254) for t when it

---

[1] The more usual London pronunciation is, however, with ʔ (§ 234).

follows a stressed vowel and is followed in turn by one of the consonants m, n, l, r, w or j. Examples: ə 'greiʔ 'mɛni (*a great many*), 'fɔːʔnait (*fortnight*), 'mʌʔn (*mutton*), 'tɔʔnəm (*Tottenham*), 'pɔːʔlənd (*Portland*), 'kwaiʔ 'rait (*quite right*), 'hav ju 'gɔʔ wʌn (*Have you got one?*), 'nɔʔ 'jɛt (*not yet*). This is done by many whose speech cannot be considered dialectal.

§ 234. In many varieties of dialectal speech the glottal stop is used in place of RP t not only in cases like the above but also finally and before vowels and before other consonants. Examples: raiʔ (*right*), jɛʔ (*yet*), 'bɛʔə (*better*), 'kriʔisaiz (*criticize*), 'gɛʔin (*getting*), 'streiʔ ə'wei (*straight away*), əig 'gɔʔ ə soʔ ə 'bɔʔl (*he'd got a sort of bottle*), 'ðaʔ s əbɛəʔ 'oːl (*that's about all*),[1] əi 'gɔʔ iz 'fuʔ 'koʔ n ðə 'fɛns (*he got his foot caught in the fence*).[1] This use of ʔ is very common, particularly in London, the Eastern Counties and Scotland. It is of course often combined with the use of vowels differing from those of RP, as explained in the sections on vowels. (ʔ is often an alternative to the d and r sounds in the cases mentioned in § 232).

§ 235. Written *t* is often not sounded if it would occur in a medial sequence of consonants, and particularly when the first consonant is s. Examples: 'lisn (*listen*), 'kaːsl (*castle*), 'mʌsnt (*mustn't*). This also happens very commonly at word junctions and in compound words, e.g. 'nɛks 'krisməs (*next Christmas*), 'pousmən (*postman*), 'weiskout or 'wɛskət (*waistcoat*), 'mous piːpl (*most people*). Note also the word *often* which is pronounced in eight different ways: 'ɔfn, 'ɔfən, 'ɔftən, 'ɔftn, 'ɔːfn, 'ɔːfən (like *orphan*), 'ɔːftən, 'ɔːftn.

§ 236. Sometimes t is dropped before d in rapid speech. For instance RP speakers may be heard to say in conversation

---

[1] Examples heard by the author in London.

'si 'daun, 'wɔ d juː 'wɔnt instead of 'sit 'daun (*sit down*), 'wɔt d juː 'wɔnt (*What do you want?*).

§ 237. t is inserted by some in *fifth* and *sixth*: fiftθ, sikstθ instead of fifθ, siksθ. There is always a t in *eighth* (eitθ). *Eighty* is usually pronounced in the North as 'eitti, with a 'doubled' (lengthened) t. In the South it is 'eiti.

§ 238. In American speech t is generally inserted between n and s in such words as tɛnts (*tense*), wʌnts (*once*). In England the pronunciation is more usually tɛns, wʌns.

§ 239. d. The most usual variety of d in English is a voiced or partially voiced alveolar plosive. It has the same tongue position as t (Fig. 19), but it is generally uttered with less force than t. Examples: 'ɔːdə (*order*), diːd (*deed*).

§ 240. d is fully voiced when it occurs between voiced sounds, as in 'ɔːdə (*order*), 'stɛdi (*steady*), ə'diʃn (*addition*). In other situations it is partially voiced or with many speakers completely voiceless (ḍ, see § 385). These varieties are found particularly in initial and final positions as when words like daːk (*dark*), driːm (*dream*), haːd (*hard*), ould (*old*) are said by themselves. They also occur next to breathed consonants, as in 'bəːθdei[1] (*birthday*). When such a word as daːk is preceded by a voiced sound in a sentence, it has a fully voiced d; for instance the d is fully voiced in in ðə 'daːk (*in the dark*), though not in ðis 'daːk 'pasidʒ (*this dark passage*). Similarly the d of haːd is fully voiced in 'haːd inʌf (*hard enough*), though not in 'haːd 'stoun (*hard stone*).

§ 241. In RP d has lateral plosion before l, as in 'midl (*middle*). It has a nasal plosion before n, as in 'sʌdn (*sudden*). A variety with dental articulation is used before θ and ð, as in widθ[2]

---

[1] Pronounced 'bəːθdi by some.
[2] Also pronounced witθ.

(*width*), and a variety with post-alveolar articulation before r, as in drɔː (*draw*).

§ 242. Sometimes in the North a dental articulation is employed (d̪) before r or ər, thus d̪rɔp (*drop*), 'lad̪ər (*ladder*). This pronunciation sounds rather as if ð were inserted after the d; these words sound something like dðrɔp, 'ladðər.

§ 243. Written *d* is often not sounded if it would occur in a medial sequence of consonants, and particularly when next to a nasal consonant. Examples: 'kainnis (*kindness*), 'granmʌðə (*grandmother*). The word *and* is very commonly pronounced without a d; examples: 'brɛd n 'bʌtə (*bread and butter*), 'tuː ən 'siks (*two and six*).

§ 244. k. Breathed velar plosive. The tongue position of an average k is shown in Fig. 20. Examples: keik (*cake*), ə'kaunt (*account*). It will be observed that the place of articulation varies according to the nature of adjacent vowels; for instance the k in kiŋ (*king*) has a 'fronter' articulation than that in 'kɔtidʒ (*cottage*). (See also § 395.)

§ 245. When k commences a strongly stressed syllable, it is somewhat 'aspirated' in Southern speech. This means that there is a little puff of breath, i.e. a slight h-sound, immediately following the plosion and preceding the vowel. In very minute transcription this may be shown by a small ʰ or by the sign ʼ; thus 'kʰʌbəd (*cupboard*), ə'kʰaunt (*account*) or 'kʼʌbəd, ə'kʼaunt. As with p and t the amount of aspiration differs with different speakers. In the North k is often not aspirated at all.

§ 246. In weakly stressed syllables k has little or no aspiration in Southern speech, e.g. 'beikə (*baker*), 'tɔːkiŋ (*talking*). Nor is there much aspiration when s precedes in a strongly stressed syllable, as in 'skɔlə (*scholar*).

§ **247.** k is sometimes inserted in the words lɛŋθ or lɛŋkθ (*length*), strɛŋθ or strɛŋkθ (*strength*). Alternative pronunciations lɛnθ, strɛnθ may be heard in dialectal speech, particularly in Scotland. On the other hand k is often omitted from ɑːskt (*asked*), especially when one says rapidly such an expression as

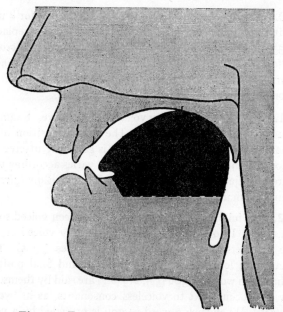

Fig. 20. Tongue position of average k and g.

hiː ˈɑːst im wɛər i wəz ˈgouiŋ (*he asked him where he was going*). This usage has given rise to a form ɑːst for ɑːsk in dialectal speech: in London one sometimes hears ai l ˈɑːst im for ai l ˈɑːsk im (*I'll ask him*).

§ **248.** Some people use t for k before l, at the beginning of syllables, as in tliːn (*clean*), kənˈtluːʒn (*conclusion*). This looks on paper like a very curious pronunciation, but in speaking

4-2

it passes almost unnoticed. It is a case where two different articulations have very similar sounds.

§ **249.** In careless speech a g terminating a syllable is sometimes used in place of k when a vowel follows, e.g. 'tʃigin for 'tʃikin (*chicken*), 'teig id ə'wei for 'teik it ə'wei (*take it away*).

§ **250.** Many people substitute the glottal stop (ʔ) for k under conditions similar to those in which this sound replaces t (§§ 233, 234). Examples: 'tʃɔʔlit for 'tʃɔk(ə)lit (*chocolate*), 'brɛʔfəst for 'brɛkfəst (*breakfast*), 'tɛʔnikl for 'tɛknikl (*technical*), 'θaʔəri for 'θakəri (*Thackeray*). This pronunciation is common in London, the Eastern Counties and Scotland.

§ **251.** g. Voiced or partially voiced velar plosive. Examples: ə'griː (*agree*), gou (*go*), ɛg (*egg*). The tongue position of g is the same as that of k, but the sound is generally uttered with less force than k. Like k its articulation varies according to the nature of adjacent vowels; for instance the g in giv (*give*) has a fronter articulation than the g in gɔt (*got*).

§ **252.** g is fully voiced when it occurs between voiced sounds as in ə'griː. In other situations it is partially voiced or, with some speakers, completely voiceless (g̊, see § 385). These varieties are found particularly in initial and final positions, as when such words as gou (*go*), big (*big*) are said by themselves. They also occur next to voiceless consonants, as in 'wɛsgeit (*Westgate*). When such a word as gou is preceded by a voiced sound in the sentence, it has a fully voiced g; for instance fully voiced g is used in 'wɛn ai 'gou (*when I go*), though not in 'dount 'gou (*don't go*). Similarly the g is fully voiced in 'big inʌf (*big enough*), though not in 'ɛgkʌp (*egg-cup*).

§ **253.** Careless speakers sometimes drop the g of 'rɛkəgnaiz (*recognize*). Americans generally add a g in the word *suggest*, pronouncing səg'dʒɛst in place of sə'dʒɛst which is the usual form in England.

§ 254. ʔ. Glottal plosive (more usually known as the 'glottal stop'). Formed by closing the glottis completely (i.e. bringing the vocal cords into contact) and suddenly opening it (i.e. separating the cords). By its nature this sound is neither breathed nor voiced.

§ 255. This consonant in an exaggerated form is the explosive sound heard in coughing. A cough may be represented in phonetic transcription; a common kind is ʔəhəʔəh.

§ 256. The glottal stop used in language is usually a weak variety. It is often prefixed to an initial vowel when the syllable needs emphasis, e.g. it wəz 'ʔabsəluːtli im'pɔsəbl (*it was absolutely impossible*), it wəz ði 'ʔounli wei tə gɛt it 'dʌn (*it was the only way to get it done*). Some people prefix ʔ to medial syllables beginning with vowels, when speaking emphatically: they will pronounce for instance *physiology* as fizi'ʔɔlədʒi instead of the normal fizi'ɔlədʒi, and they will say wɛn'ʔɛvər ai gou ðɛə, hiː z 'aut (*whenever I go there, he's out*).

§ 257. Others insert ʔ to avoid certain sequences of vowels, and particularly those which are capable of having a 'linking r' or an 'intrusive r' between them. They will pronounce 'wɛsminstə 'ʔabi, jɔː 'ʔɛg (*Westminster Abbey, your egg*) avoiding the pronunciation 'wɛsminstər 'abi, jɔːr 'ɛg with linking r. They will also say və'nilə 'ʔais, vaiə ʔɔs'tɛnd, 'tʃainə 'ʔɔːnəmənts (*vanilla ice, via Ostend, china ornaments*), avoiding the common pronunciation with intrusive r, və'nilər 'ais, vaiər ɔs'tɛnd, 'tʃainər 'ɔːnəmənts, etc.

§ 258. As has already been pointed out in §§ 234 and 250, in dialectal speech ʔ often replaces weakly stressed t and k. In London it may also be heard as a substitute for weakly stressed p, e.g. 'piːʔl for 'piːpl (*people*), 'paiʔə for 'peipə (*paper*), 'drɔʔ iʔ for 'drɔp it (*drop it*). It may occasionally replace other RP sounds. For instance the author has heard a distinguished public man say sʌ̃ʔĩ 'ɔːfu (for *something awful*).

AFFRICATES

§ 259. For the nature of affricate consonants see § 56 (ii). Most people consider affricates to be 'single sounds', but it is convenient to represent each affricate phonetically by a digraph consisting of a symbol for a plosive followed by the symbol for the corresponding (or 'homorganic') fricative. (See, however, § 268.)

§ 260. tʃ. Breathed palato-alveolar affricate. Examples: tʃəːtʃ (*church*), fɛtʃ (*fetch*). In making this consonant the tip and blade of the tongue are placed against the teeth-ridge and front part of the hard palate making complete contact (Fig. 21); the air behind is compressed by pressure from the lungs, then the contact is released in such a manner that a short corresponding fricative ʃ is heard. The tongue-tip is placed in a position differing a little from that of the ordinary English t. That the position is not quite the same can be felt by preparing to articulate t and comparing the feeling of this with the feeling of preparing to articulate tʃ (compare Figs. 19 and 21).

§ 261. The position taken up by the lips during the pronunciation of tʃ varies with individual speakers in the same way as that of ʃ (see § 342).

§ 262. tʃ may have a little aspiration as well as affrication, especially when beginning a strongly stressed syllable. Thus 'tʃɑːtə (*charter*) may have a slightly aspirated tʃ ('tʃʰɑːtə), but there is no perceptible aspiration in 'lɛktʃə (*lecture*).

§ 263. tʃ retains its affrication in all situations. For instance it is pronounced in full in fɛtʃt (*fetched*), 'wɔtʃtʃein (*watch-chain*). In this respect affricates differ from plosive consonants (see § 387).

§ 264. The affricate **tʃ** must be distinguished from the sequence **t+ʃ** which sometimes occurs. In phonetic transcription a hyphen is inserted to show the sequence **t+ʃ**. Examples: **'kɔːt-ʃip** (*courtship*), **'hat-ʃɔp** (*hat-shop*).

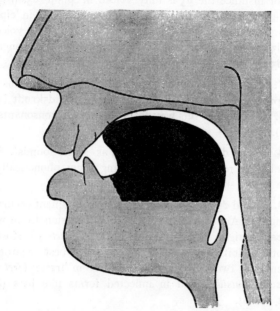

Fig. 21. Tongue position of tʃ and dʒ.

§ 265. dʒ. Voiced or partially voiced palato-alveolar affricate. Examples: **dʒʌdʒ** (*judge*), **peidʒ** (*page*). The articulation and lip position are similar to those of **tʃ** (§§ 260, 261).

§ 266. dʒ is fully voiced when it occurs between voiced sounds, as in **'meidʒə** (*major*). In other situations it is partially voiced or, with many speakers, completely voiceless (see § 386). These varieties are found particularly in initial and final positions as when words like dʒam (*jam*) and ɛdʒ (*edge*) are said by themselves. They also occur next to breathed consonants, as in fits'dʒɛrəld (*Fitzgerald*). When such a word as dʒam is preceded by a voiced sound in the sentence, it has a fully voiced dʒ; for instance the dʒ is fully voiced in 'plʌm 'dʒam (*plum jam*), though only partially voiced or even unvoiced in 'eiprikɔt dʒam (*apricot jam*). Similarly the dʒ of ɛdʒ is fully voiced in ði 'ɛdʒ əv ðə 'peivmənt (*the edge of the pavement*), though not in 'ɛdʒ tu 'ɛdʒ (*edge to edge*).

§267. dʒ retains its affrication in all situations. For instance it is pronounced in full in ə:dʒd (*urged*), 'steidʒkrɑ:ft (*stagecraft*). It differs in this way from the plosive consonants (see § 387).

§ 268. tʃ and dʒ are best considered as 'single sounds'. Some phoneticians recommend representing them phonetically by single letters such as c, ɟ.[1]

§ 269. tʃ and dʒ are the only affricates of frequent occurrence in English. Another affricate ts occurs occasionally in words of foreign origin, e.g. the first ts of 'tsɛtsi (*tsetse*).[2] Most ts's except the initial ones of such words are best regarded as sequences of two sounds: such are those in 'frɛtsɔ: (*fret-saw*), 'aut'said (*outside*), and in inflected forms like hats (*hats*), weits (*waits*).

§ 270. The Southern English tr and dr seem to be intermediate between single affricates and sequences of two distinct

---

[1] c and ɟ are the International Phonetic symbols for the palatal plosive consonants (§ 485). They can, however, generally be employed without inconvenience as single symbols to denote the affricates tʃ and dʒ, since it rarely happens that the palatal plosives and these affricates occur as separate phonemes (§§ 492 ff.) in the same language or dialect.

[2] Some people avoid this initial ts, and pronounce this word 'tɛtsi.

sounds. Examples: triː (*tree*), əˈtrakt (*attract*), drɔː (*draw*), ˈlɔːndri (*laundry*). Medially they more often sound like sequences, as in ət ˈrandəm (*at random*), ˈnaitreit (*nitrate*),[1] ˈhɛrəldri (*heraldry*), but occasionally they sound more like affricates, e.g. in əˈtrouʃəs (*atrocious*), ˈbɛdrum (*bedroom*), ˈɔːdri (*Audrey*). The distinction, which is often difficult to perceive, is shown phonetically by the position of the stress-mark, when there is one. It may be indicated by a hyphen where there is no stress-mark; thus if we wish to be very precise, we may write ˈhɛrəld-ri. Further examples of distinctions of this type will be found in the author's article *The Hyphen as a Phonetic Sign* in the *Zeitschrift für Phonetik*, Vol. 9, Part 2, 1956 (Berlin); also in Chap. XXXII of the author's *Outline of English Phonetics* (Heffer, Cambridge, 1956 and subsequent editions).

NASAL CONSONANTS

§ **271.** m. Voiced bilabial nasal. Examples: meik (*make*), muːv (*move*), θʌm (*thumb*).

§ **272.** The sound m is sometimes syllabic, e.g. in ˈprizm̩ (*prism*), ˈkazm̩ (*chasm*). Alternative pronunciations of such words with ə preceding the m are also common, thus ˈprizəm, ˈkazəm, etc. Syllabic m occurs too as the result of elision of ə in rapid pronunciation of such a word as ˈklapm̩, for the more usual ˈklapəm (*Clapham*).

§ **273.** In rapid speech m is sometimes used in place of n before or after p and b. Examples: ˈoupm̩ for ˈoup(ə)n (*open*), iˈlɛvmpəns for iˈlɛvnpəns (*elevenpence*), ˈkʌpm ˈsɔːsə for ˈkʌp(ə)n ˈsɔːsə (*cup and saucer*). Note also the common pronunciation ˈgʌvm̩mənt for ˈgʌvənmənt (*government*). These substitutions are examples of 'assimilation' (§§ 400 ff.). Other assimilations involving the use of m in place of n may be heard in very

---

[1] This word is distinct from ˈnait-reit (*night rate*). See § 504.

careless or in dialectal speech. ['ebm] is a London dialect pronunciation for 'hɛv(ə)n (*heaven*), and ['aipmi], ['grɛmfɑːvə] may be heard in London for 'heip(ə)ni (*halfpenny*), 'granfɑːðə (*grandfather*).

§ 274. The breathed consonant corresponding to m is represented phonetically by m̥. It is a useful exercise to practise making this sound by itself and in combinations such as m̥ɑː, ɛm̥, ʌm̥i.

§ 275. The sound m̥ occurs occasionally in speech. It is used in the interjections m̥m, mm̥m (generally written *hm*, *ahem*). It also occurs fairly often in rapid speech as a substitute for p or t in the neighbourhood of nasal consonants. Examples: ə'kʌmm̥nimənt, 'damm̥nis for ə'kʌmp(ə)nimənt, 'dampnis (*accompaniment*, *dampness*), 'ai doumm̥ 'maind for 'ai dount 'maind (*I don't mind*).

§ 276. n. Voiced alveolar nasal. Examples: nau (*now*), nain (*nine*). The position of the tongue and soft palate is as shown in Fig. 22.

§ 277. n is frequently syllabic especially after t, d, tʃ, dʒ, s, z, ʃ, ʒ. Examples: 'mʌtn (*mutton*), 'sʌdnli (*suddenly*), 'məːtʃnt (*merchant*), 'sɑːdʒnt (*sergeant*), 'beisn (*basin*), 'riːzn (*reason*), 'peiʃns (*patience*), ə'keiʒn (*occasion*), 'eitn'siks (*eight and six*), 'wɔtn̩iks'piəriəns (*What an experience!*). After s, z, ʃ, ʒ there is generally an alternative pronunciation with ən; for instance one often hears 'beisən, 'peiʃəns, etc. This alternative is less common after t and d.

§ 278. If it is desired to indicate in transcription that the sound is syllabic, this is done by writing n̩. As a rule it is not necessary to complicate the transcription by introducing the syllabic mark, because it is not easy to say such a sequence as 'beisn without making the n syllabic. When, however, a syllabic n is followed by a vowel, the mark must be used. See §§ 421 and 422.

§ **279.** The fact that the indefinite article ə (*a*) has an alternative form ən (*an*) used before vowels has had the effect of subtracting n from some nouns which formerly had it. The old form min or mɑin (*mine*) used in place of mi or mɑi (*my*) before

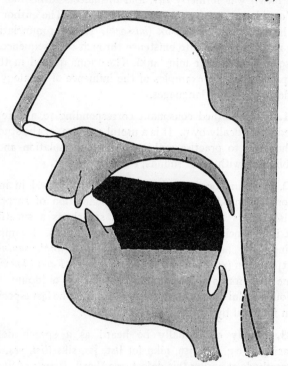

Fig. 22. Tongue position of alveolar n.

vowels has no doubt also contributed to this change. 'eiprən (*apron*) comes from Early French *naperon* (now pronounced [napʀɔ̃]); for ə 'neiprən and mɑi 'neiprən are barely distinguishable from ən 'eiprən, mɑin 'eiprən. Similarly with 'adə (*adder*) which was formerly *nadder*, 'ɔrindʒ (*orange*) from

83

Spanish *naranja* [naˈraŋxa]. Some people for the same reason pronounce *nought* (zero) as ɔːt.

§ **280.** Less frequently one meets with the reverse process. njuːt (*newt*) was formerly *ewt*, and in dialects forms like nɛg and ˈnʌŋkl are used for ɛg (*egg*), ˈʌŋkl (*uncle*).[1] The author has also heard ˈnasək for ˈhasək (*hassock*). These pronunciations have no doubt come into existence through such sequences as ən ˈɛg, main ˈʌŋkl or min ˈʌŋkl. The forms quoted in these two paragraphs are examples of the influence of 'analogy' in the development of languages.

§ **281.** The breathed consonant corresponding to n is represented phonetically by ̥n. It is a useful exercise for the student of phonetics to practise making it both in isolation and in combination with other sounds, e.g. ̥nuː, ɛ̥n, li̥nt.

§ **282.** ̥n occurs occasionally in speech. It is used in interjectional sounds, such as ̥n̥n̥n (an exclamation of surprise). It also occurs fairly often in rapid speech as a substitute for t in the neighbourhood of nasal consonants. Examples: əˈpɔin̥nmənt (*appointment*), ʌnˈplɛzn̥n̥nis (*unpleasantness*), ˈməːtʃən̥nmən (*merchantman*). The expression *I don't know* has as one of its forms ai ˈdoun̥n ˈnou. Others are ai ˈdount ˈnou, ai ˈdou ˈnou, ˈai dou ˈnou, ˈaidəˈnou, ˈaid̥nou (the last especially when followed by words like ˈwɔt or ˈhau).

§ **283.** ̥n may occasionally be heard as a speech defect, replacing s: e.g. li̥nt, jɛ̥n, ̥niki̥n for list, jɛs, siks (*list, yes, six*). For methods of curing this defect, see Ward, *Defects of Speech, their Nature and Cure* (Dent), p. 27.

§ **284.** ŋ. Voiced velar nasal. Examples: sɔŋ (*song*), iŋk (*ink*). ' The average position of the tongue and soft palate is shown in

---

[1] See Shakespeare, *King Lear*, Act II, Sc. 4 and elsewhere, where the Fool is represented as saying *nuncle* for *uncle*.

Fig. 23. The place of articulation varies to some extent according to the nature of adjoining vowels; thus the contact is further forward in siŋ (*sing*) than it is in sɔŋ (*song*).

§ **285.** ŋ is sometimes syllabic after k and g, especially in rapid speech. Examples: 'teikŋ (*taken*), wiː kŋ 'gou ðɛə tə'mɔrou (*we can go there to-morrow*), 'ɛg ŋ 'beikŋ (*egg and bacon*). In slower speech the pronunciation is with ən or n: 'teikən or 'teikn, etc.

§ **286.** In dialectal pronunciation the suffix -iŋ (*-ing*) is often pronounced -in. One may often hear in London and elsewhere 'kʌmin, 'gouin, 'weitin ə'baut, etc., for 'kʌmiŋ (*coming*), 'gouiŋ (*going*), 'weitiŋ ə'baut (*waiting about*), etc. This way of pronouncing is popularly known as 'dropping one's *g*'s'—an inaccurate way of expressing this substitution of one sound for another.[1]

§ **287.** Another dialectal pronunciation is to use -iŋ for final -in in some words, e.g. 'kitʃiŋ for 'kitʃin (*kitchen*). This probably originated as a reaction against the use of -in for *-ing* mentioned in the previous paragraph.

§ **288.** In London dialectal speech k is added to ŋ in the words compounded with *-thing*: ['nafiŋk, 'enifiŋk], etc., for 'nʌθiŋ (*nothing*), 'ɛniθiŋ (*anything*), etc.

§ **289.** In most parts of the English-speaking world the sequence ŋg occurs medially in various words, such as 'fiŋgə (*finger*), 'aŋgə (*anger*), 'lɔŋgə (*longer*), 'jʌŋgist (*youngest*), while

---

[1] In the late eighteenth and early nineteenth centuries this pronunciation was considered correct, at any rate in many words. See the remarks on this subject in the introduction to John Walker's *Critical Pronouncing Dictionary*, 1791 (p. 42 of the 1825 edition). It is known to have been common in the speech of people of education in the sixteenth century.

ŋ is used medially in other words, such as 'siŋə (*singer*), 'lɔŋiŋ (*longing*). In the Midlands, however (roughly from Birmingham to Manchester), the distinction is commonly ignored. People in these districts often use ŋg in words of the second category

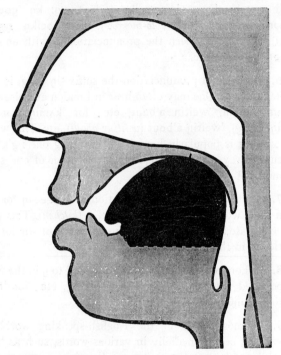

Fig. 23. Tongue position of an average ŋ.

('siŋgə, 'lɔŋgiŋg) and finally (siŋg, lɔŋg, etc.) as well as in the words of the first category. Less frequently they pronounce words of the first category with ŋ or a doubled ŋ: 'fiŋə or 'fiŋŋə, 'lɔŋə or 'lɔŋŋə. The forms 'lɔŋə, 'lɔŋist, etc., are common in Wales, but apart from the comparatives and superlatives of adjectives the usage in Wales is generally as in Southern England.

§ 290. The voiceless consonant ɬ̥ exists, but does not often occur in speech. ɬ̥ŋɬ̥ is a variant of the interjectional sound ŋ̍nŋ̍ mentioned in § 282, and ɬ̥ may occasionally be heard in place of **k** between two nasal consonants, as in 'drʌŋɬ̥n for 'drʌŋk(ə)n or 'drʌŋkŋ̍ (*drunken*), 'blaŋɬ̥nis for 'blaŋknis (*blankness*).

LATERAL CONSONANTS

§ 291. l. Voiced alveolar lateral. Examples: liːv (*leave*), lɑːf (*laugh*), bɛl (*bell*), 'litl (*little*).

§ 292. There are many varieties of l. In most of those used in English the primary articulation is by the tip of the tongue against the teeth-ridge. Contact is in the centre of the ridge, but an aperture is left on one or both sides through which the air passes out. It makes no appreciable difference to the sound if it is produced unilaterally or bilaterally. But the quality of the sound is very much affected by the position of the main body of the tongue behind the tip. The main body of the tongue may be raised in front or at the back or may take up various other positions. Three of these are shown in Fig. 24 (*a*), (*b*) and (*c*).

§ 293. These positions are analogous to the positions of vowels, and the student will find by experimenting that the different kinds of l have in fact considerable resemblance to vowel sounds. An l formed with simultaneous raising of the front of the tongue (Fig. 24 (*a*)) has a certain degree of acoustic resemblance to i, and one articulated with a depression of the front of the tongue (behind the articulating tip) and a raising at the back (Fig. 24 (*c*)) has an u-like quality or 'u-resonance' as it is often called. It is a useful exercise to practise making l's with different vowel resonances, for instance with resonances of i, e, ɑː, ɔː, u, ə; this is done by holding the tongue-tip continuously against the teeth-ridge and then producing l-sounds, at the same time trying to make them sound like the various vowels. The fact that different l-sounds have

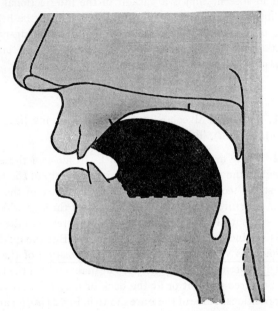

Fig. 24 (a)–(c). Tongue position of three l-sounds.
(a) Clear l.

different vowel resonances may be utilized for teaching students of speech to make particular kinds of l. l-sounds with i or e resonance are said to be 'clear'; those with back vowel resonances are called 'dark' varieties. An l with resonance of ə is a 'neutral' variety.

§ 294. It should be noticed that it is possible to make all these varieties of l dentally (i.e. articulating against the teeth) as well as when the tongue-tip is in its usual English position against the teeth-ridge. The precise place of articulation has little or no effect on the quality of the l, but the position taken up simultaneously by the main body of the tongue affects the quality considerably. Thus a dental l with u-resonance is

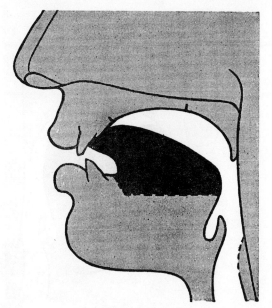

Fig. 24 (b). Neutral l.

indistinguishable in sound from an alveolar l with u-resonance. And so on with other varieties.

§ 295. When it is desired to indicate in phonetic transcription that l-sounds have particular resonances, the sounds may be symbolized thus: lⁱ, lᵘ, lᵊ, etc. A less precise way of transcribing is to use the ordinary letter l to represent 'clear' l-sounds and the special symbol ł to denote any kind of 'dark' l (§ 293).

§ **296.** Several varieties of l are found in RP. They nearly all have approximately the same primary articulation against the teeth-ridge,[1] but they differ in resonance. Two chief varieties are distinguished, a fairly 'clear' l with resonance approximating to i, and a 'dark' l with resonance approximating to u.

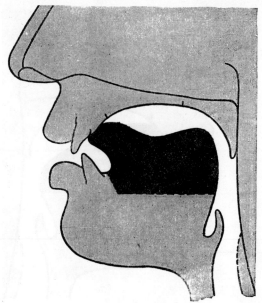

Fig. 24 (c). Dark l.

Fairly clear l's are used when a vowel or j follows, as in liːv (*leave*), list (*list*), lɛt (*let*), 'lʌki (*lucky*), lɔt (*lot*), luːz (*lose*), 'fɔlou (*follow*), 'kuːlə (*cooler*), 'valjuː (*value*). The degree of clearness of the l varies to some extent with the following vowel; it is less clear when the following vowel is a back one. Definitely

---

[1] The primary articulation is more dental when θ or ð follows, as in hɛlθ (*health*).

dark varieties of l are used finally and before consonants, as in fiːl (*feel*), bil (*bill*), ʃɛl (*shell*), dɔl (*doll*), kɔːl (*call*), kuːl (*cool*), fiːld (*field*), bild (*build*), 'aldʒibrə (*algebra*), 'ɔːltə or 'ɔltə (*alter, altar*), kuːld (*cooled*). An ə-glide may often be perceived between the vowel and the l, thus fiːᵊl, biᵊl, etc., but it is an incidental transitory sound which need not be symbolized in phonetic transcripts. A particularly dark variety of l is used when the sound is syllabic, as in 'piːpl (*people*), 'sɛtld (*settled*), 'sɛtlmənt (*settlement*).

§ 297. In Southern English, when a word ending in l is followed by a word beginning with a vowel, a rather clear variety is generally used. For instance though bil said by itself has a dark l, 'bil əv iks'tʃeindʒ (*bill of exchange*) has a clear l. So also when a suffix such as -*ing* or -*er* is added to a word; kuːl has a dark l, but 'kuːlə (*cooler*) a clear l. Even syllabic l's lose much of their darkness when a vowel follows: 'sɛtliŋ (*settling*) and 'sɛtl it (*settle it*) generally have syllabic l's which are rather clear.[1]

§ 298. There are considerable variations both in the quality and the use of l-sounds in different parts of the English-speaking world. Occasionally one meets with people in the South of England who do not differentiate between clear l's and dark l's to the extent mentioned in the preceding paragraphs. Their clear l's may have a resonance between i and ə, and their dark l's are not particularly dark. On the other hand in the distinctive London pronunciation, the dark l's are very dark indeed, the resonance being a kind of ɔ or o rather than u. In London dialectal speech the dark l is often replaced by a vowel of the ɔ or o type; *field, milk* are pronounced fiŏd, miŏk, and *railway* is 'raiŏwai or 'raiŏwai.

§ 299. In London dialectal speech, and in other regions where l final or preceding a consonant is particularly dark, vowels

---

[1] *Settling* is also sometimes pronounced 'sɛtliŋ with a non-syllabic l.

preceding the dark l (or the vocalic sound which replaces it) are considerably influenced by it. The iː of RP in a word like *field* is replaced by the opener i (fiɫd or fiŏd), and *twelve, bulb, result, bowl, school* sound like twe̜ɫv or twa̧ɫv or twe̜ŏv or twa̧ŏv, bɔɫb or bɔŏb, ri'zɔɫt or ri'zɔŏt, bɔuɫ or bɔŏ, sko̧ːɫ or sko̧ːŭ.

§ **300.** Noticeably distinct shades of vowel sound are thus often heard according as a dark or a clear l follows. For instance in London it is common to hear differences of vowel quality in *bowl* and *bowling* (bouɫ or bɔuɫ, 'böüliŋ), *rule* and *ruling* (ruːɫ or ro̧ːɫ and something approaching 'rüːliŋ or 'rəüliŋ), *calculate* and *callous* ('kɑlkjuleit and 'kaləs).

§ **301.** In Scotland l's are as a rule dark in all positions. So it is usual to hear Scottish people pronounce for instance [ɫif] (*leaf*), [ɫ ̟ft] (*lift*), [ɫʌik] (*like*), ['pɫɛnte] (*plenty*), ['vaɫju] (*value*), etc. In continuous transcriptions of Scottish speech it is unnecessary to use the special letter ɫ; ordinary l can be written with the convention that it always denotes a dark variety.

§ **302.** In American English a dark l is likewise generally used in all positions.

§ **303.** In English as spoken in Ireland l is always clear; clear l is for instance used by Irish people in such words as milk, 'piːpl as well as before vowels. This pronunciation may also be heard in Liverpool; its existence there is probably due to Irish influence.

§ **304.** There has been a tradition among teachers of voice production and singing that dark l is an undesirable sound and that it should be replaced by clear l. This view cannot be supported on acoustic or other physical grounds. It probably originated in the fact that the training of singers was for a long period chiefly carried on by foreign teachers to whom the English dark l was a strange sound which they were unable to make, and which they did not recognize as being a kind of l. The tradition still persists, however, and in consequence such words as milk, 'piːpl are usually pronounced with clear l by singers; this artificial pronunciation may also often be heard on the stage.

§ 305. Many of those who speak with RP sometimes omit dark l altogether before another consonant in rapid or careless speech. Examples: fu'fil for ful'fil (*fulfil*), 'ɔːmoust or 'ɔːməst for 'ɔːlmoust or 'ɔːlməst (*almost*), 'ɔː'rait for 'ɔːl'rait (*all right*), 'wɛə ʃ wi 'gou for 'wɛə ʃl wi 'gou or 'wɛə ʃəl wi 'gou (*Where shall we go?*).

§ 306. A partially voiceless l is used after initial p, k, f and s, as in pliːz (*please*), kliːn (*clean*), flou (*flow*), slip (*slip*). Sometimes the devoicing is complete, especially after p and k; the pronunciation with completely devoiced l may be represented thus: pl̥iːz, kl̥iːn, etc. A voiceless l with strong friction is the sound of Welsh *ll*. It is usual to represent this sound phonetically by the special symbol ɬ. The pronunciation of *Llangollen* and *Machynlleth* may therefore be written ɬanˈgoɬen, maˈxənɬeθ, or l̥anˈgol̥en, maˈxənl̥eθ.

§ 306 *a*. ļ is heard fairly frequently as an individual speech defect, replacing s: e.g. liļt, jɛļ, ļikļ (for *list, yes, six*). For methods of remedying this see Ward, *Defects of Speech, their Nature and Cure*, pp. 25, 26.

§ 307. In the dialectal speech of Bristol and the neighbourhood the l of the termination -əl is often dropped; for instance *rascal* is pronounced 'raːskə. And final syllabic l is replaced by ə; for instance *Bristol* is pronounced 'bristə.

§ 308. This usage has had a curious repercussion. Many Bristolians, having no doubt been taught that l should be sounded in such words, or seeing that there is an *l* in the spelling, are uncertain about the presence or absence of final l's. In consequence they not unfrequently insert an 'intrusive' l

after a final -ə. They will for instance pronounce *Nova Scotia*
as 'nouvəl 'skouʃəl (for RP 'nouvə 'skouʃə), and say ai'di:əl
for ai'diə.

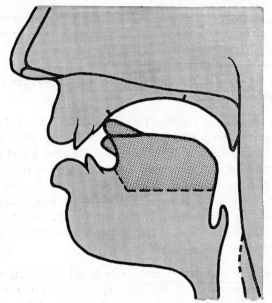

Fig. 25. Tongue position of lingual rolled r.

ROLLED CONSONANTS

§ **309.** Rolled sounds can hardly be said to occur in RP. It is,
however, good practice for students of speech to learn to make
'rolled r'. This is a voiced sound made by causing the tongue-
tip to vibrate against the teeth-ridge after the manner shown
in Fig. 25.

§ **310.** Some people can make this sound quite easily and
without practice. Others find it very difficult. There are no
infallible rules for teaching it to those who at first are unable

to make it. One method is to place the tongue-tip in position for **d**, and then force out air with a strong sudden jerk. After a few attempts, repetitions of this exercise will often result in **drrrdrrrdrrr**....[1] Some learners find it easier to learn a breathed **r̥** first, by a similar exercise: **tr̥r̥tr̥r̥tr̥r̥**.... Then the student must learn to detach the **d** (or **t**): this will give **rrr**... (or **r̥r̥r̥**...). Sometimes it is necessary to adjust the tongue first at one point of the teeth-ridge and then at another until the learner hits upon the position in which he can get the tongue-tip to make some sort of vibration. When once the tongue can be made to vibrate at all, it is a matter of practice —sometimes long practice—to learn to make a clean roll. A student cannot be said to have a mastery of the sound unless he can make it without special preparation, and hold it on as long as his breath lasts.

§ 311. Another method that sometimes succeeds is the following: pronounce first a *dental* **t**, that is to say a variety of **t** articulated against the edge of the upper teeth (phonetically **t̪**). Add **ə** to it, making **t̪ə**, and then add the syllable **da:** said with an ordinary English (alveolar) **d**: thus **t̪əda:**. Then repeat this sequence **t̪əda:t̪əda:t̪əda:**... at first slowly and then with gradually increasing speed. When this is pronounced very fast, and if the tongue is kept as relaxed as possible, the **d** tends to turn into a 'single flap **r**' (§ 317). When once a single flap **r** has been acquired in this way, the action can be extended so as to produce the fully rolled **r** of several taps.

§ 312. Rolled lingual **r** is a common sound in Scotland and in Wales. In these regions it is the usual sound of the letter *r* when a strongly stressed vowel follows. Examples: Scottish [rʌit] (*right*), [ʌ'raev] (*arrive*), [krak] (*crack*), ['rabɪt] (*rabbit*),

---

[1] **rrr** is here used to mean a long sustained continuous rolled **r**.

95

['frizɪŋ] (*freezing*). The number of taps of the tip of the tongue does not as a rule exceed three; it is sometimes only two and sometimes only one (i.e. a flapped r, § 317). In positions of weak stress and when consonants follow, a single flap r is usually employed in Scottish English. Scottish people also sometimes use a fricative r (§ 347) in these positions.

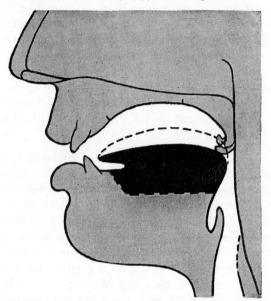

Fig. 26. Tongue position of uvular rolled r (ʀ).

§ 313. Another rolled sound which it is a useful exercise to learn to make is the 'uvular rolled r' (phonetically ʀ). This is formed by a particular kind of raising of the back part of the tongue, which is adjusted in such a manner that the air as it passes out causes the uvula to vibrate as shown in Fig. 26. It is believed that in the articulation of this sound the tongue is held in such a way that there is a groove down the centre, and that the uvula lies in this groove. The height of the sides of the tongue is shown by the dotted line in the figure.

§ 314. To learn to make ʀ, start from the breathed velar fricative sound which we represent phonetically by x—the Scottish sound in lɔx (*loch*). Most people can make this easily;

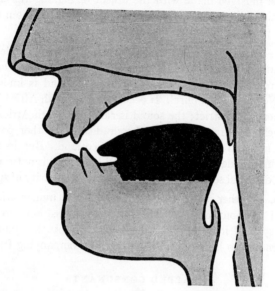

Fig. 27. Tongue position of uvular fricative r (ʁ).

but in cases of difficulty it may be arrived at by placing the tongue in the k position and forcing the air through in a continuous stream. The next step is to add voice to this. This gives the voiced velar fricative, which is represented phonetically by ɣ. There are several varieties of ɣ distinguished by different degrees of friction and by the presence or absence of accompanying uvular vibration and 'scrape'. (In the absence of indication to the contrary the letter ɣ means the fricative corresponding exactly to g, without any accompanying uvular vibration or scrape.) What usually emerges when practising as directed above is a variety of ɣ with considerable scrape and with intermittent vibration of the uvula. Then, in order to arrive at ʀ, various adjustments of the back of the tongue must be made with the object of making the uvular vibrations regular and eliminating the scrape. It often needs much practice to find the right adjustment.

§ 315. In parts of Northumberland and Durham a rolled ʀ is in common use in place of the r of RP. *Really, dry, Durham* are pronounced 'ʀiːli, dʀɑi, 'dɣʀəm. The sound is known as the 'Northumbrian burr'. It occurs also in South Africa in the Malmesbury district; the sound is called in South Africa 'the Malmesbury bray'. ʀ is heard sporadically in other parts of England, and rather frequently in Scotland. But in Great Britain outside Northumberland and Durham ʀ is not a recognized dialectal sound, but is an individual peculiarity of speech.

§ 316. Another variety of the 'burr' is a uvular fricative sound (without roll). It has the tongue position shown in Fig. 27, and it is represented phonetically by the symbol ʁ. One may also hear a uvular roll with accompanying friction.

FLAPPED CONSONANTS

§ 317. A flapped consonant has the same kind of action as a rolled consonant, but it consists of only a single tap of the vibrating organ instead of several taps. Flapped lingual r is formed in the same sort of way as rolled lingual r, but consists of only a single tap of the tip of the tongue against the teeth-ridge. (In very precise transcription it may be denoted phonetically by a special symbol, ɾ.) Similarly, there exists a flapped uvular ʀ—a single flap of the uvula made in the manner shown in Fig. 26. Flapped consonants are sometimes called 'semi-rolled'.

§ 318. Flapped lingual r is used by some RP speakers in place of fricative r in some words. See § 352.

§ 319. In Scottish speech a flapped r is generally used finally and before consonants and before weakly stressed vowels. (See § 312.) Examples: [far] (*far*), [mor] (*more*), ['ɛvɩr] (*ever*), [fɔrm] (*form*), [wʌrld] (*world*), ['vɛre] (*very*), ['piriʌd] or ['pireʌd] (*period*). Similarly in English as spoken in Wales.

§ 320. The Northumbrian burr (§§ 313–315) sometimes consists of only a single flap of the uvula.

§ 321. Completely or partially voiceless varieties of rolled or flapped r or ʀ are found before and after other voiceless consonants. For instance in Scotland the word *thirty* is generally pronounced in a way that would be written in precise transcription ['θɩr̥te]. In Newcastle the word *tree* is pronounced tʀ̥iː.

FRICATIVES

§ 322. f. Breathed labio-dental fricative with strong breath force. Examples: fut (*foot*), seif (*safe*), 'ɔfə (*offer*).

§ 323. When f is followed by θ, there is a variant pronunciation with p. Examples: 'difθɔŋ or 'dipθɔŋ (*diphthong*), ɔf'θalmïə or ɔp'θalmïə (*ophthalmia*). Some use f for v in *nephew*, pronouncing 'nɛfjuː instead of the historically justifiable 'nɛvjuː. 'nɛfjuː is a modern 'spelling pronunciation'.

§ 324. In careless speaking many people drop the f of *half* in the expression *half past*. They pronounce for instance 'hɑːpəs 'twɛlv for 'hɑːf pɑːs 'twɛlv (*half past twelve*).

§ 325. In South-Western dialects the f of RP is replaced by v. For instance in Cornwall one may hear *fire* pronounced as vʌiɹ.

99

§ **326.** **v.** Voiced or partially voiced labio-dental fricative. Examples: vein (*vain, vein*), muːv (*move*), 'klɛvə (*clever*). In initial and final positions the voicing is generally only partial. The voicing may in fact disappear altogether in these positions; the sound is then v̥, which differs from f only in being pronounced with weak breath force.

§ **327.** In rapid speech the v's of *of* and *have* are often dropped before another consonant and especially before the word *the*. People say for instance 'aut ə ðə 'wei (*out of the way*), z 'matr ə 'fakt (*as a matter of fact*), juː 'ʃudnt ə bin sou 'sili (*you shouldn't have been so silly*). Examples like this latter one have given rise, by analogy, to ungrammatical forms like if iː 'hadnt ə bin 'ðɛə (for *if he hadn't been there*), if iː d ə 'wɔntid tu (for *if he had wanted to*). This form of expression is considered incorrect, but it is quite commonly used by speakers influenced by dialect.

§ **328.** In London dialectal speech final -v(ə)n is commonly replaced by bm. Examples: 'sebm, i'lebm, 'ebm for RP 'sɛvn (*seven*), i'lɛvn (*eleven*), 'hɛvn (*heaven*).

§ **329.** **θ.** Breathed dental fricative (see Fig. 28). Examples: θin (*thin*), brɛθ (*breath*), 'mɛθəd (*method*).

§ **330.** In careless speaking θ is sometimes weakened to a kind of h between vowels, e.g. 'nou 'haŋk ju for 'nou 'θaŋk ju (*No thank you*). When θ occurs between two consonants it is sometimes dropped or replaced by t, e.g. sikss for siksθs (*sixths*), mʌns or mʌnts for mʌnθs (*months*). In *asthma* the *th* is generally not pronounced ('asmə), but 'asθmə and 'astmə may sometimes be heard.

§ **331.** In London dialect the θ of RP is often replaced by f. One hears for instance [frəi] for θriː (*three*), ['nafiŋk] for 'nʌθiŋ (*nothing*).

§ **332.** **ð.** Voiced or partially voiced dental fricative. The tongue position is the same as for θ (see Fig. 28). Examples:

ðɛn (*then*), briːð (*breathe*), wið (*with*), ˈʌðə (*other*). In initial and final positions the voicing is often only partial. The voicing may in fact disappear altogether in these positions; the sound is then ð̣, which differs from θ only in being uttered with weak breath force.

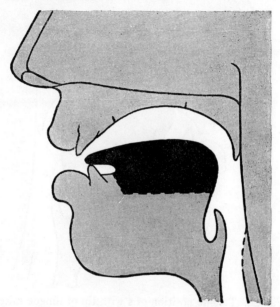

Fig. 28. Tongue position of θ and ð.

§ 333. *Clothes* is pronounced klouðz. There existed until recently another form without ð (klouz); this is now old-fashioned and seems likely to go out of use. In words compounded with *with*, such as *withdraw, withhold, therewith,* some RP speakers use ð and others θ: wiðˈdrɔː or wiθˈdrɔː, wiðˈhould or wiθˈhould, ðɛəˈwið or ðɛəˈwiθ. This does not, however, apply to *within* and *without* which in the South always have ð (wiˈðin, wiˈðaut).

§ **334.** In Scotland θ is used in some words where the South has ð. *With* is regularly [wιθ], *though* is [θo], and *smooth* is [smuθ]. *With* is also pronounced with θ in the North of England.

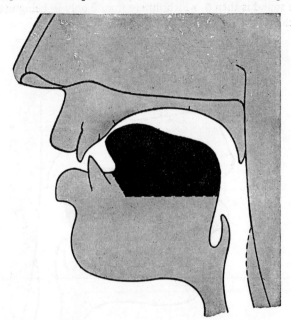

Fig. 29. Tongue position of s with tip of tongue raised.

§ **335.** In London dialect the ð of RP is commonly replaced by v. *Then* and *father* are pronounced [ven], ['fɑ:və].

§ **336. s.** Breathed alveolar fricative with very narrow aperture for the air to pass through; it is generally said with considerable breath-force. Examples: si:s (*cease*), 'asid (*acid*). Some articulate this sound with the tip of the tongue and others with the blade (keeping the tip down near the lower teeth). See Figs. 29, 30. The manner of articulation depends largely on the shape of the individual speaker's teeth and palate. The degree of hissing varies with individuals; with some it is physically impossible to make a very penetrating hiss. The student of speech should observe how he places his tongue when he says **s**, and should see whether he can make an

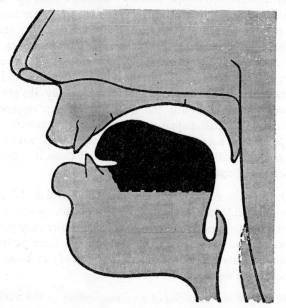

Fig. 30. Tongue position of **s** with tip of tongue lowered.

equally distinct one with the tip of his tongue in a position different from that to which he is accustomed. He should also compare the acoustic quality of his **s** with that of others.

§ 337. A variety of **s** which is fairly common in the South of England is one in which the tongue articulation is accompanied by an articulation by the lower lip against the upper teeth. The acoustic quality of this kind of **s** differs noticeably from the normal **s** described above. The student should ascertain whether he makes any lip-movement when he pronounces his **s**, and whether he is able to make a satisfactory **s** without any lip action.

§ 338. In South-Western country dialects **s** next to voiced sounds is replaced everywhere by **z**, e.g. one may hear zɛnd for sɛnd (*send*). Apart from this the use of **s** does not vary greatly in the English-speaking world. It is noteworthy, however, that the termination *-sive* is generally pronounced with **s** in the South of England but with **z** in the North and in Scotland: for instance *explosive, persuasive* are more usually iks'plousiv, pə'sweisiv in the South but [ɛks'plozɪv], [pɪr'swezɪv] in Scotland. A word that appears to be changing its pronunciation is *opposite*; the normal Southern pronunciation is 'ɔpəzit, but it is not unusual now to hear 'ɔpəsit, and there is a London dialect form ['ɔpəsait].

§ 339. z. Voiced or partially voiced alveolar fricative. Examples: ziːl (*zeal*), tʃuːz (*choose*), 'mʌzlin (*muslin*). In initial and final positions the voicing is generally only partial. The voicing may even disappear altogether in these positions; the sound is then ᶎ, which differs from **s** solely in being pronounced with weaker breath force.

§ 340. There are varieties of **z** corresponding to the varieties of **s** mentioned in §§ 336, 337.

§ 341. ʃ. Breathed palato-alveolar fricative. Examples: ʃeip (*shape*), 'ʃugə (*sugar*), 'eiʃə (*Asia*), 'mouʃn (*motion*). The sound is not articulated in exactly the same way by everybody. Its manner of formation depends to some extent upon the shape of the speaker's teeth and palate. More usually the tongue-tip is raised in the position shown in Fig. 31, but some keep the tongue-tip down near the lower teeth as shown in Fig. 32. The student should observe how he places his tongue when he makes the sound ʃ, and should experiment and see whether he can make an equally distinct one with his tongue-tip in a position different from the one to which he is accustomed.

§ **342.** With many the articulation of ʃ is accompanied by protrusion of the lips. With others the lips are in a neutral

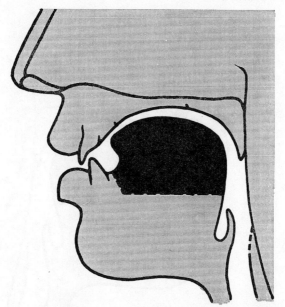

Fig. 31. Tongue position of ʃ with tip of tongue raised.

position. The sounds formed with and without lip-protrusion are acoustically distinct from each other. The student should observe the position of his lips when he says his ʃ, and should compare the acoustic quality of his ʃ with that of others.

§ **343.** In a few words ending in *-ciate*, *-ciation* the pronunciation varies, some people using **s** and others ʃ. Such are *associate* (ə'souʃieit or ə'sousieit), *appreciation* (əpriːʃi'eiʃn or əpriːsi'eiʃn). The pronunciation with ʃ is commoner in some words and the pronunciation with s is more usual in others. Many people, for instance, use ʃ in *associate* but s in *association* (ə'souʃieit but əsousi'eiʃn). ə'priːʃieit is probably more usual than ə'priːsieit.

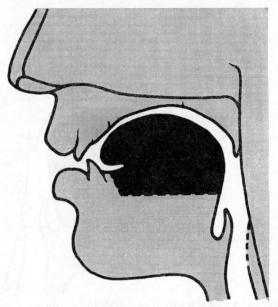

Fig. 32. Tongue position of ʃ with tip of tongue lowered.

§ **344.** Note pronunciations like 'paːʃl (*partial*) but paːʃi'aliti (*partiality*), 'ouʃn (*ocean*), ouʃi'anik (*oceanic*). Occasionally one may hear 'eiʃïə, 'eiʃjə, 'eiʒïə, 'eiʒjə, or 'eiʒə for RP 'eiʃə (*Asia*), 'rʌʃïə or 'rʌʃjə for RP 'rʌʃə (*Russia*), 'pəːʒə for the more usual 'pəːʃə (*Persia*). These pronunciations are common in the North. i'kweiʒn seems to be gradually superseding the older pronunciation i'kweiʃn (*equation*), which is still the only pronunciation shown in most dictionaries.

§ 345. 3. Voiced or partially voiced palato-alveolar fricative. Examples: 'mɛʒə (*measure*), ruːʒ (*rouge*). In final positions the voicing is generally only partial, and may even disappear altogether. The sound is then ʒ̥, which differs from ʃ solely in being pronounced with weaker breath force.

§ 346. The remarks on the articulation of ʃ and its varieties (§§ 341, 342) apply equally to ʒ.

§ 347. *Fricative* r. This is a voiced post-alveolar sound, formed by the tongue-tip against the back part of the teeth-ridge, the 'front' part of the tongue being to some extent depressed as shown in Fig. 33. A certain amount of friction is heard as the air passes through the fairly narrow space between the tongue-tip and the teeth-ridge.

§ 348. A variant of this without perceptible friction is used by many. The absence of friction is due either to a slight widening of the aperture between the tongue and the teeth-ridge or to a diminution of breath force or to a combination of the two. The sound so made is called *frictionless continuant* r.

§ 349. Many people use a variety of r in which the tongue articulation is accompanied by a certain degree of lip-protrusion. This is particularly common among those who use a frictionless continuant r. The student should observe what degree of lip protrusion he uses, if any, and should compare his r with those of others.

§ 350. In the speech of many, both fricative and frictionless r occur, the fricative variety being used after t and d and the frictionless in other situations.

§ 351. When it is desired to distinguish in transcription fricative or frictionless continuant r from rolled r (§ 309), the

5-2

letter ɹ may be employed to denote the fricative or frictionless continuant, the ordinary form r being reserved for representing the rolled sound. Generally speaking, however, the ordinary letter r can be used without ambiguity, if it is stated once for all what kind of sound is meant in the form of language transcribed.

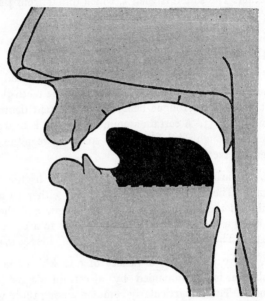

Fig. 33. Tongue position of fricative tongue-tip r.

§ 352. Fricative r (or, alternatively, frictionless continuant r) is the usual sound given by Southern speakers to the written *r* when a vowel follows. Examples: rɛd (*red*), 'brʌðə (*brother*), ə'reindʒ (*arrange*), 'hiəriŋ (*hearing*). Some, however, use a flapped lingual r (§ 317) between vowels, as 'hiəriŋ, ə'raiv (*arrive*), and a few do the same after θ and ð, as in θriː (*three*), 'brɛðrin (*brethren*). After n, as in 'hɛnri (*Henry*), the sound is almost always frictionless. After initial p, t or k, r is voiceless or partially so (ɹ̥), e.g. in print (*print*), trai (*try*), kraun (*crown*).

§ 353. As already mentioned in § 315, some people have as a speech defect for r a uvular sound (rolled or fricative or a combination of the two). A normal r may be taught to those who have this defect by showing them that ordinary fricative r (ɹ) is allied to ʒ (§ 345), and that a near approach to it can be arrived at by endeavouring to sound ʒ with the jaws wide apart. When the learner can do this, a correct ɹ can be obtained by making adjustments of the tongue-tip.

§ 354. Another fairly common defective r is a sound made with little or no tongue action but by an articulation of the lower lip against the upper teeth. The sound differs from v in having no perceptible friction. It is denoted in International Phonetic transcription by the symbol ʋ. Examples: 'vɛʋi for 'vɛri (*very*), kʋɑud for krɑud (*crowd*). Those who have this defect may learn to make fricative r by the method mentioned in § 353; they must take care to keep the lower lip out of the way when practising the sound.

§ 355. When written *r* is final or followed by a sounded consonant, it does not have any consonantal value in ordinary South-Eastern English. *Farm* is pronounced fɑːm; *purse, nor, pair, fire, poor* are pəːs, nɔː (like *gnaw*), pɛə, 'faiə, puə or pɔː (like *paw*). *Stork* and *stalk* have identical pronunciation (stɔːk). In other parts, however, the written *r* has a distinct value in such words. In Scotland it is generally a single flap: [farm], [pʌrs], [nɔr], [per], ['faeɪr], [pur]. In the West Country and in the North-West and in America either the letter is sounded as ɹ or the vowel has what is called 'retroflex modification' or 'r-colouring'. 'r-colouring' means giving an r-like effect simultaneously with the pronunciation of the vowel. This effect is generally produced by 'inverting' the tongue, i.e. curling the

tip of the tongue backwards towards the hard palate as shown
in Fig. 34. The same effect can be, and often is, produced by
retracting the whole body of the tongue, keeping the tip down
and away from the lower teeth as shown in Fig. 35. The effect
can be amplified by 'lateral contraction' of the tongue (§ 489).

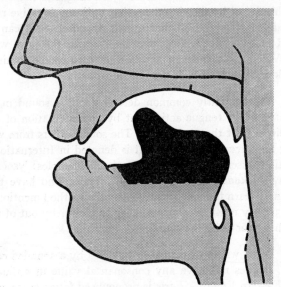

Fig. 34. Tongue position of 'r-coloured' ɑ
(variety with retroflexed tongue).

§ 356. 'r-colouring' may be represented phonetically either by
use of digraphs (ɑɹ, ɔɹ, əɹ, etc.) with a convention as to their
values, or by superposing ɹ (thus ɑ̇, ɔ̇, ə̇, etc.) or by attaching
a hook to the vowel letters (ɑ̡, ɔ̢, ə̢,[1] etc.). West Country
pronunciation of the words quoted in the last paragraph may
therefore be written phonetically in any of the following three
ways: (i) faɹm (less usually fɑɹm), pəɹs, nɔːɹɹ, pɛːɹ, 'faiəɹ, puəɹ,

---

[1] The symbol ə̢ has an alternative form ꜱ.

representing either the pronunciation with vowel+ɹ or the pronunciation with r-coloured vowels; (ii) fáːm (also fɑ̇ːm), pə́ːs,[1] nɔ̇ː, pɛ́ː (also pɛɘ̇), 'faiɘ̇, puɘ̇, denoting the pronunciation with r-coloured vowels; (iii) fɑ̱ːm (also fɑ̱ːm), pə̱ːs,[1] nɔ̱ː, pɛ̱ː

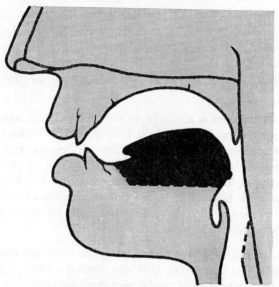

Fig. 35. Tongue position of 'r-coloured' ɑ (variety with tip of tongue down and retracted).

(also pɛɘ̱),[2] 'faiɘ̱, puɘ̱, also denoting the pronunciation with r-coloured vowels. American examples will be found in Text No. 18.

§ 357. *Linking* r. When a word ending with *r* in ordinary spelling is followed in the sentence by a word beginning with a vowel, it is usual in RP to insert a consonantal r-sound. The following are examples showing the difference between words

---

[1] pə́ːs and pɑ̱ːs may also be written pɹːs.
[2] pɛɘ̇ and pɛɘ̱ are other ways of writing pɛːɹ.

pronounced by themselves and the same words said with a
vowel following:

fɑː (*far*)	but	'fɑːr ə'wei (*far away*)
ɔː (*or*)	,,	ɔːr 'ɛls (*or else*)
fɔː (*four*)	,,	'fɔːr 'auəz (*four hours*)
'nɛvə (*never*)	,,	'nɛvər ə'gɛn[1] (*never again*)
pɛə (*pair*)	,,	ə 'pɛər əv 'ʃuːz (*a pair of shoes*)
hiə (*here*)	,,	'hiər i 'tiz (*here it is*)
'wɛsminstə (*Westminster*)	,,	'wɛsminstər 'abi (*Westminster Abbey*)

§ 358. This usage is a relic of an old pronunciation when all
written *r*'s were sounded. It is believed that r began to be
dropped before consonants in the fifteenth century, and that
this pronunciation became usual in the speech of cultured
southern people in the course of the seventeenth. The dropping
of *final* r's is believed to have followed somewhat later.[2] In
instances such as those quoted in the second column of § 357
the r was preserved by the following vowel.

§ 359. In the RP of the early part of the twentieth century
and for a long time before that, the usage described in § 357
seems to have been quite regular, and there were probably only
two cases of this description where the r was not as a rule
inserted before a vowel, namely: (i) where the words are not in
close grammatical connexion, and (ii) when the last syllable of
the first word begins with r. Examples of (i): hiː 'oupənd ðə
'dɔː ənd 'wɔːkt 'in (*he opened the door and walked in*), ai ʃəd
'laik ðə 'peipə if juː v 'finiʃt wið it (*I should like the paper if you*

---

[1] Or ə'gein.
[2] See H. C. Wyld's *History of Modern Colloquial English*
(Blackwell, Oxford), pp. 298–300; also p. 41 of *English
Pronunciation through the Centuries* (published by the Linguaphone Institute).

have finished with it), 'kʌm bak 'hiə in ə 'fjuː 'minits (*come back here in a few minutes*). Examples of (ii): ə 'rɔː əv 'lɑːftə (*a roar of laughter*), ðɛə z ən 'ɛrə in it (*there is an error in it*), ði inˈtiəriə əv ðə 'haus (*the interior of the house*).

§ 360. In recent years this pronunciation has been changing, and a great many Southern people may now be found who do not use linking r at all or who restrict its use to very common expressions. They pronounce 'fɑː əˈwei, ɔː 'ɛls, 'fɔː 'auəz, 'hiə i 'tiz, ə 'pɛə əv 'ʃuːz, 'wɛsminstə 'abi, etc. (see also § 365). In common expressions like *for instance, after all*, the r is still generally sounded, but some omit it even here. Many of the younger generation of Londoners insert a glottal stop: 'fɑː ʔəˈwei, fə 'ʔinstəns, etc.

§ 361. *Intrusive r.* Many Southern people insert r when words spelt with final -*a* are followed by words beginning with a vowel. They pronounce for instance

soda and milk	as	'soudər ən 'milk
China and Japan	,,	'tʃainər ən dʒəˈpan
vanilla ice	,,	vəˈnilər 'ais
he is in Persia at the moment	,,	hiː z in 'pəːʃər ət ðə ˌmoumənt
he put his umbrella up	,,	hiː 'put (h)iz ʌmˈbrɛlər ʌp
the idea of it	,,	ði aiˈdiər əv it
a cinema organ	,,	ə 'sinimər ɔːgən

This pronunciation has been in use quite a long time. It has evidently been brought about by *analogy* and dates no doubt from the time when r ceased to be sounded in final positions (probably towards the end of the seventeenth century). The existence of intrusive r was mentioned by some late eighteenth-century writers, who called it a vulgarism (see Jespersen's *Modern English Grammar*, vol. I, § 13·42). H. Sweet, writing in 1890, stated that most educated speakers of Southern English used it in rapid speech (*Primer of Spoken English*, p. viii).

§ 362. Some people use intrusive r not only after ə but also after ɑː and ɔː. They pronounce for instance

the Shah of Persia	as	ðə 'ʃɑːr əv 'pəːʃə
Is papa in?	,,	'iz pə'pɑːr in?
awe-inspiring	,,	'ɔːr-in‚spaiəriŋ
I saw it there	,,	ai 'sɔːr it ðɛə
sawing	,,	'sɔːriŋ (like *soaring*)

It is not used after any other vowels.

§ 363. The use of intrusive r is the result of *analogy*. Since in Southern pronunciation words like 'ɑːftə, 'ɛvə have variant forms with r added when the next word begins with a vowel, it is natural to treat words like 'soudə and 'tʃainə similarly.

§ 364. Some people, instead of looking upon intrusive r as an interesting illustration of analogy, regard it as a 'bad' pronunciation on the ground that it does not correspond to spelling. There has therefore been a tendency among many to avoid it, particularly after ɑː and ɔː, and the efforts to avoid it have been attended by a considerable measure of success. The result is that cases where intrusive r would be natural are treated in one of two ways: either the terminal ə or ɑː or ɔː is run on to the following vowel without break, or a glottal stop is inserted. So we now hear very commonly pronunciations like

'soudə‿ən 'milk	or	'soudə ʔən 'milk
və'nilə‿'ais	,,	və'nilə 'ʔais

The first of these seems to be generally considered preferable.

§ 365. The avoidance of intrusive r is no doubt responsible for the now common failure to use 'linking r' appropriately, as mentioned in § 360. This is again an instance of change of pronunciation by analogy. Those who have accustomed themselves to pronouncing ˈsoʊdə ən ˈmilk, etc., are naturally prone to say ˈnɛvə əˈgɛn,[1] etc.

§ 366. It is probable that the pronunciation which gives the greatest general satisfaction is that of speakers who use 'linking r' consistently and who do not use 'intrusive r' at all. We have no statistics as to the number of people who speak in this way, but the number is probably comparatively small.

§ 367. When there are in RP two consecutive weakly stressed syllables beginning with r, careless speakers are liable to omit the first one, e.g. to say

ˈlaibəri	for RP	ˈlaibrəri (*library*)
ˈtɛmpəri	„	ˈtɛmp(ə)rəri (*temporary*)
ˈfɛbjuəri	„	ˈfɛbruəri (*February*)
(dialectally		
also ˈfɛbjuɛri)		

The pronunciation ˈfɛbjuəri is no doubt encouraged by analogy with ˈdʒanjuəri (*January*).

§ 368. In dialectal speech ə is sometimes inserted before r in ˈɛnəri (for RP ˈhɛnri, *Henry*), ʌmbəˈrɛlə (for RP ʌmˈbrɛlə, *umbrella*), dʒibəˈrɔːltə (for RP dʒiˈbrɔːltə, *Gibraltar*).

§ 369. h. Breathed glottal fricative. Examples: hɑːd (*hard*), huː (*who*), hit (*hit*). It is the sound heard when air passes out through the open glottis and the mouth is held in position for a vowel. There are as many varieties of h as there are vowels. In English the variety used in any particular case is that corresponding to the vowel which follows. Thus the h in hɑːd is a kind of voiceless ɑ, and so on.

§ 370. In RP, written *h* is often not sounded in weakly stressed positions. In particular, the words *him, her, his, have,*

---

[1] Or əˈgein.

had, *who* have weak forms without h (im, ə:, iz, əv and v, əd and d, u: and u) as well as their strong forms him, hə:, hiz, hav, had, hu:. Examples:

'giv im iz 'kout (*give him his coat*)
'giv ə:r ə: 'kout (*give her her coat*)[1]
ai 'ʃudnt əv 'θɔ:t sou (*I shouldn't have thought so*)
'ðouz u(:) (ə)v 'finiʃt mei 'gou (*those who have finished may go*)

§ 370 a. Words beginning with *h*, when the first syllable has weak stress, are similarly treated. For instance, it is usual to pronounce ɔn ði ə'raizn (*on the horizon*), ət ði ou'tɛl (*at the hotel*).

§ 371. ət 'houm (*at home*) has a variant pronunciation ə'toum, like *a tome*. This is probably the only case in RP where h is omitted in a strongly stressed syllable.

§ 372. h is not used at all in a great many genuine dialects including that of London, and the pronunciation of such words as *hard*, *hook*, *hit* without h may often be heard from people whose speech is influenced by such dialects. This 'dropping of *h*'s' has long been looked upon as a sign of lack of education. Consequently, a reaction has set in, due no doubt in part to spelling, and the use of h as in RP is now fairly general. In fact it is not uncommon now to hear h sounded in weakly stressed positions such as those mentioned in § 370. There is also a tendency among non-literary people to insert h where there is none in RP. The author has for instance heard hiŋk for iŋk (*ink*) from a dialectal speaker.

§ 373. There exists a 'voiced h' (phonetic symbol ɦ). It is an easy sound to make, though its precise mode of formation is somewhat obscure. It is as if one pronounced a vowel using

---

[1] Compare 'giv ə:r ə 'kout (*give her a coat*).

a stronger current of air than is necessary for a vowel, the superfluous air causing a simultaneous frictional sound in and around the glottis.

§ **374.** ɦ may often be heard in English as a variant of h between voiced sounds, i.e. in such words as 'bɔihud (*boyhood*), əd'hiə (*adhere*), in'habit (*inhabit*), 'moulhil (*mole-hill*). In some types of English, and notably with many South African speakers, the ordinary h of RP is not used at all, but voiced h replaces it in all positions.

SEMI-VOWELS

§ **375.** j. Palatal semi-vowel (§ 56 (viii)). The sound starts at or near i and immediately moves in the direction of some other vowel. Examples: jɑːd (*yard*), jʌŋ (*young*), 'miljən (*million*), kjuːb (*cube*). In such a word as jiːld (*yield*) the tongue starts in the position of a very close i and moves to a slightly opener one.

§ **376.** The sequence hj is replaced in the speech of some by the breathed palatal fricative (phonetic symbol ç). They pronounce, for instance, *huge* as çuːdʒ in place of the more usual hjuːdʒ.

§ **377.** j tends to have an effect on a preceding s or z, causing them to change to ʃ and ʒ or sounds resembling these. Thus many people pronounce *this year, Is your box ready?, Are these your books?*, as 'ðiʃ jəː, 'iʒ jɔː 'bɔks ˌrɛdi, ə 'ðiːʒ jɔː 'buks, rather than 'ðis jəː, 'iz jɔː 'bɔks ˌrɛdi, ə 'ðiːz jɔː 'buks. Sometimes variant pronunciations of words have arisen from a coalescence of sj into ʃ and zj into ʒ. For instance 'isjuː (*issue*) has alternative pronunciations 'iʃuː, and 'iʃjuː, and 'frizjən (*Frisian*) is sometimes pronounced 'friʒjən or 'friʒ(ə)n. See also § 401 (iii).

§ 378. There is also a tendency to replace tj and dj by tʃ and dʒ in many words. Many people for instance pronounce *tube* (RP tjuːb) as tʃuːb, *don't you* as 'dountʃu(ː) rather than 'dountju(ː), *did you* as 'didʒu(ː) rather than 'didju(ː). In dialectal speech one may also hear 'indʒən for RP 'indjən (*Indian*). See also § 401 (iv).

§ 379. w. Labio-velar semi-vowel. The sound starts at or near an u position (i.e. with lip-rounding and a raising of the back of the tongue) and immediately moves in the direction of some other vowel. Examples: win (*win*), weit (*wait, weight*), wɔːk (*walk*). In such a word as wuːnd (*wound*) the lips and tongue start in the position of a very close u and move to a slightly opener one.

§ 380. Words written with *wh*[1] are commonly pronounced with w in the South of England. Examples: witʃ (*which*, like *witch*), wɛn (*when*), wɔt (*what*). In Scotland, Ireland and the North of England and in America these words are pronounced with hw: hwitʃ, hwɛn, hwɔt.[2] This pronunciation is now adopted also by many in the South. In these regions a labio-velar breathed fricative (phonetic symbol ʍ) may often be heard as an alternative: ʍitʃ, ʍɛn, ʍɔt, etc. There are also sounds intermediate between hw and ʍ, and it is not always easy to analyse a speaker's pronunciation with precision. In transcriptions it is generally adequate to write hw, since this digraph can be used conventionally to mean ʍ or any particular intermediate sound between ʍ and the sequence hw.

---

[1] Except *who, whom, whose, whole* which are pronounced with h: hu(ː), huːm, huːz, houl. *Whelk* is also an exception; it is pronounced wɛlk in Scotland and no doubt also in other parts where most *wh*'s are pronounced hw. If the pronunciation hwɛlk exists at all, it is a recent spelling-pronunciation.

[2] American hwət, hwʌt or hwɑt.

§ **381.** Note that *will* and *would* have weak forms without **w**, namely **l** and **əd** or **d**. Examples: 'ðat l 'duː (*that will do*), hiː l kʌm (*he will come*), it əd bi ə 'gud 'θiŋ (*it would be a good thing*), ðei d 'laik it (*they would like it*).

VII. THEORY OF PLOSIVE CONSONANTS

§ **382.** A completely pronounced plosive consonant has (i) contact of the articulating organs, and (ii) release of these organs. Thus in pronouncing **p** the lips must be first closed and then opened. The period of contact is termed the *stop*; the release gives a sound known as a *plosion*. A completely pronounced plosive is necessarily followed by another sound; this may be a vowel (sometimes a very short one which is hardly recognized as such) or an 'aspiration' (which may vary in amount). In **biː** (*bee*) the **b** is followed by the vowel **iː**; in **lip** (*lip*), said in isolation, the **p** is followed by a weak aspiration or slight **h**, so that the word might be represented in a minutely accurate phonetic transcription thus, **lipʰ** or **lip'**. In **ɛg** (*egg*), when said by itself, the **g** is finished off by a very short vowel (**ɛgə**) or by a weak aspiration (**ɛgʰ**), depending on the speaker; the second alternative is the commoner in English. It is possible to pronounce words like **pin** (*pin*), **pɛə** (*pair*), **paːk** (*park*) in such a manner that the vowel follows immediately upon the plosion of the **p**; this is in fact done by many Northern speakers. In the South, however, an aspiration is inserted, giving a pronunciation which may be represented in a minute transcription thus: **pʰin**, **pʰɛə**, **pʰaːk**.

§ **383.** Plosives may also be followed by various consonants. Consonants following breathed plosives are in English generally breathed or partially so. In **lips** (*lips*) the **p** is followed by **s**, a breathed consonant. In **pliːz** (*please*) and **print** (*print*) the **l** and **r** are only partially voiced; they begin breathed and end voiced. This could be shown by a minute notation thus: **pl̥iːz**, pr̥int. Some people use completely voiceless l and r in such words, thus pl̥iːz, pr̥int.

§ 384. In voiced plosive consonants such as b, d, there may be voice continuing throughout the 'stop', or there may be voice during part of it. The amount of voice depends, in English, on the position which the consonant occupies in the word or sentence and on the nature of the sounds next to it. Between voiced sounds, as in 'prɔbləm (*problem*), 'ʌndə (*under*), ə'baut (*about*), the stop is voiced throughout. Initially and finally such sounds do not as a rule have much voice. Initially, as the b in bak (*back*) when the word is said by itself, only the latter part of the stop is voiced. Finally, as the d in haːd (*hard*) when the word is said by itself, only the beginning part of the stop is voiced. Stops of voiced plosive consonants are likewise only partially voiced when next to breathed consonants. For instance, the g of 'bagpaip (*bagpipe*), and the b of əb'tein (*obtain*) have voice only during the initial part of their stops, while the b of 'futbɔːl (*football*) and the g of 'skeipgout (*scapegoat*) have voice only during the latter part of their stops.

§ 385. Many English people do not voice the stops of b, d, g at all, except between voiced sounds. In the other situations mentioned in § 384 they use 'voiceless b, d, g' (phonetically, b̥, d̥, g̊). These sounds resemble p, t, k, in having no voice during their stops, but they differ from them in being articulated with weaker force; their plosions are less strong, and the aspirations they have in final positions are weaker than those of p, t, k. Those who speak in this way pronounce 'ʌndə, ə'baut, 'prɔbləm, etc., with fully voiced b, d, etc., but they pronounce the other words quoted in § 384 as b̥ak,[1] haːd̥,[1] b̥ag̊paip,[1] əb̥'tein, 'futb̥ɔːl, 'skeipg̊out.

---

[1] When said in isolation. But ðə 'bak, ə 'bag̊paip, 'haːd 'lʌk, would have fully voiced b and d.

§ 386. What has been said concerning the voicing of the plosives b, d, g, applies equally to the affricate dʒ. A voiceless variant ʤ̥ may often be heard initially and finally and next to breathed consonants. Thus in the speech of some people, words like *journey, lodge* are pronounced 'ʤ̥əːni, lɔʤ̥ when said in isolation or in combinations such as *that journey, lodge-keeper* ('ðat 'ʤ̥əːni, 'lɔʤ̥ˌkiːpə). Between voiced sounds, as in ðə 'dʒəːni (*the journey*), 'lɔdʒiŋ (*lodging*), dʒ is fully voiced.

§ 387. Plosive consonants are sometimes not fully articulated; under certain conditions they may be reduced to stops only, without plosions. This generally happens in English when a plosive is immediately followed by another plosive. For instance in the usual pronunciation of words like fakt (*fact*), lukt (*looked*), the tongue does not leave the roof of the mouth in passing from the k to the t. There is no plosion to the k; only the stop is pronounced. *Act two* is usually pronounced 'akt 'tuː, the k and the first t having no plosions; the first t is in fact only indicated by a silence in this expression. Similarly in bɛgd (*begged*) there is as a rule no plosion to the g. Other examples illustrating lack of plosion are apt (*apt*), rɔbd (*robbed*), 'iŋkpɔt (*inkpot*), 'noutbuk (*note-book*), 'big 'bɛn (*Big Ben*), and cases of 'double consonants' as in 'ðat 'taim (*that time*),[1] 'bukkeis (*book-case*),[2] and sequences of corresponding voiced and breathed consonants as in 'ðat 'dei (*that day*),[1] 'bɛdtaim (*bed-time*), 'ɛgkʌp (*egg-cup*), 'skrapbuk (*scrap-book*), 'bakgraund (*background*).

§ 388. Plosive consonants may also have *lateral plosion* and *nasal plosion*. Lateral plosion occurs when t or d is followed

---

[1] Pronunciations like 'ðatʰ 'taim, 'ðatʰ 'dei may sometimes be heard. They sound unnatural, and are probably artificially acquired.

[2] Some people pronounce this word 'bukeis with only a single k.

by l as in 'litl (*little*), 'mɛtl (*metal, mettle*),[1] 'niːdl (*needle*), 'pɛdl (*pedal*). In pronouncing such words the tongue-tip remains stationary against the teeth-ridge during the pronunciation of

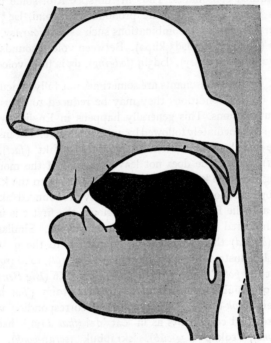

Fig. 36. Diagram illustrating the movement dn.

the tl and dl, and the plosion consists in releasing the contact of one or both sides of the tongue. It is very unusual to pronounce such words with the ordinary central plosion, which would give pronunciations like 'litəl, 'pɛdəl, etc. Nasal plosion occurs

---

[1] Reference is here made to the pronunciation of those who do not use the glottal stop (§ 233).

when a plosive consonant is immediately followed by a nasal, as in 'ðat 'nait (*that night*), 'tɔpmoust (*topmost*), 'ʌtmoust (*utmost*),[1] 'sʌdnli (*suddenly*). In such words the plosion is caused not by release of the articulating organs in the mouth but by a descent of the soft palate. Fig. 36 illustrates the movement by which the dn of 'sʌdnli is produced; the tongue remains stationary throughout, but the soft palate is raised for the d and lowered for the n.

VIII. NASALIZATION

§ 389. The term 'a nasalized sound' is used to denote a sound, other than the nasal consonants m, n, ŋ, etc., pronounced with lowering of the soft palate. All vowels and many consonants can be nasalized. Thus it is possible to pronounce a nasalized ɑ or i or ɛ or l or v. The symbol of nasalization is a superposed ~ ; these sounds would therefore be denoted phonetically by ɑ̃, ĩ, ɛ̃, l̃, ṽ.

§ 390. There are degrees of nasalization. The exact method of producing different degrees is not fully known,[2] but for present purposes we may consider weak nasalization to be caused by a very slight withdrawal of the soft palate from the back wall of the pharynx, and strong nasalization to be caused by full lowering of the soft palate (see Fig. 37).

§ 391. Strongly nasalized sounds are not used by those who speak with RP. Careful observation shows, however, that vowels are nasalized to a certain extent when next to nasal consonants. There is, for instance, some nasality in the latter

---

[1] Reference is here made to the pronunciation of those who do not use the glottal stop (§ 233).

[2] See R. Curry's *Mechanism of the Human Voice* (J. and A. Churchill, London), pp. 97, 98 and 116.

part of the diphthong in faind (*find*) and perhaps also at the beginning of the vowel in such a word as muːv (*move*). Such partial nasalization passes practically unnoticed.

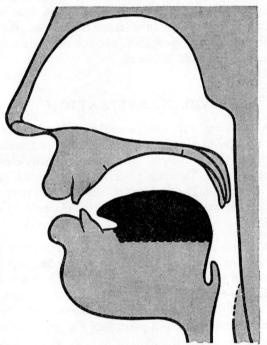

Fig. 37. Diagram illustrating the mechanism of partial and complete nasalization.

§ 392. Many people may be met with who speak in most respects with RP but who nasalize strongly their vowels when nasal consonants are adjacent. They pronounce definitely fãĩnd, mũːv, 'fʌ̃nĩ (*funny*), etc. This obscures their speech to a certain extent, and in the interests of clear speaking it is well to avoid it. Strong nasalization is also to be heard in dialectal speech. In RP the expression *Aren't you coming?* is pronounced ˈɑːnt ju(ː) ˈkʌmiŋ, and there may be slight, hardly perceptible, nasalization of the vowels ɑː, ʌ, i consequent upon the proximity of the nasal consonants. With London dialect speakers, however, a pronunciation like [ˈãĩnt ʃə ˈkãmĩn] may be heard, with strong nasalization of the vowels marked with ~. Some people nasalize their vowels even when there is no adjacent nasal consonant; this kind of nasal speech is probably individual and is not a characteristic of any particular dialect.

§ **393.** Those who nasalize their vowels and desire to rid themselves of this manner of pronouncing often find difficulty in doing so. The following method of practice will be found helpful. Start by pronouncing a sound which cannot easily be nasalized. z is such a sound; for if z is nasalized, the resulting sound has very little resemblance to z. Try to nasalize it purposely; the result will be a sound more like n than z. Try the experiment of nasalizing and denasalizing z several times, thus z:z̃:z:z̃:..., and see if you can feel the downward and upward movement of the soft palate. Then try the same experiment with a close iː, thus iː:ĩː:iː:ĩː:..., and then with a close uː, thus uː:ũː:uː:ũː:.... If there is difficulty in pronouncing iː without nasalization, prefix z to it, thus ziː:ziː:ziː:.... When iː and uː can be said without nasalization, try similar experiments with opener vowels, which may be found more difficult. Try for instance purposely nasalizing and denasalizing such vowels as ɑː and ɔː, thus ɑː:ɑ̃ː:ɑː:ɑ̃ː:..., ɔː:ɔ̃ː:ɔː:ɔ̃ː:..., endeavouring to feel the muscular sensation in the soft palate. When all the isolated vowels can be pronounced without nasality, easy words should be practised. The greatest difficulty will probably be found in words in which the vowel is preceded or (especially) followed by a nasal consonant, e.g. ran (*ran*), kʌm (*come*), faind (*find*). In practising them a complete break should at first be made between the vowel and the consonant, thus ra-n, kʌ-m, fai-nd, etc. This break may then be reduced in length until the sounds of the words are linked together in the normal way.

IX. SIMILITUDE, ASSIMILATION, ELISION

§ 394. It often happens in connected speech that in a place where one would expect to hear one of the normal sounds of a language, another sound rather like it but partaking of some characteristic of an adjoining sound, is actually employed. When this occurs, the sound actually used is said to show *similitude* with the adjoining sound. The following are some examples of similitude.

§ 395. (i) There is an 'ordinary' k, i.e. the sound which one would utter if asked to say it in isolation. This 'ordinary' k is used in such a word as 'kəːtn (*curtain*). There are also 'varieties' of k. The sound in kiː (*key*) can be heard and felt to be different from that in 'kəːtn. It has a 'fronter' articulation, thus partaking to some extent of the front articulation of iː. The k of kiː is therefore said to show similitude with the iː. The k of 'kɔːnə (*corner*) is again different. It has a 'backer' articulation than 'ordinary' k. This backer k is used, to the exclusion of ordinary k, whenever the sound ɔː follows; it shows similitude with the ɔː, which is a back vowel.

§ 396. (ii) The l of leis (*lace*) is the l ordinarily used in Southern English before most vowels. But the l of pleis (*place*) is different; it is voiceless or partially so, and has this voiceless-ness in common with the preceding p. It is a variety of l showing similitude with the p. Similitudes of the same nature are seen in the r of trɑi (*try*), the j of kjuː (*queue, cue*), the m of smɔːl (*small*), and so on.

§ 397. (iii) Ordinary English n is an alveolar sound. But the n of mʌnθ (*month*) is articulated dentally like the θ following it. It shows similitude with the θ.

§ 398. (iv) Some people use a labio-dental nasal (ɱ) in such a word as 'kʌɱfət (*comfort*). This may be regarded as a particular variety of m conditioned by the following f. In other terms, the sound shows similitude with the f.

§ 399. (v) Ordinary English ʌ is formed as described in § 131. But when a dark l follows, e.g. in such a word as ri'zʌlt (*result*), many people use a retracted variety of ʌ, which may be represented by the notation ʌ̠ (ri'zʌ̠lt). In some types of dialectal speech a variety of ɔ replaces ʌ in this situation (see § 299). These modified ʌ's come about because dark l has a secondary back articulation (§ 293 and Fig. 24 (*c*)). The modified ʌ used by these speakers shows similitude with the dark l; it is nearer in articulation to dark l than the normal ʌ is.

§ 400. When in the course of the historical development of a language a change occurs, by which a sound is replaced by another which is nearer to a neighbouring sound in the word or sentence, an *assimilation* is said to have taken place. It is convenient to call this type of assimilation *historical assimilation*, so as to distinguish it from other types mentioned in §§ 402 and 404. Changes of this sort may be expressed by the formula 'sound *A* has been replaced by sound *B* under the influence of sound *C*'. The following are some examples of historical assimilation.

§ 401. (i) There is reason to think that in the English of 500 years ago and earlier every final s was pronounced s—that the plurals of words like *dog, thing, bone* were 'dɔgəs, 'θiŋgəs, 'bɔːnəs (generally spelt in Middle English *dogges, thinges* or *thynges, bones* or *boones*). At a later date the ə ceased to be pronounced. When this happened, the s of these words was brought into contact with the preceding voiced consonant and is believed to have been replaced immediately by the voiced sound z, giving the modern pronunciation dɔgz, θiŋz, bounz. According to the formula, 's has been replaced by z under the

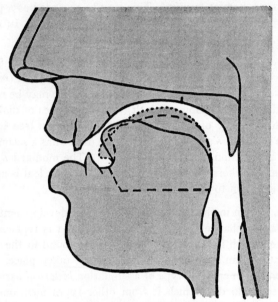

Fig. 38. Approximate tongue positions of s, j and ʃ,
illustrating the process of assimilation sj > ʃ.
——— s ••••• j ------ ʃ.

influence of the voiced sounds g, ŋ[1] and n '. Note that there has probably never been any assimilation in such words as kats (*cats*), nɛks (*necks*); the final sound has, as far as we can tell, always been s.

---

[1] The date of the disappearance of the g from words like θiŋg is not precisely known. It still exists in Midland speech (§ 289).

ASSIMILATION

(ii) The usual modern pronunciation 'rɑːzb(ə)ri (*raspberry*) may be presumed to be derived from an older form 'rɑːspˌbɛri. If this is so, there has been a historical assimilation: the p has been elided and 's has been replaced by z under the influence of the b'.

(iii) A former sj has become in modern English ʃ in many words. For instance *sugar* and *nation* were undoubtedly pronounced 'sjugəɹ, 'nɛːsjən at one time; now they are 'ʃugə, 'neiʃn. This coalescence of sj illustrates the process of assimilation. sj has been replaced by ʃ, the two sounds s and j influencing each other. The process is illustrated in Fig. 38.[1]

(iv) Words like *nature, furniture* were doubtless formerly pronounced with tj. They are pronounced so to-day by many; for instance the present-day Scottish pronunciation is ['netjʌr], ['fʌrnɪtjʌr]. The usual Southern pronunciation is with tʃ ('neitʃə, 'fəːnitʃə). Here tj has been replaced by the affricate tʃ, the two sounds t and j influencing each other.[2]

(v) Some people pronounce *width* as witθ. widθ, which may also be heard, is presumably the older form. witθ, therefore, exemplifies a historical assimilation: 'd has been replaced by t under the influence of the breathed sound θ'.

(vi) *Handkerchief* was presumably once pronounced 'handˌkəːtʃif. If this was so, the ŋ of the present-day pronunciation 'haŋkətʃif exemplifies a historical assimilation; the

---

[1] Occasional spellings with *sh* show that this coalescence began in the fifteenth century. The forms with ʃ probably became fairly general in the sixteenth, but statements by seventeenth-century grammarians indicate that pronunciations with sj were still used in Elizabethan times by some people.

[2] Some assimilations of this type which were formerly made have now been discontinued. For instance *bestial, odious* used to be pronounced 'bɛstʃəl, 'oudʒəs; this pronunciation was shown by the notations *bes'chal, ŏ'dzhus* in Sheridan's *Dictionary* (1790). We have now reverted to the unassimilated forms 'bɛstjəl, 'oudjəs.

d has been elided, and 'the n has been replaced by ŋ under the influence of the k'. The reverse process has produced the form lɛnθ, which is a common variant of lɛŋθ (*length*) in Scotland. Here 'ŋ has been replaced by n under the influence of θ'.

(vii) In recent times assimilation has given rise to the common modern pronunciation of *used* (accustomed, was accustomed). Being habitually followed by tu or tə (*to*), the older pronunciation juːzd has given place to juːst: most southern people say, for instance, hiː z 'juːst tu it (*he is used to it*), hiː 'juːst tə liv in 'lʌndən (*he used to live in London*). The formula expressing this assimilation is 'zd has been replaced by st under the influence of the following t'. It is noteworthy that the form juːst has now come to be the common form when no tu (tə) follows. People may be heard to say not only hiː 'juːs(t) tə 'liv ðɛə (*he used to live there*), but also 'juːst hiː tə 'liv ðɛə? (*Used he to live there?*), 'jɛs hiː 'juːst (*yes, he used*), 'nou hiː 'juːsnt (*no, he usedn't*). In the North this assimilation has not taken place; the pronunciation is still as a rule juːzd (in Scotland [juzd]).

§ **402.** When the process of putting words together to form sentences or compound words results in the replacement of a sound by another one having greater resemblance to an adjoining sound, a different type of assimilation takes place. It may be called *contextual assimilation*. Changes of this sort may be expressed by the formula 'sound *A* is replaced by sound *B* under the influence of sound *C*'. The following are some examples of such assimilations.

§ **403.** (i) When hɔːs (*horse*) and ʃuː (*shoe*) are put together to make *horse-shoe* the pronunciation is usually 'hɔːʃʃuː. There is contextual assimilation by which the s of hɔːs is replaced by ʃ under the influence of the following ʃ. The same applies to such pronunciations as 'dʌʃʃiːt, 'dʒʌʃ 'ʃʌt ðə 'dɔː, which are fairly common variants of the more precise 'dʌst-ʃiːt, 'dʒʌst 'ʃʌt ðə 'dɔː (*dust-sheet, just shut the door*).

(ii) When dʌz (*does*) is followed by ʃiː (*she*), the usual pronunciation of the sequence is 'dʌʒ ʃi(ː); ' the z of dʌz is replaced by ʒ under the influence of the ʃ'. Similarly in 'butʃəʒ 'ʃɔp (*butcher's shop*).

(iii) The change of z to ʒ before j, to which reference was made in § 377, also illustrates contextual assimilation.

(iv) When people say ai 'douŋk 'kɛə for ai 'dount 'kɛə (*I don't care*), there is contextual assimilation: 'nt is replaced by ŋk under the influence of the following k'. And when they pronounce ai 'doum(p) 'bliːv it for ai 'dount bi'liːv it (*I don't believe it*), there is likewise contextual assimilation by which 'nt is replaced by m(p) under the influence of b'.

(v) The common pronunciation 'faifpəns which results from compounding faiv (*five*) and pɛns (*pence*) illustrates a contextual assimilation involving change from voice to breath: 'v is replaced by f under the influence of the following p'.

§ 404. We may distinguish a third kind of assimilation which may be termed *negligent assimilation*. It takes place when words are said carelessly and with modified pronunciation. Some of these assimilations may perhaps be regarded as particular cases of historical assimilations, on the assumption that the unassimilated forms are older. Others are particular cases of contextual assimilations.

§ 405. Examples of assimilations of this type are seen in the negligent pronunciations 'oupm for 'oupən (*open*), 'gʌvm̩mənt for 'gʌv(ə)nmənt (*government*), 'stam-pɔint for 'stan(d)pɔint (*standpoint*), ɔm 'pəːpəs for ɔn 'pəːpəs (*on purpose*), 'kʌpm 'sɔːsə for 'kʌp ən 'sɔːsə (*cup and saucer*), where n is replaced by m under the influence of p or m. Others are the substitution of b for d in the careless pronunciation juːb 'bɛtə for juːd 'bɛtə (*you'd better*), of p for t in 'fupbɔːl for 'futbɔːl (*football*), or ʃ for s in 'kwɛʃʃn for 'kwɛstʃən (*question*), of k for t in 'gɛk 'gouiŋ for 'gɛt 'gouiŋ (*get going*).

§ **406.** Assimilations are due to 'economy of effort'. They take place and pass almost unnoticed as long as the words concerned remain easily intelligible. Some assimilations, and especially very negligent ones, make words less easily intelligible than the unassimilated forms. In that case the speech is said to be 'careless' or 'slovenly' or 'slipshod'.

§ **407.** The difference between similitude and assimilation must be clearly observed. A *similitude* is the use of a certain variety of sound at the present time. An *assimilation* is a process, i.e. the process of replacing one sound by another under particular conditions (in the course of history or when putting words together in forming sentences).

§ **408.** Some similitudes can be shown to have arisen through a process of assimilation. mʌnθ, for instance (§ 397), is derived from an early English word written *moneth* and in other ways containing a vowel letter after the *n*; the pronunciation in Old English was probably 'moːnəθ. The dental n now used in mʌnθ was no doubt brought into being when the vowel of the second syllable disappeared. The case is therefore one in which a similitude has come into being through assimilation.

§ **409.** On the other hand there is no means of showing that the voiceless or partially voiceless l of pleis (§ 396) has been arrived at by any process of assimilation. We cannot prove that at one period the l of such a word was fully voiced and subsequently became devoiced; in fact the evidence, such as it is, indicates that the sound has been voiceless or partially voiceless ever since it entered the language. This is therefore a case where a similitude has not come into being through assimilation.

§ **410.** Some assimilations lead to similitudes, as in the case of mʌnθ (§§ 397, 408), but most do not. There are for instance no similitudes in the examples quoted in § 401 and § 403. What the assimilations have done in all those cases is to cause one normal sound of a language to be replaced by another.

§ 411. *Elision* is the dropping of a sound which once existed or which still exists in precise speech.

§ 412. The following are some examples to illustrate elision. (i) It is clear from the derivation that such a word as 'mouʃn (*motion*) used to have a vowel before the n in the second syllable. Some people still sound one, at any rate in precise speaking ('mouʃən). The common pronunciation therefore shows elision of the sound ə.

(ii) Such expressions as 'tuː ən 'siks (*two and six*), 'weit n 'siː (*wait and see*) show elision of the d of (ə)nd (weak form of *and*). The common form 'ai dou'nou (*I don't know*) shows elision of nt.

(iii) Compound words like 'krisməs (*Christmas*), 'tʃɛsnʌt (*chestnut*), 'pousmən (*postman*), 'dʌsbin (*dust-bin*) may be considered to show elision of the t's which the first elements have when said by themselves. Similarly the derived form commonly pronounced 'kainnis (*kindness*) may be considered to show elision of the d of kaind.

§ 413. Elisions, like assimilations, are due to 'economy of effort'. If a word or expression remains perfectly intelligible without a certain sound, people tend to omit that sound. If the elision of a sound makes a word or expression difficult to recognize, we say that the pronunciation is 'slipshod', etc.

§ 414. Some elisions may be regarded as particular kinds of assimilation, the formula being: 'sound *A* is replaced by zero under the influence of sound *C*.' The elision of d in 'kainnis is one of this nature, since d in such a position would naturally tend to become nasalized; and nasalized d = n, which would naturally disappear in such a position. 'd is replaced by zero under the influence of the adjoining nasal consonants.'

X. SYLLABLES

§ 415. In every word made up of more than a single sound at least one of the sounds is heard to be more 'prominent' than the other(s). If there is only one such 'prominent' sound, the sequence is said to consist of a single *syllable*. If there are two, three, or more sounds which stand out more prominently than their immediate neighbours, the sequence is said to consist of two, three, or more syllables. The sequences θin, praiz, fɛns, for instance, constitute single syllables; 'θinist, 'praiziz, di'fɛns contain two syllables each, 'dɛfinit, sə'praiziz, di'fɛnsiv contain three syllables, and so on.

§ 416. Some sounds are more 'sonorous', i.e. have greater carrying power, than others. The reason why certain sounds are prominent in words and sentences generally is that they are adjacent to less sonorous sounds. The 'peaks' of the syllables quoted in § 415 owe their prominence to this cause.

§ 417. When there is no great variation of air-pressure, vowels are more sonorous than consonants, open vowels are more sonorous than close vowels, voiced nasal and lateral consonants are more sonorous than other voiced consonants, and these are more sonorous than breathed consonants.

§ 418. Length and stress also play a certain part in making sounds prominent. The longer a sound is the more prominent it becomes, and, other things being equal, strong stress produces greater prominence than weak stress.

§ 419. The most prominent sound in a syllable is said to be *syllabic*. Syllabic sounds are generally vowels or the more prominent parts of diphthongs, as in the examples in § 415. Consonants may, however, also be syllabic. l and n are so in such words as 'piːpl (*people*), 'ritn (*written*), where they are preceded by less sonorous consonants.

§ 420. When it is desired to show in a phonetic transcript that a consonant is syllabic, this is done by placing the mark ˌ under the consonant symbol. Thus we might write 'piːpl̩, 'ritn̩. There is as a rule no need to use this mark, since the situation of syllabic consonants is generally such that they cannot be otherwise than syllabic.

§ 421. It does, however, occasionally happen that the situation does not show this, and in such cases the use of the syllabic mark is necessary to avoid ambiguity in the phonetic writing. Instances are when a syllabic consonant is followed by a vowel, as in 'glʌtn̩i¹ (*gluttony*), 'kɔtn̩i (*cottony*),² 'kɔdl̩iŋ (*coddling*), 'laitn̩iŋ (*lightening*). These words should be compared with words like 'tʃʌtni (*chutney*), 'kɔkni (*Cockney*), 'kɔdliŋ (*codling*), 'laitniŋ (*lightning*), 'simpli (*simply*). It will be noticed that in the instances just quoted the consonants are rendered syllabic by means of *length* (§ 418); the l of 'kɔdl̩iŋ is longer than the non-syllabic l of 'kɔdliŋ, etc. (There is not much difference in *sonority* between n and l and i.)

§ 422. It is noteworthy that many words can be pronounced with either syllabic or non-syllabic n or l. For instance, *threatening, settler* are sometimes pronounced 'θretn̩iŋ, 'setl̩ə and sometimes 'θretniŋ, 'setlə. But in other words alternatives are rare or non-existent. It is for instance probable that *simplest* is always pronounced with non-syllabic l ('simplist or 'simpləst) and that *ficklest* is generally said with syllabic l ('fikl̩ist or 'fikl̩əst). This question is discussed at length in an article by the author entitled *The use of Syllabic and Non-*

---

¹ Alternative pronunciation of 'glʌtəni.
² As in *a cottony material*.

Syllabic l *and* n *in Derivatives of English Words ending in Syllabic* l *and* n published in the *Zeitschrift für Phonetik und allgemeine Sprachwissenschaft*, vol. xii, parts 1-4, Berlin, 1959 (Calzia Festgabe).

§ 423. It is generally easy to count how many syllables a word contains by noticing the peaks of prominence. But it is often difficult and sometimes impossible to determine precisely where a syllable begins or where it ends. More often than not a consonant, or more than one consonant, intervenes between syllabic sounds, as in the examples of two and three syllable words in § 415. Sometimes the beginning of a syllable is marked by the onset of a strong or moderate stress, as in kri'eit or kriː'eit (*create*), 'biːˌiːtə (*bee-eater*), hai'iːnə (*hyena*). Sometimes the mere glide from one prominent sound to another suffices to indicate the separation of syllables; this is the case in such words as 'siːiŋ (*seeing*), 'bluːiʃ (*bluish*), and in words where a syllabic consonant is followed by a vowel such as those mentioned in § 421.

XI. DURATION

§ 424. Most speech sounds[1] are capable of being continued during a longer or a shorter period. The actual lengths of sounds in connected speech vary greatly. For the purpose of practical linguistic training it is generally sufficient to distinguish two or at most three degrees of duration: *long* and *short*, or *long*, *half-long* and *short*.

§ 425. The chief principles of duration followed in RP may be taken to be as follows (see, however, § 429).

§ 426. (i) iː, ɑː, ɔː, uː and əː are fully long when final, e.g. when such words as siː (*see*), kɑː (*car*), rɔː (*raw*), tuː (*two*), fəː (*fur*) are said by themselves or are final in a sentence;

---

[1] Except the plosions of plosive consonants.

(ii) they are also fully long when a voiced consonant follows and the syllable is final in a sentence, e.g. when such words as siːd (*seed*), hɑːm (*harm*), kɔːz (*cause*), smuːð (*smooth*), bəːd (*bird*) are said by themselves or are final in a sentence;

(iii) they are less long in similar positions when weakly stressed, e.g. in ˈlinsiːd (*linseed*), ˈspriŋbɔːd (*spring-board*);

(iv) they are less long, often not more than half-long, when weakly stressed syllables follow, e.g. in iˈmiːdjətli (*immediately*), ɔpəˈtjuːniti (*opportunity*), ˈtuː əv ðəm (*two of them*), ˈfəːnitʃə (*furniture*);

(v) they are half-long when a breathed consonant follows in the same syllable, e.g. in siːt (*seat*), hɑːf (*half*), ʃɔːt (*short*), luːs (*loose*), fəːst (*first*);

(vi) they are half-long, or even less than half-long, in weakly stressed positions preceding a strong stress, e.g. in iːˈkɔnəmi (*economy*),[1] ɔːˈdeiʃəs (*audacious*), ɔːˈθɔriti (*authority*).[2]

§ **427.** i, ɛ, a, ɔ, u, ʌ and ə may be considered as short, but their actual lengths vary to a limited extent in the same way as those of iː, ɑː, etc. For instance the vowels of bit (*bit*), lɛt (*let*), fut (*foot*) are shorter than those of bid (*bid*), lɛd (*led, lead*), wud (*wood*); and though the i of big (*big*) may be considered short,[3] the i of igˈnɔː (*ignore*) is generally shorter.

§ **428.** Diphthongs vary in length in the same way as the 'long' vowels. Thus fully long diphthongs are heard in words like hai (*high*), nau (*now*), slou (*slow*), haid (*hide*), laud (*loud*), reiz (*raise*) when said by themselves; but the diphthongs are less long in such words as ˈprimrouz (*primrose*), ˈtaidinis (*tidiness*), aiˈdɛntiti (*identity*), hait (*height*), moust (*most*).

---

[1] Also pronounced with i (iˈkɔnəmi).

[2] Also pronounced əˈθɔriti.

[3] It is *relatively* short, i.e. short as compared with what iː would be under similar conditions, as for instance in liːg (*league*). The *actual* length of the vowel in big is about the same as the half-long iː of biːk (*beak*).

THE PRONUNCIATION OF ENGLISH

§ 429. There is a modern tendency in South-Eastern English to lengthen some or all of the traditionally short vowels i, ɛ, a, ɔ, u and ʌ in many situations. The speech of those who pronounce in this way needs a different style of transcription from that used throughout the greater part of this book. In this manner of speaking, words like *fit* and *feet*, *cot* and *caught*, *wood* and *wooed* are, or may be, distinguished by vowel quality only, instead of by a complex of duration and quality. Consequently, all the qualities must be represented by separate symbols. This involves the introduction of three additional letters, namely ɩ[1] for open i, ɒ for open ɔ and ɷ[1] for open u.

§ 430. In the speech of those referred to in the preceding paragraph there is no constant relationship between the qualities and lengths of vowels. Whether a vowel is long or short depends upon the stress and the position of the vowel in the word or sentence. The most noteworthy case in which the traditionally short vowels are lengthened is when the syllable is strongly stressed and is final in the sentence. Thus it is common in South-Eastern England to hear such pronunciations as

[ðɛə wər 'ounlɩ 'sɩːks]	*There were only six*
['wɒt dju θɩŋk əv 'ðɩːs]	*What do you think of this?*
[ai hadnt 'θɔːt əv 'ðaːt]	*I hadn't thought of that*
[ðə 'flɔː wəz 'ɔːl 'wɛːt]	*The floor was all wet*
[ɩ'tɩznt 'baːd]	*It isn't bad*
['lɒk ət ðat 'dɒːg]	*Look at that dog*
[ɩt 'fɛl ɒn mi 'fɷːt]	*It fell on my foot*

§ 431. In common Scottish speech too there are no relationships between quality and length. The lengths of vowels are

---

[1] The forms ɩ and ɷ were recommended by the International Phonetic Association in 1943. Prior to this the less satisfactory letters ɪ and ʊ had been used. They continue to be recognized alternatives.

determined in most cases by the phonetic context, and in a few cases differences of length without accompanying differences of quality distinguish one word from another. The usage differs considerably from that of the Southern speakers referred to in § 429. The traditionally long vowels are pronounced short except in final position. For instance *week, food, caught* are pronounced in Scotland [wik], [fud], [kɔt] (like *cot*) with very short vowels, but in *bee* [bi], *two* [tu], *blow* [blo] the vowels are fairly long. Vowels are long before inflectional endings such as -d and -z. For instance, the following words have long vowels: ʌ'griːd (*agreed*), bruːd (*brewed*), roːd (*rowed*), friːz (*frees*), bruːz (*brews*), roːz (*rows*), and are thus distinguished from [grid] (*greed*), [brud] (*brood*), [rod] (*road*), [friz] (*freeze*), [bruz] (*bruise*), [roz] (*rose*). The Scottish usage in regard to length involves introducing a special symbol (ɩ) for the transcription of the traditionally short i. No other extra symbols are needed, since no differences are made corresponding to the Southern English differences a/ɑː, ɔ/ɔː, u/uː. In Scotland *Sam* and *psalm* have identical pronunciation [sam]; so also have *cot* and *caught* [kɔt], *pull* and *pool* [pul].

§ **432.** In American speech too there is as a rule no constant relationship between qualities and lengths of vowels. Consequently, it is necessary to make use of the symbols ɩ and ɷ[1] (though probably not ɒ) in transcribing what has been called 'General American'.[2] For details, readers are referred to J. S. Kenyon's *American Pronunciation*.[3]

---

[1] Or the older symbols ɪ, ʊ.

[2] Some of the words containing short ɔ in British RP have [ɔ] in American English (e.g. *long, coffee, Boston*), others have ɑ (e.g. *top, hot, solid, economy*). *What* has ə in the speech of many Americans (see § 117); others use ɑ in this word, and some use ʌ. In many words American pronunciation varies; see Kenyon and Knott's *Pronouncing Dictionary of American English* (G. and C. Merriam Company, Springfield, Mass.).

[3] Published by George Wahr, Ann Arbor, Michigan.

§ **433.** Consonants vary in length to some extent according to their surroundings. When final they may be observed to be longer after short vowels than they are after long vowels. Compare the final n's of siːn (*seen*) and sin (*sin*) or the l's of fiːl (*feel*) and fil (*fill*). Their lengths are also affected, like vowels, by the nature of following consonants. For instance it is easy to hear that the n in bɛnt (*bent*) is much shorter than that in bɛnd (*bend*) and that the l in gʌlp (*gulp*) is shorter than that in bʌlb (*bulb*).

§ **434.** The principles enunciated in §§ 426–8 are only approximate. It is not difficult to distinguish five or six degrees of duration if we wish, and experiments with apparatus reveal many more than these. Thus the iː in siːn (*seen*) can be heard to be shorter than that in siːd (*seed*) but longer than that in siːt (*seat*); the ɔː in skɔːld (*scald*) is shorter than the fully long ɔː in sɔː (*saw*) but longer than the half-long ɔː in hɔːlt (*halt*); the ə in ˈmanəz (*manners*) is longer than that in ˈkaləs (*callous*), but is hardly half-long. The principles mentioned are, however, sufficiently near the mark for the purposes of ordinary practical study of English pronunciation.

§ **435.** Special length is sometimes given to sounds in order to emphasize words. Thus the meaning of the word iˈnɔːməs (*enormous*) can be intensified by saying it with an extra long ɔː. ˈsplɛnːdid with a very long n is an intensified form of *splendid*; and ˈlitːl with a lengthened t means 'very little'. Added point can also be given to a whole sentence by lengthening a sound of one of the important words. For instance *I never heard of such a thing* can be emphasized either by pronouncing həːd with an unusually long vowel or by lengthening the v of *never* (ai ˈnɛvːə ˈhəːd əv sʌtʃ ə θiŋ). When this sentence is emphasized by the second method, the vowel of ˈhəːd is not very long on account of the presence of the following weakly stressed syllables (§ 426 (iv)).

XII. STRESS

§ 436. The degree of force with which a speaker pronounces a sound or a syllable is called its *stress*. This force is conceived chiefly as pressure from the chest wall affecting the air-stream, but in reality the pressure extends to other parts of the body, and may often be observed in accompanying gestures especially of the head and hands. Degrees of stress are generally, though not always, perceived by hearers as degrees of loudness.

§ 437. Stress varies from syllable to syllable. Syllables which are pronounced more forcibly than neighbouring syllables are generally said to be *stressed*, or more accurately *strongly stressed* or *pronounced with strong stress*. Syllables which are pronounced without much force are commonly called *unstressed*; it is more accurate to say that they are *weakly stressed* or *pronounced with weak stress*, since they must have some degree of stress.

§ 437 a. Stress is not the same as 'prominence' (§§ 415–418); stress is one of the factors that may cause or help to cause a sound or syllable to be 'prominent'.

§ 438. It is commonly thought that several degrees of stress are distinguishable. For instance many of us would have no difficulty in accepting the statement that the word *opportunity* contains five degrees of stress—that if we use the figure 1 to denote the strongest stress, 2 to denote the second strongest, etc., the notation $\overset{2}{\mathrm{o}}\overset{4}{\mathrm{p}}\mathrm{ə}'\overset{1}{\mathrm{t}}\mathrm{j}\overset{5}{\mathrm{u}}\mathrm{ː}\overset{3}{\mathrm{n}}\mathrm{i}\mathrm{t}\mathrm{i}$ represents correctly the grading of stress in this word. Detailed investigation of this and other long words reveals, however, that the estimation of degrees of stress is less easy than may at first sight be supposed. What is clear in the case of the word *opportunity* is that its vowels have different degrees of *prominence* corresponding to the above numbers. It would seem, however, to be impossible to prove that the prominences in this word are accounted for solely by degrees of push from the chest wall; prominence is often accounted for by other features of speech, mainly inherent sonority, length and intonation. The uː in ɔpəˈtjuːniti undoubtedly bears a real strong stress (push from the chest wall); the ɔ too probably has a fairly strong stress, though in regard to this sound it must be remarked that its considerable sonority (§ 416) would make it prominent without the aid of stress. As to the remaining vowels, the extreme shortness of the ə and the first i suffices to make them non-prominent, and the final i necessarily has a certain degree of prominence by reason of its situation. We cannot therefore be certain that the above grading of these vowels is strictly in accordance with differences in chest pressure.

§ **438 a.** It is instructive to examine the prominences in long words and in sentences, and to estimate the extent to which they are attributable to true stress (push from the chest wall) and how far they are caused by inherent sonority, length and intonation.

§ **438 b.** Notwithstanding uncertainties such as those mentioned in § 438, which arise from possible confusions of stress with prominence, we may with due reserve make subjective estimates which are sufficiently near the mark for practical linguistic studies and for marking stresses in phonetic transcriptions. When we do this, it seems possible to distinguish up to four degrees of stress. This number is, however, rarely essential. It is often possible to manage sufficiently well with three degrees, and sometimes even with only two. When two degrees are distinguished, the syllables are said to be *strongly stressed* (or simply *stressed*) and *weakly stressed* (or *unstressed*). When three degrees are distinguished, the intermediate degree is called *medium stress* or *secondary stress*; the strong stress is then called *primary stress*.

§ 439. Strongly stressed syllables are shown in international phonetic transcription by the mark ' placed at the beginning of the syllable. The words *father, arrive, opportunity* are thus written 'fɑːðə, ə'raiv, ɔpə'tjuːniti, and the sentences *What shall we do?, it's time to go home* are written 'wɔt ʃ(ə)l wi: 'duː (or wɔt 'ʃal wi(:) duː), it s 'taim tə gou 'houm. Extra strong stress may be denoted by ".

§ 440. Secondary stress is shown by the mark ‚. It is chiefly needed in words having three or more syllables preceding the primary stress, and in compound words. Examples are ‚vʌlnərə'biliti (*vulnerability*), ‚sivilai'zeiʃn[1] (*civilization*), ig‚zami'neiʃn (*examination*), ris‚pɔnsə'biliti (*responsibility*), 'tin‚oupnə (*tin-opener*), 'taipdi‚zainiŋ (*type-designing*).

§ 441. The situation of the strong stresses in words is called *word-stress*. The manner of giving appropriate degrees of stress to words in sentences is called *sentence-stress*.

§ 442. The stressing of some words varies according to localities and sometimes with individuals in the same locality. The following stressings may for instance be heard in the North: kriti'saiz (*criticize*), rɛkəg'naiz (*recognize*), rɛkən'sail (*reconcile*), intə(r)'vjuː (*interview*), 'dʒuːlai (*July*), 'magəziːn (*magazine*), 'vaibreit (*vibrate*), kɔn'sɛntreit (*concentrate*), i'lʌstreit (*illustrate*). The usual Southern forms are 'kritisaiz, 'rɛkəgnaiz, 'rɛkənsail, 'intəvjuː, dʒuː'lai, magə'ziːn, vai'breit, 'kɔnsɛntreit or 'kɔns(ə)ntreit, 'iləstreit. in'kwaiəri (*inquiry*) is sometimes pronounced ['ɪŋkwəri] in America.

§ 443. In London dialectal speech strong stress is sometimes given to syllables which have weak stress in RP. Thus one

---

[1] Also ‚sivili'zeiʃn.

may hear in London 'ɛks'tɛnʃn (for iks'tɛnʃn, *extension*), 'miu'niʃnz (for mju(ː)'niʃnz, *munitions*), 'nɛsə'sɛri (for 'nɛsis(ə)ri, *necessary*), 'fɛbju'ɛri (for 'fɛbruəri, *February*), 'riː'kɔːdiŋ (for ri'kɔːdiŋ, *recording*).

§ **444.** In the following words different stressings may be heard from different people in the South who speak on the whole with RP. Those in the second column are probably of recent introduction in the South; some of them may be due to northern influence:

'hɔspitəbl (*hospitable*)	hɔs'pitəbl
'aplikəbl (*applicable*)	ə'plikəbl
'ɛkskwizit (*exquisite*)	ɛks'kwizit
in'ɛksplikəbl (*inexplicable*)	'iniks'plikəbl
'fɔːmidəbl (*formidable*)	fɔː'midəbl
'diridʒəbl (*dirigible*)	di'ridʒəbl
'kɔntrəvəːsi (*controversy*)	kən'trɔvəsi
'intristiŋ or 'intrəstiŋ or 'intərestiŋ } (*interesting*)	intə'rɛstiŋ
'intrikit (*intricate*)	in'trikit
'dʒʌstifaiəbl (*justifiable*)	dʒʌsti'faiəbl

§ **445.** When words of more than two syllables are used as names of ships, they sometimes have a stress different from that which they have as ordinary words. Such are ə'rabik (*Arabic*), 'houmərik (*Homeric*) instead of 'arəbik, hou'merik. *Formidable* as a name of a ship is generally pronounced fɔː'midəbl, but it appears that an attempt is being made at the present time to introduce the pronunciation 'fɔːmidəbl.

§ **446.** Particular words and sentences are not always stressed in the same way. Sometimes special stressings are needed to make the meaning clear or to give emphasis for intensity or for contrast (§§ 450 and 452). The word *injudicious*, for instance, is pronounced normally ˌindʒuː'diʃəs or sometimes 'indʒuː'diʃəs. But when used in contrast with *judicious*, it is pronounced 'indʒuːˌdiʃəs: e.g. 'ðat wəz 'vɛri dʒuː'diʃəs (*that was very judicious*); answer 'nɔt ə'tɔːl, 'ai ʃəd kɔːl it vɛri 'indʒuːˌdiʃəs (*not at all, I should call it very injudicious*). Similarly people sometimes say 'ɔˌfɛnsiv ən 'diːˌfɛnsiv (*offensive and defensive*) as being more distinct than ə'fɛnsiv ən di'fɛnsiv.

§ **447.** In some words the position of the strong stress varies according to the stresses of neighbouring words in the sentence. This is particularly the case with words which have two strong stresses when said by themselves—*double-stressed* words, as they are called. When such words are in close grammatical connexion with a following strongly stressed word the second strong stress is weakened; and conversely when they are in close grammatical connexion with a preceding strongly stressed word, the first strong stress is weakened. The word *unknown*, for instance, is a double-stressed word, i.e. when said by itself both syllables generally have strong stress. It would also have double stress in such a sentence as 'θiŋz laik 'ðat ər 'ʌn'noun in 'ðis kʌntri (*things like that are unknown in this country*). But in *an unknown land* the stress on -*known* is weakened; people generally pronounce ən 'ʌnnoun 'land. And in *quite unknown* it is the stress on *un-* which is weakened; people generally pronounce this expression as 'kwait ʌn'noun. Similarly with *fifteen*. By itself it is usually pronounced 'fif'tiːn, but *fifteen men* and *just fifteen* are pronounced 'fiftiːn 'mɛn, 'dʒʌst fif'tiːn. So also we say 'wɛəz mai ˌindjə'rʌbə (*Where's my india-rubber?*), but ən 'indjəˌrʌbə 'bɔːl (*an indiarubber ball*).

§ **448.** The stressings of words in sentences vary according to the degrees of emphasis one wishes to give to particular words. There are nearly always some words in a sentence which are of greater importance than others. Some words can be slurred over;

some are of such small importance that people leave them out altogether in telegrams. The more important words are generally the nouns, adjectives, demonstrative pronouns, adverbs and principal verbs, but it is not possible to give any hard and fast rule as to this. (All words are 'important' which give the hearer a new piece of information, and which therefore in a sense are in a kind of contrast.)

§ 449. The following are some sentences in which there is no special emphasis on any particular word:

fou'nɛtiks iz ən im'pɔːtənt 'eid tə ðə 'praktikəl 'stʌdi əv 'laŋgwidʒ

Phonetics is an important aid to the practical study of language.

ðə 'fəːst 'rɛkwizit əv ə 'gud 'alfəbit iz ðət it ʃəd bi 'keipəbl əv biːiŋ 'ritn ənd 'rɛd wið 'iːz ənd 'ritn wið 'mɔdərit 'kwiknis

The first requisite of a good alphabet is that it should be capable of being written and read with ease and written with moderate quickness. (Henry Sweet.)

'kliə 'spiːtʃ, laik 'lɛdʒəbl 'hand-raitiŋ, iz 'laːdʒli ə (')kwɛstʃən əv 'gud 'manəz—əv kənsidə'reiʃn fə ðə 'kʌmfət ən(d) kən'viːnjəns əv 'ʌðəz

Clear speech, like legible handwriting, is largely a question of good manners—of consideration for the comfort and convenience of others. (P. B. Ballard.)

§ 450. Words can be emphasized either for *intensity* or for *contrast* or for both in combination. Emphasis for intensity is applicable when there can be different degrees of the meaning of a word. Words such as *magnificent, splendid, tiny, quantities, squeeze* are susceptible of degrees of their meaning, and are therefore capable of being emphasized for intensity. Greater degrees than the ordinary are often indicated in speech by prefixing adverbs (*very, extremely,* etc.) to adjectives or verbs, or by prefixing adjectives (*great, enormous,* etc.) to nouns. But another method which is often more effective is to give extra prominence to the strongly stressed syllable. When this method is adopted, the extra prominence is generally effected by extra strong stress. For instance, the meaning of mag'nifisnt (*magnificent*) is intensified if we put extra strong stress on the second syllable (mag''nifisnt). Special intonations generally contribute to giving the required special prominence, and extra length is also sometimes employed (§ 418).

§ **451.** Sometimes emphasis for intensity is shown by giving strong stress to a syllable which normally has weak stress. For instance 'absəluːtli (*absolutely*) and 'rɑːðə (*rather*) have emphatic forms 'absə'luːtli,[1] 'rɑːˈðəː.

§ **452.** Emphasis for contrast is mainly conveyed by special intonations, but in addition the emphatic word generally has a stronger stress than neighbouring words which are important enough ordinarily to have strong stresses. Alternatively, the emphatic word may have an ordinary strong stress and the neighbouring words may have their stress reduced to a medium or even a weak degree. To illustrate this let us take the sentence *He didn't mean to go*. Said ordinarily, without special emphasis on any particular word, the pronunciation is

hiː 'didnt 'miːn tə 'gou.

But if *he* is emphasized for contrast, the pronunciation may be one of the following combined (usually) with an intonation of the type ＼. . . . . (a variant of the 'emphatic fall-rise', § 463):

'hiː 'didnt 'miːn tə gou,
"hiː 'didnt 'miːn tə 'gou,
'hiː ˌdidnt ˌmiːn tə ˌgou,
'hiː didnt miːn tə gou.

---

[1] With some speakers 'absəluːtli and 'absə'luːtli have different meanings, 'absəluːtli denoting 'completely' and 'absə'luːtli denoting 'certainly'.

§ 453. Similarly if the same sentence is said with contrast-emphasis on *mean* (with some such implication as 'but he couldn't help himself'), the pronunciation is any one of the following combined with an intonation of the type

(another variant of the 'emphatic fall-rise'):

>   hiː 'didnt 'miːn tə gou,
>   hiː 'didnt ''miːn tə 'gou,
>   hiː ˌdidnt 'miːn tə 'gou,
>   hiː didnt 'miːn tə gou.

§ 454. The following are some further examples illustrating the functions of sentence-stress:

>   'wɔt ʃ(əl) wiː¹ 'duː,   *What shall we do?*
>   wɔt 'ʃal wiː¹ 'duː,
>   'wɔt ʃəl 'wiː duː,
>   ai 'kaːnt 'faind ˌɛniθiŋ,   *I can't find anything.*
>   'ai kaːnt 'faind ˌɛniθiŋ,
>   ai 'kaːnt faind 'ɛniθiŋ.

XIII. BREATH-GROUPS, SENSE-GROUPS

§ 455. Pauses occur at frequent intervals in speaking. They are made: (i) for the purpose of taking breath, (ii) for the purpose of making the meaning clear.

§ 456. Sequences without pause which end at a point where breath is or may be taken are called *breath-groups*. Sequences without pause which end at a point where a pause is or may be made without detriment to the sense, or to make the sense of the words clear, are called *sense-groups*. A breath-group may consist of one or more sense-groups.

---

¹ Also pronounced, in this connexion, wi.

§ **457.** The ends of breath-groups are generally shown in writing by full stops. The ends of sense-groups are often shown by commas, but commas do not *necessarily* indicate divisions between sense-groups. Portions of a sentence written with a comma or full stop at the end are often divisible into more than one sense-group. And occasionally a comma is written where no pause would be made in speaking. If it is desired to show accurately in writing the limits of breath-groups and sense-groups, special marks have to be used for this purpose. The marks generally adopted to show the ends of breath-groups and sense-groups are ‖ and | respectively.

XIV. INTONATION

§ **458.** The pitch of the voice with which a voiced sound is pronounced is called its *intonation*. In connected speech the voice-pitch is continually rising and falling. These variations produce intonations which may be described as ‘tunes’ or ‘patterns’ or ‘contours’.[1]

§ **459.** When the pitch of the voice rises we have a *rising intonation*; when it falls we have a *falling intonation*; when it remains on one note for an appreciable time, we have *level intonation*.

§ **460.** The range of intonation is extensive. When people speak, their intonation often touches notes both higher and lower than they can sing. The range is often wider in the

---

[1] The fact that some speech sounds are breathed does not interfere materially with the tunes. In connected speaking only about one sound in every five is a breathed one. Consequently sentence-intonation may be regarded for practical purposes as continuous.

declamatory style of speech than in conversation. In declamatory style, as heard for instance on the stage, it is not unusual for a man with an ordinary voice to use a range of intonation

of over two octaves, rising to F 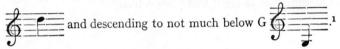 or even higher,

and descending so low that the voice degenerates into a sort of growl without recognizable pitch. In the case of women's voices the range of intonations is generally rather less than two octaves, rising (in declamatory style) to not much above D and descending to not much below G[1]

§ 461. Intonation may be conveniently shown graphically by placing dots and lines in appropriate places on a stave, each dot or line representing the pitch of a syllable. The dots represent level or nearly level pitches; rising or falling lines represent syllables in which a rising or falling pitch is clearly perceptible. The graphic representation is generally best placed immediately above the phonetic transcription of the words, but sometimes, and especially in showing the intonation of short sentences, it is convenient to place the marks after the words. In the examples which follow, dots and lines are printed thick when the syllables to which they refer are strongly stressed; they are printed thin when the syllables are weakly stressed.

§ 462. Various shades of meaning can be conveyed by intonation. This may be illustrated by the following ways of pronouncing the word *yes*:

---

[1] Though notes lower than this may often be observed in the speech of women with noticeably low voices.

jɛs	Meaning 'that is so',
jɛs	„ 'of course it is so',
jɛs	„ 'most certainly',
jɛs	„ 'is it really so?',
jɛs	„ 'yes, I understand what you have said; please continue' (the telephone *yes*),
jɛs	„ 'it may be so',

or by pronouncing the single sound m with various intonations:

m   m   m   m   etc.

And compare the following ways of pronouncing *What a beautiful day!*

wɔt ə 'bjuːtəfl 'dei   said perfunctorily;

wɔt ə 'bjuːtəfl 'dei   said enthusiastically;

'wɔt ə 'bjuːtəfl 'dei   said sarcastically.

151

Compare also the various ways of saying *What are you doing?* shown in §§ 464 (iii) and 471.

§ **463.** Several 'intonation patterns' are used in Southern English. The four commonest may be symbolized as follows:

the simple fall

the simple rise

the normal fall-rise

the emphatic fall-rise

These typical patterns are extended or contracted according to the number of syllables in the clause. The following are examples of contracted forms:

simple fall   or   or

simple rise   or   or

normal fall-rise   or

emphatic fall-rise   or

§ **464.** Falling intonations generally denote finality. They are accordingly used in commands, of complete statements not implying any continuation known to the speaker, of questions containing a specific interrogative word, and of the last alternative in alternative questions. The following are examples:

(i) Commands:

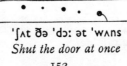

'ʃʌt ðə 'dɔː ət 'wʌns
Shut the door at once

152

'duː wɔt ai 'tɛl ju
Do what I tell you

'kʌm 'hiə
Come here

hiə
Here

(ii) Complete statements:

wiː v 'dʒʌst kʌm 'bak frəm 'taun
We have just come back from town

hiː 'finiʃt it 'jestədi
He finished it yesterday

it s 'dʒʌst 'rɛdi
It is just ready

it s 'reiniŋ
It is raining

153

(iii) Questions containing a specific interrogative word:

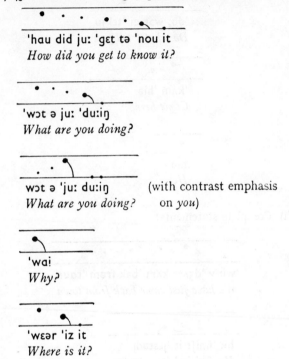

'hɑu did juː 'gɛt tə 'nou it
How did you get to know it?

'wɔt ə juː 'duːiŋ
What are you doing?

wɔt ə 'juː duːiŋ   (with contrast emphasis
What are you doing?   on *you*)

'wai
Why?

'wɛər 'iz it
Where is it?

(iv) The last alternative in an alternative question:

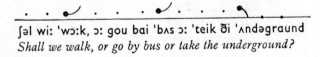

ʃəl wiː 'wɔːk, ɔː gou bai 'bʌs ɔː 'teik ði 'ʌndəgrɑund
Shall we walk, or go by bus or take the underground?

§ 465. The rising intonations are generally employed in sense-groups which are not final, i.e. when a continuation of some sort is expressed or implied. The simple rise is exemplified in the first two clauses of the example in § 464 (iv). It may also be heard in enumerations, such as:

wʌn	tu:	θri:	fɔ:	faiv
one,	*two,*	*three,*	*four,*	*five*

The normal fall-rise is illustrated in the two following examples, where the continuation is expressed:

ju: məst 'sain ðis 'peipə, ən 'ðen giv it 'bak tə mi:
You must sign this paper, and then give it back to me

it wəz 'fain 'jɛstədi, bət 'wɛt ðə dei bi'fɔ:
It was fine yesterday, but wet the day before

The emphatic fall-rise is illustrated in the following examples, where the continuation is implied:

ai 'θiŋk sou   (implying 'but I'm not quite sure')
I think so

'ðat s nɔt wɔt ai mɛnt   (implying 'What I meant was some-
That is not what I meant   thing quite different')

'ðat s nɔt wɔt 'ai mɛnt   (implying 'though it may be what
That is not what I meant   you intended')

155

```
  .    •   .   .   ⌣
```

ðat s 'nɔt wɔt ɑi 'mɛnt   (implying 'though it may have
That is not what I meant   sounded as if I meant it'[1])

```
  .      •   .   .   ⌣
```

ɑi l 'duː it if ɑi 'kan   (implying 'though I'm doubtful if
I'll do it if I can   I shall be able to manage it'[1])

```
  .     •   .    ⌣
```

ənd 'if juː 'dount—   (implied threat[1])
And if you don't—

In the last three examples the whole of the emphatic fall-rise is compressed into a single syllable.

§ **466.** Questions requiring the answer *yes* or *no* are particular cases of implied continuation. They have rising intonation (simple rise or normal fall-rise) because 'or not' or something equivalent is implied. Examples:

```
  •    .   .   •    ⁄
```

'ʃal wiː gou 'aut nɑu
Shall we go out now?

```
  .    .      •    ⁄
```

ʃəl wiː 'gou aut 'nɑu   (implying 'or not', 'or later on',
Shall we go out NOW?   etc.)

```
  .    .    •   ⁄
```

wud juː 'laik sə'mɔː
Would you like some more?

---

[1] mɛnt, kan and dount in these examples have the intonation termed the 'snake' in Palmer's *New Classification of English Tones*.

§ **467.** A request is an imperative sentence implying a continuation, namely giving the person addressed an option of not complying. Requests therefore end with a rise. Examples are:

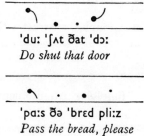

'du: 'ʃʌt ðat 'dɔ:
Do shut that door

'pɑːs ðə 'brɛd pliːz
Pass the bread, please

§ **468.** Sentences are often divisible into two or more 'intonation groups'. The sections are generally the same as sense-groups (§ 456), but they may on occasion be shorter than sense-groups. The last section may have a rise or a fall according to the principles already enunciated. Preceding sections generally end with a rise.

§ **469.** The following are examples where all the sections are sense-groups. The groups are separated by | in the transcriptions.

hiː 'stɑːtid 'ʌp | 'snatʃt ʌp (h)iz 'kout | ənd 'ran aut əv ðə 'haus
He started up   snatched up his coat   and ran out of the house

wɛn ðə 'wəːk s 'finiʃt | hiː l kʌm 'bak
When the work is finished, he will come back

See also the first three examples in § 465.

§ **470.** In the following there are intonation-groups which are shorter than sense-groups. The ends of these groups are shown by | on the intonation stave.

'wiː v dʒʌst kʌm 'in   (implied contrast with 'I am just going
We have just come in   out'—a double contrast)

'aː juː 'gouiŋ   (implying astonishment—two rises)
Are you going?

it wəz 'absəluːtli im'pɔsəbl   (rejoinder to someone who
It was absolutely impossible   thought the thing could be
done—two falls)

§ **471.** The tunes often undergo modifications which have effects of suggesting shades of meaning or the mood of the speaker. The following are examples:

wɔt 'aː juː 'duːiŋ   (expressing great curiosity; compare the
What are you doing?   ordinary, less emphatic way of asking
this question, § 464 (iii))

'wɔt ə juː 'duːiŋ   (expressing anger)
What are you doing?

wɔt ə 'vɛri 'fʌni 'θiŋ   (implies greater astonishment than
What a very funny thing!   )

158

'teik it ə'wei   (an encouraging form of intonation often used
Take it away   in speaking to children—a high rise followed
             by a lower one[1])

§ 472. A rise-fall of the following type is sometimes used:

It generally implies contrast or surprise. Examples are:

bət ɑi 'wɔntid tə kʌm   (rejoinder to 'How kind of you to
But I wanted to come   have come')

'iz it   (said with some surprise)
Is it?

ou   (expression of surprise)
Oh!

§ 473. The effect of an emphatic intonation may be intensified by saying the initial consonant of the emphatic syllable with a pitch opposite to that of the stressed part of the syllable (i.e. low when the stressed part is high, and high when the stressed part is low). In the following examples this manner of reinforcing the intonation is shown by the part of the curve preceding the dot which marks the position of the strong stress.

---

[1] The intonation termed the 'swan' in Palmer's *New Classification of English Tones.*

159

(i)

it wəz ə 'riəl 'plɛʒə
It was a real pleasure

hau 'nais əv ju:
How nice of you!

ai d 'laik tə du it   (='On the contrary, it will be a
I'd like to do it   pleasure to me to do it')

nɔt 'nau   (='Not now surely')
Not now

nou
No

(ii)

dju: 'riəli wɔnt it
Do you really want it?

'riəli
Really?

nau   (='Do you really mean now?')
Now?

When the emphatic syllable begins with a breathed consonant or without a consonant, these 'preparatory' pitches, as they may be called, are barely audible. It is possible, however, for the speaker to perceive them subjectively. The effect is sufficient for the hearer to be aware of it.

§ **474.** For fuller information concerning the intonation of Southern English, readers are referred to the specialized books on the subject.[1]

§ **475.** In other parts of the country forms of intonation are often used which differ considerably from those commonly employed in the South.

§ **476.** For instance English as spoken in Wales is noteworthy for the use of a high falling tone on final syllables with weak stress. In fact the Welsh employ the rise-fall described in

---

[1] Armstrong and Ward, *Handbook of English Intonation* (Heffer, Cambridge).

H. E. Palmer, *English Intonation with Systematic Exercises* (Heffer, Cambridge).

H. E. Palmer, *A New Classification of English Tones* (International Phonetic Association, Department of Phonetics, University College, London, W.C. I).

Chapter 31 of D. Jones's *Outline of English Phonetics* (Heffer, Cambridge, 1956 and subsequent editions).

R. Kingdon, *The Groundwork of Intonation* (Longmans).

R. Kingdon, article on *Tonetic Stress Marks for English* in *Le Maître Phonétique*, Oct. 1939. (Illustrates 60 possible intonations of the sentence 'I can't find one'.)

R. Kingdon, *English Intonation Practice* (Longmans).

O'Connor and Arnold, *Intonation of Colloquial English* (Longmans).

M. Schubiger, *English Intonation, its form and function* (Niemeyer, Tübingen).

M. Schubiger, *The Role of Intonation in Spoken English* (Fehr'sche Buchhandlung, St Gall, Switzerland).

W. R. Lee, *An English Intonation Reader* (Macmillan).

W. Jassem, *Intonation of Colloquial English* (Wrocław, Poland).

§ 472 in circumstances where it would not be used in Southern England. Examples:

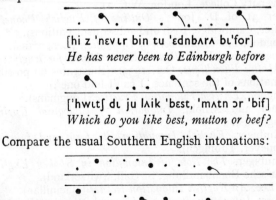

ai m 'goiŋ tu ɬa'nɛɬi
I'm going to Llanelly

it wəz 'vɛri ri'markəbl
It was very remarkable

The ordinary Southern intonation of this last sentence would be

or (more emphatically)

§ **477.** In Scotland intonation varies considerably according to locality. A succession of high falling tones is characteristic of the speech of Edinburgh and the East of Scotland generally. Examples:

[hi z 'nɛvɪr bin tu 'ɛdnbʌrʌ bɪ'for]
He has never been to Edinburgh before

['hwɪtʃ dɪ ju lʌik 'bɛst, 'mʌtn ɔr 'bif]
Which do you like best, mutton or beef?

Compare the usual Southern English intonations:

Often also in Scotland the final stressed syllable of a sentence has a high pitch with a very slight fall. The words [bɪˈfor], [ˈbif] in the preceding examples could be pronounced so. Other illustrations are

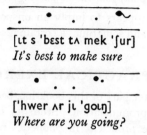

[ɪt s ˈbɛst tʌ mek ˈʃur]
It's best to make sure

['hwer ʌr jɪ 'goɪŋ]
Where are you going?

§ 478. A characteristic feature of American speech is that the simple rise is commonly employed where in England we should use a fall-rise. Thus Americans will say

[kant ju ˈfaɪnd ɪt]
Can't you find it?

where in England we should more usually say

kaːnt juː ˈfaind it

§ 478 a. Another frequent intonation in American English is to end a sentence with a high-pitched fall-rise which is quite distinct from the Southern English fall-rise shown in the last three examples in § 465. Example:

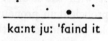

[wi ˈsʌtnli ˈkan]   (said in reply to a question
We certainly can   'Can you come here?')

163

[wi 'hapnd tə bɪ 'pasɪŋ ə'lɔŋ]
We happened to be passing along

This intonation appears to imply an unspoken continuation, with friendliness and sometimes a certain hesitancy on the part of the speaker.

XV. PRACTICAL EXERCISES

§ **479.** The greater part of this book has been concerned with descriptions of pronunciation. Students of speech cannot, however, become proficient in phonetics merely by reading such descriptions. They must also perform practical exercises. A few such exercises have already been suggested (see for instance §§ 15, 25, 36, 44, 172, 274, 281, 293, 309, 313, 314), but many more are required.

§ **480.** In the first place the learner is recommended to devote a considerable amount of time to practising cardinal vowels, and particularly the eight primary cardinal vowels (§§ 45 ff.). When he is thoroughly familiar with these, he should take each English vowel, establish precisely what value he gives to it and compare it with the nearest cardinal vowels, and then make himself proficient in pronouncing all the variants indicated in this book. He should say these variants in isolation and should also practise using them in words in place of the vowels to which he is accustomed. For instance when he is studying vowel No. 3 of RP (§ 88), he should practise saying words like *pen* and *head* with various shades of sound ranging between cardinal 2 and cardinal 3.

§ **481.** It is also a good exercise to learn to make some vowels and consonants which do not exist in English at all. Foremost among these are the 'front rounded' vowels, the chief of which are represented phonetically by the letters y, ø and œ. The secondary cardinals **y** and **ø** (which may be numbered 9 and 10) have the tongue positions of **i** and **e** respectively combined with close lip-rounding. Cardinal **œ** (No. 11) has the tongue position of **ɛ** combined with open lip-rounding.

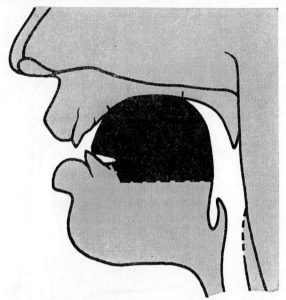

Fig. 39. Tongue position of **c** and **ɟ**.

§ **482.** It is also important to learn to make the sound which we have represented by **ü** (§ 123). The cardinal variety of this (No. 18) is half-way between cardinal **u** and cardinal **y**. For its mode of formation see Fig. 17.

§ **483.** Another useful exercise is to familiarize oneself with 'unrounded u', the phonetic symbol for which is **ɯ** (§ 119). The cardinal unrounded **u** (No. 16) has the tongue position of cardinal **u** and the lip position of **i**. (The variety referred to in § 119 has the tongue position of English short **u**.) When **ɯ** has been mastered, the sound ï which is half-way between ɯ and i should be practised. This sound may also be acquired by unrounding an ü.

§ **484.** For consonant practice students are recommended to learn particularly the following sounds: (i) the palatal plosives,

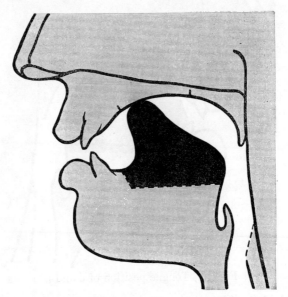

Fig. 40. Tongue position of t̪ and ɖ.

which are represented phonetically by c and ɟ, (ii) the retroflex plosives t̪ and ɖ, (iii) the uvular plosives q and ɢ, (iv) the bilabial fricatives ɸ and β, (v) the velar fricatives x and ɣ. They should also learn to make the breathed sounds m̥, n̥, ŋ̊, l̥, r̥ both in isolation and in various difficult combinations, such as ɑːm̥ɑː, n̥ɑi, ɛŋ̊k, l̥ikl̥ (a not uncommon defective pronunciation of *six*), r̥iŋ (the Old English form of *ring*).

§ **485.** Figs. 39, 40 and 41 show how the above-mentioned plosives are formed. c is a very 'forward' k. It has a j-glide following it; this can be seen from Fig. 39, which shows that it is not possible to pass from the position c to any vowel without performing the action of j. c may be acquired by starting from kj and trying to pronounce this with a very forward tongue articulation and as nearly as possible as a

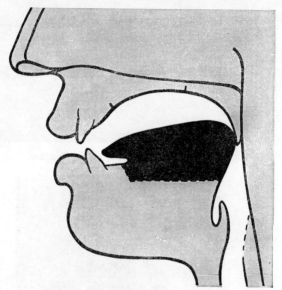

Fig. 41. Tongue position of q and ɢ.

single sound. ɟ is the corresponding voiced sound. Students can learn to make it by gabbling a j, i.e. repeating jə jə jə... very fast, and then endeavouring to make complete closure at the same place of articulation. The retroflex consonants are made by the tip of the tongue placed on the hard palate, that is to say further back than alveolar t, d (Fig. 40). q may be learnt as a very retracted variety of k (Fig. 41).

§ **486.** To learn to make φ, place the two lips nearly in contact and blow air out between them. The sound is much the same as that made in blowing out a candle. β is the corresponding voiced sound.

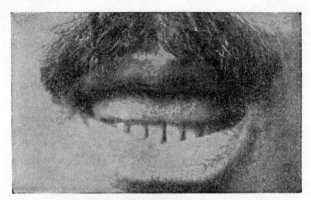

Fig. 42. Lateral spreading of the tongue.

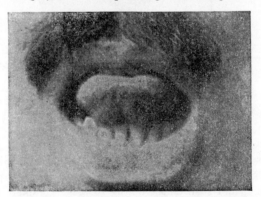

Fig. 43. Lateral contraction of the tongue.

§ **487.** The sounds x, γ, ʀ and ʁ should also be learnt. For these see §§ 313, 314 and 316.

§ **488.** Those who use completely unvoiced **v** and **z** in initial and final positions (§§ 326, 339) often have difficulty in producing fully voiced **v** and **z** in isolation. They should practise doing so. They can learn to make fully voiced **v** by starting from the vowel **ə:** and bringing the lower lip against the upper teeth while thinking all the time of this vowel. It is a good exercise to sing **v** on several notes. Similarly with fully voiced **z**.

§ **489.** For improving one's general control over movements of the tongue it is useful to practise 'lateral spreading' and 'lateral contraction' of the tongue, keeping the centre of the tip of the tongue unmoved and projecting slightly over the edge of the lower teeth. See Figs. 42 and 43.

XVI. EAR TRAINING

§ **490.** The basis of all phonetic study is the cultivation of the perception of sounds by the ear. To become a phonetician one must be proficient in recognizing sounds readily in all manner of contexts and in analysing new sounds. This proficiency is attained through systematic ear-training exercises, i.e. exercises for developing auditory memory. The method is as follows. The teacher dictates invented words made up of sounds of his pupil's mother tongue, sometimes in sequences which are familiar to him and sometimes in unfamiliar sequences. The pupil writes these words in phonetic transcription and the teacher examines his results. Most pupils make mistakes at first; they mistake one sound for another, they fail to observe some of the sounds dictated, and sometimes they put in sounds which were not in the dictation. When the pupil shows by his transcript that he has failed to hear correctly, the teacher repeats the word (or part of it) firstly in the way shown by the transcript and then in the manner originally dictated, alternating the two several times. By this means the pupil learns to recognize the sounds readily in different combinations. When he can generally recognize without fail the sounds of his mother tongue, the teacher repeats the process with more difficult words containing less familiar sounds, e.g. cardinal vowels and sounds of foreign languages. It generally requires long practice before the learner can be confident of writing correctly really difficult words containing unusual sounds.

§ 491. The following are a few examples of invented words suitable for dictation as ear-training exercises:

(i) Easy words made up of sounds of RP (mostly in familiar situations): mouˈθrɛglaʃ, viˈtəːʒənɔi, ˈlʌntəˈreiðuːp, ɛθiːˈnɑuʃɔŋ.

(ii) More difficult words made up of sounds of RP (some in unfamiliar situations): bʒouˈŋɔʃpʃʌkθ, ˈŋirtnaðˈmliːəŋ, ʌlˈθɔːbmpliərft, diːˈzjɑːθouθˈfugŋɛ.

(iii) Difficult words containing sounds not occurring in RP. (In the following examples italic letters denote sounds with values differing from those assigned to the letters in ordinary transcriptions of RP.[1] Italic vowel letters are to be taken to have cardinal values and are to be pronounced short when not followed by the length mark; italic t, d denote dental varieties; italic r denotes the rolled lingual sound. Dark l is represented by ł. Other unusual sounds are denoted by special letters or marks, as shown elsewhere in the book.) ˈɣoːpjʌˈłaːʒðɯ, ˈtrjɛbʀjɔˈsuŋac, ˈɔuvˈmiʔməˈceːli, ˈfʀãːdʒindnɔːˈxɔy, ŋaːˈβaːkŋiːʔɛːlk, ˈluːqeːɱiˈøːʃɔtʁ, ɛˈłiːympraʒˈgŋeu, ˈnəüljəɸərətʃɔ̃ĩʃ.

---

[1] In writing they may be distinguished in any way that may be found convenient, e.g. underlining or putting rings round the letters.

XVII. PHONEMES

§ 492. In §§ 58 and 395 it was pointed out that there are several different k sounds in English; that the k in kiːp is a different sound from the first k in kuk, and that the k at the end of kuk has a different articulation from the one at the beginning. (This latter difference can be easily perceived if one whispers the word.) Here, therefore, are three sounds which we are accustomed to treat as if they were one and the same; we write them in phonetic transcription with a single letter, k. We do this because the variants are determined by the phonetic context, so that no misunderstanding is possible: the English k-sound of kiːp is never used before u, nor does either of the k-sounds in kuk ever occur before iː. The treatment of the three sounds as if they were one is therefore entirely justifiable.

§ 493. When two or more sounds can, for reasons like this, be considered as constituting a single entity, that entity is called a *phoneme*.

§ 494. The following are other instances of different sounds belonging to a single phoneme. The t's in tɛn (*ten*), eitθ (*eighth*), truː (*true*), the nasally exploded t as in 'mʌtn (*mutton*), and the laterally exploded t of such a word as 'kɛtl (*kettle*) are all distinct from each other. But each one is appropriate to a particular phonetic context and cannot be exchanged for one of the others in that context; these different t-sounds, therefore, count for linguistic purposes as if they were all the same, and we write them all with the same letter, t. In other terms they 'belong to the same phoneme'.

§ 495. Clear l and dark l are two very distinct sounds, but in the speech of those who use both (§ 296) they belong to a single phoneme. This is because the conditions under which the one or the other sound is used in Southern English are prescribed by the neighbouring sounds in the word: clear l is used when a vowel follows, but dark l finally or when a consonant follows. This means that clear l and dark l belong to a single phoneme in the speech of those who pronounce in this way.

§ **496.** The sounds of ɛ illustrate the assignment of distinct vowels to a single vowel-phoneme. It is easy to hear that the vowel-sounds in the Southern pronunciation of *get* and *well* are different, the first being considerably closer than the second. A comparison of several words containing ɛ will show that its precise quality is conditioned by the kind of consonant following it, and in particular that a much opener variety is used before dark l than before other consonants.

§ **497.** The various sounds belonging to a particular phoneme are often called its *allophones*. For instance 'dark' l and the different shades of 'clear' l (§ 296) are the 'allophones' of the RP l-phoneme.

§ **498.** Those interested in details of the theory of phonemes are referred to the present author's book *The Phoneme, its Nature and Use*.[1] It may, however, be remarked here that there are at least two possible ways of regarding the phoneme. Some take it to be a family of related sounds, the members of which are used in accordance with certain rules of phonetic context in a particular language. Others think that the different sounds may be considered as physical manifestations of an abstract conception which may be called a phoneme—that one has in mind, for instance, an imaginary k which one aims at making but which appears as k_1, k_2, k_3, etc., when actually uttered next to different vowels.

§ **499.** The theory of phonemes has an important bearing on methods of constructing systems of phonetic notation. One of

---

[1] Published by W. Heffer and Sons, Cambridge.

the chief features of a 'broad' style of transcription (§ 61) is that it provides *one symbol for each phoneme* of the language or dialect transcribed. A notation of this sort is therefore often said to be 'phonemic'. Phonemic transcriptions are simple and at the same time unambiguous to everyone who knows the principles governing the use of allophones in the language or dialect transcribed. Thus klaud and fiːld are phonemic representations of *cloud* and *field*.

§ **500.** It is sometimes useful to demonstrate the occurrence of particular allophones by introducing special symbols to denote them. Forms of transcription embodying extra symbols for this purpose are called *allophonic* or *linguistically narrow*. It would, for instance, be 'allophonic' to write the word *cloud* as kl̥aud, showing in the writing that the l in it is voiceless (§§ 306, 396). (We usually transcribe this word more simply as klaud, i.e. by a 'phonemic' representation, in which the voicelessness of the l in this situation is implied by a convention.) Similarly it would be 'allophonic' to transcribe the Southern English pronunciation of *field* as fiːɫd, with the special symbol ɫ to show that the l in this word is a 'dark' variety, instead of writing simply fiːld as is done in § 296.

§ **501.** It would not be 'allophonic' to use the symbol ɫ in a transcription of usual Scottish pronunciation, because in that kind of English all the l-sounds are of 'dark' quality (§ 301).

§ **502.** When a special symbol is introduced into a transcription for the purpose of showing that a sound differs from some analogous sound in another language or dialect, the transcription is said to be *comparative* or *typographically narrow*. The introduction of a special symbol on such grounds is not necessarily allophonic. Thus it would be typographically narrow to use ɫ instead of l in transcribing Scottish English. To do this may sometimes be convenient, as it is in § 301, but this kind of narrowing is not concerned with the phoneme theory, since dark l does not stand in any phonemic relation to clear l in Scottish English.

XVIII. SYLLABLE SEPARATION

§ 503. Some points connected with the separation of words into syllables (§ 423) are to be explained by reference to the theory of phonemes. This is because special allophones (§ 497) are often required when a phoneme occurs at the beginning or end of a word, and the use of these special allophones is generally adhered to when such words are put into sequence or when they are put together to form compound words.

§ 504. The principle may be illustrated by comparing the compound words 'pleit-rak (*plate-rack*) and 'plei-trak (*play-track*). When the phoneme which we represent by t begins a word, the sound used has a strong articulation, but when this phoneme ends a word, a weakly articulated sound is employed. Thus the t's in teik (*take*) and trak (*track*) are articulated with greater force than the t's of pleit (*plate*) or fɛlt (*felt*). Again, when a word begins with the r-phoneme in English, the allophone employed is the fully voiced one; but when r follows an initial voiceless plosive, such as t, the sound used is a voiceless or partially voiceless one (§ 352). It will be seen then that 'pleit-rak and 'plei-trak are quite distinct in sound in spite of the fact that they are made up of the same phonemes. They are said with different allophones of the phonemes t and r, namely those which would be used if the constituent words were said in isolation. In 'pleit-rak the t is a weak variety and the r is fully voiced, while in 'plei-trak the t has strong articulation and the r is voiceless.

§ 505. Besides being pronounced with different allophones of the t and r phonemes, 'pleit-rak and 'plei-trak are distinguished

by the lengths of the ei's. It is easy to hear that the ei of
'pleit-rak is rather short (in accordance with the principle
formulated in §§ 426 (v), 428), but that the ei of 'plei-trak has
full length (like the words quoted in § 426 (i)).

§ 506. The following are a few further examples showing how
the use of particular allophones indicates syllable separation:
'mins-miːt (*mincemeat*) is said with a weak s and a fully voiced
m,[1] 'baŋk-reit (*bank rate*) has a weak k and a fully voiced r,[2]
'liŋks-aid (*lynx-eyed*) has a weaker s than 'baŋk-said (*Bankside*).

§ 507. The following are additional examples illustrating the
use of vowel length to show syllable separation: 'ɔː-strʌk (*awe-
struck*), 'hɔːs-trʌk (*horse-truck*), 'tou-strap (*toe-strap*), 'toust-rak
(*toast-rack*).

§ 508. Occasionally a suffix behaves as if it were the second
element of a compound word, and causes a preceding vowel to
be pronounced with full length. For instance the suffix -lis[3]
(-*less*) has this effect in 'triː-lis (*treeless*);[4] and *shyness, blueness*
can be said with longer vowels than *sinus, Eunice* ('ʃai-nis,
'bluː-nis but 'sainəs, 'juːnis).

§ 509. Conversely there are a few compound words which are
pronounced as if they were 'unit words' and not compounds.
The word *peacock* for instance is said with the shortened iː
which is usual when a voiceless consonant follows in the same
syllable (§ 426 (v)), thus 'piːkɔk, not 'piː-kɔk. It is probable
that most people pronounce similarly in the commoner com-

---

[1] If there were such a word as 'min-smiːt, it would have a
stronger s and a partially voiceless m (§ 396) and a longer n.
[2] If there were such a word as 'baŋ-kreit, it would have a
strong k and a voiceless r. The ŋ would also be longer than that
in 'baŋk-reit.
[3] Pronounced -ləs by some.
[4] Compare the shorter iː in 'fiːliŋ (*feeling*).

pounds of *tea-*: 'tiːkʌp (not 'tiː-kʌp), 'tiːpɔt (not 'tiː-pɔt), 'tiːspuːn (not 'tiː-spuːn). The less common compounds of *tea-* are, however, usually said with the fully long iː, e.g. 'tiː-sɛt (*tea-set*), 'tiː-klɔθ (*tea-cloth*), 'tiː-trei (*tea-tray*), 'tiː-streinə (*tea-strainer*). So also with *beetroot* and *bedroom*, which are generally pronounced 'biːtruːt, 'bedrum—not 'biːt-ruːt (which would have a fully voiced r) and not 'bed-rum (like 'hed-rum, *head-room*).

§ **510.** Readers desiring further information on the subject of syllable separation are referred to the author's article *The Hyphen as a Phonetic Sign* in the *Zeitschrift für Phonetik*, Vol. 9, Part 2, 1956 (Berlin), in which the subject is discussed in considerable detail and with many more examples; also to Chap. XXXII of the author's *Outline of English Phonetics* (Heffer, Cambridge, 1956).

PART 2

PHONETIC TEXTS

NOTES ON THE PHONETIC TEXTS IN PART 2

Texts Nos. 1–14 illustrate the 'Received Pronunciation' described in Part 1. The pronunciation shown is in all essentials that of the author, but a few modifications have been made in cases where he feels that his pronunciation is not the most usual.

The style of pronunciation is not the same throughout, but varies according to the type of passage transcribed. For instance, freer use is made of 'weak forms' of words in the conversational parts than in the more literary parts.

It is to be understood that many deviations from the pronunciation here shown would come within RP. Users of the book are recommended to take special note of the particulars in which their own pronunciation differs from that recorded here.

In Text No. 8 the intonation is marked by the graphic method described in § 461. Variant intonations would be possible in many places.

Text No. 15 illustrates the pronunciation of Southern speakers who lengthen the traditionally short vowels in certain situations. This style of speech should probably be regarded as a form of RP.

Texts Nos. 16–18 show other types of educated speech. Text No. 19 is an attempt at a transcript of local London dialect. It is not guaranteed to be correct in all respects.

Texts Nos. 20 and 21 are approximate reconstructions of types of pronunciation that were probably current in the fourteenth and late sixteenth centuries. For methods of ascertaining the pronunciation readers are referred to the books on Middle English and Early Modern English, and particularly to Jespersen's *Modern English Grammar*, Vol. I, Sweet's *History of English Sounds*, Ellis's *Early English Pronunciation* (especially Vol. I), Zachrisson's *The Pronunciation of English Vowels 1400–1700*, Wyld's *History of Modern Colloquial English*, Kökeritz's *Shakespeare's Pronunciation* and E. J. Dobson's *English Pronunciation, 1500–1700*.[1] See also the present author's 'Notes on the Pronunciation of English at the Time of Shakespeare' in *English Pronunciation Through the Centuries*, pp. 38–41 (Linguaphone Institute), which accompanies a double-sided record of Shakespearian English.

An asterisk (*) prefixed to a word means that it is a proper name. It is only inserted at the first occurrence of the word in a text.

1.

ai had ə moust ɛntə'teiniŋ haːf 'auə mai 'sɛkənd aːftə'nuːn. səm 'wimin ənd litl 'gəːlz wə 'biːtiŋ ə 'pail əv 'griːn stʌf ɒn ðə 'θrɛʃiŋ-flɔː dʒʌst bi'lou, 'wakiŋ it wið ə sɔːt əv 'wudn 'malit. sou ai 'ran 'aut (wið 'pɛnsl ən 'noutbuk), 'griːtid ðəm, ən 'sat 'daun bi'said ðəm ɒn ðə 'nais 'drai 'graund ənd 'wɒtʃt ðə 'houl pə'fɔːməns. ðə 'krɒp wəz ə 'smɔːl 'lɛntl ɔː 'pəːpl 'piː, ən ðə 'hiːp wəz ə 'pail əv 'plaːnts, 'stɔːks, 'ruːts, 'pɒdz ənd 'ɔːl. ðei dʒʌst 'biːt ən 'biːt til 'ɔːl ðə 'pɒdz əd 'bəːst 'oupən, 'ðɛn 'paild 'pɒdz ən 'siːdz intu ə 'big 'siv ən 'tɒst it til 'moust əv ðə 'siːdz wə 'ʃeikn 'aut. 'nɛkst ðei trans'fəːd it intu ə 'big 'flat 'trei ən 'ʃuk it 'tuː ən 'frou til ðei kəd 'skim ðə 'pɒdz ɔːf ðə 'tɒp. 'ɛvriwʌn wəz teikiŋ ə 'hand, ənd 'aːftər ai d 'dʒɒtid 'daun 'ɔːl ðə 'wəːdz ai kəd kən'viːnjəntli kə'lɛkt, ai 'tuk ðə 'vɛərĭəs 'aːtiklz in 'təːn ən kɔːzd 'mʌtʃ ə'mjuːzmənt bai 'seiiŋ 'kɛəfəli: ''ðis iz ə 'siv, ai 'tɒs ðə 'lɛntlz,' ''ðis iz ə 'trei, ai 'ʃeik it 'tuː:

[1] Viëtor's *Shakespeare's Pronunciation* indicates a style of speech which has now been shown to be much too archaic for the period.

ən 'frou,' it͵sɛtrə. ai fɛlt 'rɑːðə laik ə 'stɑː 'təːn ət ə və'raiəti
ʃou, ən 'brɔːt 'dɑun ðə 'hɑus ət ði 'ɛnd wið: ''ðis iz ə litl
'θɔːn-buʃ, ai 'swiːp ʌp ðə 'θrɛʃiŋ-flɔː.'

it s ə sɔːt əv im'pruːvd *'bəːlits mɛθəd əv 'tiːtʃiŋ jɔː͵sɛlf.
ai 'fɑund ðət wɛn mai *buruʃ'ʃaski¹ ran 'ɑut, ai kəd 'stil di'lait
ðəm bai 'tʃatəriŋ 'ɔn in 'iŋgliʃ in ə 'frɛndli 'wei. ðei 'fɛlt ðə
'gud'wil, ən ðei 'didnt 'nou ai wəz 'seiiŋ: ''juər ə 'nais-lukiŋ
litl 'miŋks, bət juː l 'luk 'bɛtə wɛn juː 'wɒʃ jɔː 'feis.' ai gɒt
'moust əv ðɛə 'neimz 'ritn 'dɑun, ən 'ðɛn wɛn ðei bi'gan tə
gɛt 'rɛdi tə gou 'houm, ai had ə 'rɒmp wið ðə 'smɔːl wʌnz, huː
'ran 'ɔːf 'skwiːliŋ wɛn ai 'traid tə 'katʃ ðəm, 'dʒʌst laik 'iŋgliʃ
͵kidiz əv ðə 'seim 'eidʒ. ai 'hadnt had sʌtʃ 'fʌn sins auər 'oun
͵jʌŋstə wəz 'smɔːl inʌf tə 'rɒmp wið.

From *Language Hunting in the Karakoram* (p. 81),
by E. O. LORIMER

2.

ai 'θiŋk *'sɑːdʒənt mʌst əv 'laikt 'tʃildrən—ɔː pə'haps hiː
'ounli 'fɑund ðəm ə 'plɛznt 'tʃeindʒ frəm ðə 'juːʒuəl, mɔː
sə'fistikeitid 'ɔkjupənts əv iz 'stjuːdiou.…'səːtnli hiː wəz
'vɛri 'peiʃnt, wud gou tu ͵ɔːlmoust 'ɛni 'trʌbl, kən͵sistənt
wið biːiŋ ə͵lɑud tə ͵peint, tu ə'mjuːz ʌs. 'wɛn ðə 'fəːst fasi'neiʃn
əv 'wɒtʃiŋ him ət 'wəːk, ə 'kʌndʒərə 'drɔːiŋ i'fɛkts aut əv ðə
'void, həd 'wɔːn 'ɔːf, wiː bi͵keim 'rɛstlis—is'pɛʃəli *sə'ʃɛvərəl
huː wəz 'ounli 'tuː jəːz 'ould. 'ɑːftər ə 'kwɔːtr əv ən 'auə, it wud
biː im'pɒsəbl fər ͵aiðə *'deivis ɔː 'miː 'ɛni 'lɒŋgə tə ris'trein hiz
'tʃaildiʃ im'peiʃns, ɔː tə kə'dʒoul him intə 'pouziŋ. bət
'sɑːdʒənt kud 'ɔːlweiz kən͵traiv tə 'hould iz ə'tɛnʃən fər ə
'fjuː 'ɛkstrə 'minits, 'aiðə bai in'dʌldʒiŋ in ə pi'kjuːliə ənd
i'labərit 'wisliŋ hiː əd ͵kʌltiveitid, laik ðat əv ə 'frenʃ *si'flœːr*

---

¹ Burushaski, the language of the Hunza people in the
extreme north of Kashmir.

əpən ðə 'mjuːzikhɔːl 'steidʒ, ɔː bai in'sɛsntli in'touniŋ ə
'limərik, witʃ 'ran:

> ðɛə 'wɔz ə jʌŋ 'leidi əv 'spein
> huː 'ɔːfn wəz 'sik in ə 'trein,
> 'nɔt 'wʌns ənd ə'gein,
> bət ə'gein ənd ə'gein
> ənd ə'gein ənd ə'gein ənd ə'gein.

wið ən ˌɛər əv 'rapt ə'meizmənt ən di'lait, sə'ʃɛvərəl wud 'lisn
tə ðis resi'teiʃn, 'ruːtid θruː'aut ðə pə'fɔːməns ɔv it tə ðə 'rait
'spɔt.... 'iːvn 'ðis, hauˌɛvə, 'didnt 'səːv tə kiːp im 'kwaiət
in'dɛfinitli, ənd 'biːiŋ sou 'jʌŋ, hiz 'fidʒitiŋ wəz 'sʌtʃ ðət
i'vɛntjŭəli ə 'dɔl had tə bi ˌmeid, əv ig'zaktli 'hiz 'saiz ən
'kʌləriŋ, sou ðət it kəd 'pouz fɔr im. 'saːdʒənt wud 'ðɛn 'peint
him fə sou 'lɔŋ əz ðə 'rɛstlis 'tʃaild wud ə'lau, ənd 'wɛn hiz
kən'tinjuiŋ tə 'sit ɛni 'lɔŋɡə biˌkeim 'aut əv ðə 'kwɛstʃən, ðis
'minjətʃə 'waksnfeist 'lei 'fiɡə, wið ðə 'seim 'fɛə 'kəːlz ən ðə
'seim 'klouðz, wud 'teik hiz 'pleis.

From *Left Hand, Right Hand,* by SIR OSBERT SITWELL

3.

hi: 'lukt 'ʌp frəm iz 'buk tə faind 'meitrən 'standiŋ in ðə
'midl əv ðə 'rum.

'ai 'did 'nɔk,' ʃi ˌsɛd, 'bət juː wə 'lɔst in jɔː 'buk.'

ʃiː 'stud ðɛə, 'slɛndə ənd ri'mout; həː 'waitkʌft 'handz
'klaːspt 'luːsli in 'frʌnt əv həː 'narou 'weist; həː 'wait 'veil
'sprediŋ itsɛlf in im'pɛriʃəbl 'digniti; həːr 'ounli 'ɔːnəmənt ðə
'smɔːl 'silvə 'badʒ əv həː di'ploumə. *'graːnt 'wʌndəd if ðɛə
wəz 'ɛniwɛər in ðis 'wəːld ə mɔːr ʌn'ʃeikəbl 'pɔiz ðən 'ðat
ə'tʃiːvd bai ðə 'meitrən əv ə 'greit 'hɔspitl.

'aiv 'teikn tə 'histri,' hi: ˌsɛd. ''raːðə 'leit in ðə 'dei.'

'ən 'admrəbl 'tʃɔis,' ʃi ˌsɛd. 'it 'puts θiŋz in pəs'pɛktiv.'
həːr 'ai 'laitid ɔn ðə 'pɔːtrit ən ʃi ˌsɛd: ''aː juː *'jɔːkɔː *'laŋkəstə?'

'sou ju(ː) 'rɛkəgnaiz ðə ˌpɔːtrit.'

''ou 'jɛs. 'wɛn ai wəz ə prə'beiʃnə ai juːst tə 'spɛnd ə 'lɔt əv
'taim in ðə *'naʃnḷ. ai had 'vɛri litl 'mʌni ən 'vɛri 'sɔː 'fiːt, ənd
it wəz 'wɔːm in ðə *'galəri ən 'kwaiət ənd it had 'plɛnti əv
'siːts.' ʃiː 'smaild ə vɛri 'litl, 'lukiŋ 'bak frəm həː 'prɛznt
'kɔnsikwəns tə ðat 'jʌŋ, 'taiəd, 'əːnist ˌkriːtʃə ʃiː 'had biːn.
'ai 'laikt ðə 'pɔːtrit ˌgaləri 'bɛst bikɔz it 'geiv wʌn ðə 'seim
'sɛns əv prə'pɔːʃn ðət 'riːdiŋ 'histri dʌz. 'ɔːl ðouz *im'pɔːtənsiz
huː əd 'meid sʌtʃ ə tə'duː ouvə sou 'mʌtʃ in 'ðɛə dei. 'ɔːl 'dʒʌst
'neimz. 'ɔːl 'kanvəs ən 'peint. ai sɔː ə 'lɔt əv 'ðat ˌpɔːtrit in
'ðouz deiz.' həːr ə'tenʃən wɛnt 'bak tə ðə 'piktʃə. 'ə moust
ʌn'hapi ˌkriːtʃə,' ʃi ˌsɛd.
  'mai 'səːdʒən ˌθiŋks it s 'poulioumaiə'laitis.'
''pouliou?' ʃiː kən'sidəd it. 'pə'haps. ai 'hadnt 'θɔːt əv it
biˌfɔː. bət tə 'miː it s 'ɔːlwəz 'siːmd tə biː in'tɛns ʌn'hapinis.
it s ðə moust 'dɛspəritli ʌn'hapi 'feis ðət ai v 'ɛvər in'kauntəd
—ənd ai v in'kauntəd ə 'greit 'meni.'

From The Daughter of Time, by JOSEPHINE TEY

<h2 align="center">4.</h2>

''ou ai 'sei, *ˌmagi,' sɛd *ˌtɔm ət 'laːst, 'liftiŋ ʌp ðə 'stand,
'wiː məs 'kiːp 'kwaiət 'hiə, ju nou. if wiː 'breik ˌɛniθiŋ misiz
*'stɛliŋ l 'meik əs 'krai *pɛ'kaːviː.[1]'
  ''wɔt s 'ðat?', sɛd ˌmagi.
  'ou, it s ðə 'latin fər ə 'gud 'skouldiŋ,' sɛd ˌtɔm, 'nɔt wiˌðaut
sʌm 'praid in iz 'nɔlidʒ.
  'iʒ ʃiː ə 'krɔs ˌwumən?', sɛd ˌmagi.
  'ai bi'liːv juː,' sɛd ˌtɔm, wið ən im'fatik 'nɔd.
  'ai θiŋk 'ɔːl ˌwimin ə 'krɔsə ðən 'mɛn,' sɛd ˌmagi. ''aːnt
*'glɛg z ə 'greit diːl 'krɔsə ðən 'ʌŋkl glɛg, ən 'mʌðə 'skouldz
miː 'mɔː ðən 'faːðə dʌz.'

---

[1] In old-fashioned pronunciation (now nearly out of date)
*pɛ'keivai.

183

'wɛl, 'juː l bi ə ˌwumən 'sʌm dei,' sɛd ˌtɔm, 'sou 'juː ˌniːdnt ˌtɔːk.'

'bət 'ai ʃl bi ə 'klɛvə ˌwumən,' sɛd ˌmagi wið ə 'tɔs.

''ou, ai 'dɛə'sei, ənd ə 'naːsti kən'siːtid 'θiŋ. 'ɛvribɔdi əl 'heit juː.'

'bət juː 'ɔːtnt tə 'heit miː, tɔm; it l bi 'vɛri 'wikid ɔv ju, fər ai ʃl 'biː jɔː 'sistə.'

''jɛs, bət if juər ə 'naːsti disə'griəbl 'θiŋ, ai 'ʃal heit ju.'

''ou bət tɔm, juː 'wount! ai 'ʃaːnt bi disəˌgriəbl. ai ʃl bi 'vɛri 'gud tə juː—ənd ai ʃl bi 'gud tu 'ɛvribɔdi. juː 'wount 'heit miː 'riəli, 'wil juː, tɔm?'

''ou, 'bɔðə, 'nɛvə 'maind! 'kʌm, it s 'taim fə miː tə 'ləːn mai 'lɛsnz. 'siː 'hiə, ˌwɔt ai v ˌgɔt tə 'duː,' sɛd ˌtɔm, 'drɔːiŋ 'magi tə'wɔːdz him ənd 'ʃouiŋ həːr iz 'θiərɛm, wail ʃiː 'puʃt əː 'hɛə bi'haind əːr 'iəz, ən pri'pɛəd əːˌsɛlf tə 'pruːv həː keipə'biliti əv 'helpiŋ im in *'juːklid. ʃiː bi'gan tə 'riːd wið 'ful 'kɔnfidəns in əːr 'oun 'pauəz, bət 'prɛzntli, biˌkʌmiŋ 'kwait bi'wildəd, həː 'feis 'flʌʃt wið iri'teiʃn. it wəz ʌnə'vɔidəbl—ʃiː məs kən'fɛs həːr in'kɔmpitənsi, ən ʃiː wəz 'nɔt 'fɔnd əv hjuːˌmili'eiʃn.

'it s 'nɔnsns,' ʃi ˌsɛd, 'ən 'vɛri ʌgli 'stʌf—'noubədi niːd 'wɔnt tə ˌmeik it ˌaut.'

''aː, 'ðɛə nau, mis 'magi!', sɛd ˌtɔm, 'drɔːiŋ ðə buk ə'wei, ənd 'wagiŋ iz 'hɛd at hə, 'juː 'siː juə 'nɔt sou 'klɛvər əz juː 'θɔːt ju wəː.'

''ou,' sɛd ˌmagi 'pautiŋ, 'ai 'dɛəsei ai kəd 'meik it 'aut if ai d 'ləːnt wɔt 'gouz bi'fɔː, əz 'juː hav.'

'bət 'ðat s wɔt ju: 'dʒʌs 'kudnt, mis ˌwizdəm,' sɛd ˌtɔm. 'fər it s 'ɔːl ðə 'haːdə wɛn juː 'nou wɔt ˌgouz bi'fɔː; fə 'ðɛn juː v gɔt tə 'sei 'wɔt "dɛfi'niʃn 'θriː" iz, ənd 'wɔt "'aksiəm 'faiv" iz. bət 'gɛt ə'lɔŋ wið juː 'nau; 'ai məs gou 'ɔn wið 'ðis. 'hiə z ðə 'latin 'gramə. 'siː wɔt juː kən 'meik əv 'ðat.'

From *The Mill on the Floss*, by GEORGE ELIOT

5.

ðə 'tɛligrɑːf iks'pleind

tu iks'plein 'simpli ðə 'wəːkiŋ əv ðə 'tɛligrɑːf iz ə 'pʌzl fə ðə
fiˈlɔsəfə; ən nou 'wʌndə 'simpl fouks 'kʌm tə 'griːf ouvə ðə
ˌtɑːsk. ðə 'fɔlouiŋ iz ði ɛksplə'neiʃn 'givn tu iz 'fɛlou bai ən
i'taljən 'pɛznt.

''dju: 'si: ðouz 'poulz ən 'waiəz ðət 'rʌn ə'lɔŋ bə ðə 'said
əv ðə 'reilwei?'

'ai 'nou ðat s ðə 'tɛligrɑːf. bət 'hau dəz it 'wəːk?'

''nʌθiŋ mɔː 'simpl. ju: v 'ounli tə 'tʌtʃ 'wʌn ˈɛnd əv ðə
'waiə, ən 'klik—ði 'ʌðər ɛnd 'raits it 'daun 'dʒʌst ðə 'seim əz
ə 'pɛn.'

''stil, ai 'dount kwait 'si: hau it s 'dʌn.'

''lɛt mi: 'trai tə ˌmeik it 'plein. 'hav ju: gɔt ə 'dɔg?'

''jɛs.'

''wɔt dəz iː 'duː if ju: 'pintʃ iz 'teil?'

'wai, 'bɑːk, tə bi ˌʃuə.'

''wɛl ðɛn, sə'pouziŋ jɔː 'dɔg wə 'lɔŋ inʌf tə 'riːtʃ in 'bɔdi
frəm *'flɔrəns 'hiə tə ðə 'kapitl.'

''wɛl?'

'it s 'kliə, ðɛn, ðət if ju: 'pintʃ iz 'teil in 'flɔrəns, hi: l 'bɑːk
in *'roum. ən 'ðat s ig'zakli hau ði i'lɛktrik 'tɛligrɑːf wəːks.'

Anecdote from *Engelsk Läsebok*, by JESPERSEN and RODHE

6.

ðə 'streindʒə, 'miːnwail, həd bin 'iːtiŋ, 'driŋkiŋ ən 'tɔːkiŋ
wi'ðaut sɛ'seiʃn. ət 'ɛvri 'gud 'strouk hi: iks'prɛst iz satis'fakʃn
ənd ə'pruːvl əv ðə 'pleiəz in ə moust kɔndi'sɛndiŋ ən 'patrənaiziŋ
'manə, witʃ 'kudnt 'feil tu əv bin 'haili 'gratifaiiŋ tə ðə 'pɑːti
kən'səːnd; wail ət 'ɛvri 'bad ə'tɛmt ət ə 'katʃ, ənd 'ɛvri 'feiljə
tə 'stɔp ðə 'bɔːl, hi: 'lɔːnʃt hiz 'pəːsnl dis'plɛʒə ət ðə 'hɛd əv
ðə di'voutid indi'vidjŭəl in 'sʌtʃ dinʌnsi'eiʃnz az ''ɑː, 'ɑː !—

'stjuːpid'—'ˈnɑu, 'bʌtəfiŋgəz'—'ˈmʌf'—'ˈhʌmbʌg'—ən 'sou
fɔːθ—idʒakjuˈleiʃnz witʃ 'siːmd tu isˈtabliʃ him, in ði əpinjən
əv 'ɔːl əˈrɑund, əz ə moust 'ɛkslənt ənd ʌndiˈnɑiəbl 'dʒʌdʒ əv
ðə 'houl 'ɑːt ən 'mistəri əv ðə 'noubl 'geim əv 'krikit.

   'ˈkapitl 'geim'—'wɛl 'pleid'—'sʌm 'strouks 'admrəbl,' sɛd ðə
ˌstreindʒə, əz 'bouθ 'saidz 'krɑudid intə ðə 'tɛnt ət ðə kən-
'kluːʒn əv ðə 'geim.

   'juː v 'pleid it, sə?' inˌkwaiəd mistə *'wɔːdl, huː əd bin
'mʌtʃ əˈmjuːzd bai hiz ləˈkwasiti.

   'ˈpleid it | 'θiŋk ai 'hav—'θɑuznz əv taimz—'nɔt 'hiə—
'wɛst 'indiz—ikˈsaitiŋ 'θiŋ—'hɔt 'wəːk—'vɛri.'

   'it 'mʌs bi rɑːðər ə 'wɔːm pəˌsjuːt in 'sʌtʃ ə 'klaimit,'
əbˌzəːvd mistə *'pikwik.

   'ˈwɔːm—'rɛd'hɔt—'skɔːtʃiŋ—'glouiŋ. 'pleid ə 'matʃ 'wʌns
—'siŋgl 'wikit—'frɛnd ðə 'kəːnl—sə *'tɔməs *'bleizou—'huː ʃd
get ðə 'greitist 'nʌmbr əv 'rʌnz.—'wʌn ðə 'tɔs—'fəːst 'iniŋz—
'sɛvn əˈklɔk 'ei 'ɛm—'siks 'neitivz tə luk 'aut—'wɛnt 'in—
'kɛpt in—'hiːt in'tɛns—'neitivz 'ɔːl 'feintid—'teikn əˈwei—'frɛʃ
'hɑːf'dʌzn 'ɔːdəd—'feintid 'ɔːlsou—'bleizou 'bouliŋ—səˈpɔːtid
bai 'tuː 'neitivz—'kudnt boul miː 'aut—'feintid 'tuː—'kliəd
əˌwei ðə 'kəːnl—'wudnt giv 'in—'feiθfl əˈtɛndənt—*'kwaŋkou
*'sambə—'lɑːst man 'lɛft—'sʌn sou 'hɔt, 'bat in 'blistəz—
'bɔːl 'skɔːtʃt 'brɑun—'faiv ˌhʌndrəd n 'sɛvnti 'rʌnz—'rɑːðər
igˈzɔːstid—'kwaŋkou 'mʌstəd ʌp 'lɑːst riˈmeiniŋ 'strɛŋθ—
'bould miː 'aut—'had ə 'bɑːθ n 'wɛnt 'aut tə 'dinə.'

   'ən 'wɔt biˌkeim əv 'wɔtsizneim, sə,' inˌkwaiəd ən 'oul
'dʒɛntlmən.

   'ˈbleizou?'

   'ˈnou—ði 'ʌðə ˌdʒɛntlmən.'

   'ˈkwaŋkou 'sambə?'

   'ˈjɛs, sə.'

   'ˈpuə 'kwaŋkou—'nɛvə riˈkʌvəd it—'bould 'ɔn ɔn 'mai
əkaunt—'bould 'ɔːf ɔn iz 'oun—'daid, sə.' 'hiə ðə 'streindʒə
'bɛrid iz 'kauntinəns in ə 'brɑun 'dʒʌg, bət 'wɛðə tə 'haid

iz i'mouʃn ɔːr im'baib its 'kɔntɛnts, wiː 'kanɔt dis'tiŋktli
ə'fəːm. wiː 'ounli 'nou ðət iː 'pɔːzd 'sʌdnli, 'druː ə 'lɔŋ ən
'diːp 'brɛθ, ənd 'lukt 'aŋʃəsli 'ɔn, əz 'tuː əv ðə 'prinsəpl
'mɛmbəz əv ðə *'diŋli 'dɛl 'klʌb ə'proutʃt mistə 'pikwik, ən
'sɛd—

'wiər ə'baut tə pɑː'teik əv ə 'plein 'dinə ət ðə 'bluː 'laiən,
sə; wiː 'houp 'juː ənd jɔː 'frɛnz l 'dʒɔin əs.'

'əv 'kɔːs,' sɛd mistə 'wɔːdl, 'ə'mʌŋ auə 'frɛnz wiː in'kluːd
mistə——', ənd iː 'lukt təwɔːdz ðə 'streindʒə.

'*'dʒiŋgl,' sɛd ðat 'vəːsətail 'dʒɛntlmən, ''dʒiŋgl—*'alfrid
'dʒiŋgl isˌkwaiə, əv 'nou 'hɔːl, 'nouwɛə.'

'ai ʃl bi 'vɛri 'hapi, ai m 'ʃuə,' sɛd mistə 'pikwik.

''sou ʃl 'ai,' sɛd mistər 'alfrid 'dʒiŋgl, ˌdrɔːiŋ 'wʌn 'ɑːm θruː
mistə 'pikwiks, ənd ə'nʌðə θruː mistə 'wɔːdlz, az iː 'wispəd
kɔnfi'dɛnʃəli in ði 'iər əv ðə 'fɔːmə ˌdʒɛntlmən:—

''dɛvliʃ 'gud 'dinə—'kould bət 'kapitl—'piːpt intə ðə 'rum
ðis 'mɔːniŋ—'faulz n 'paiz n 'ɔːl 'ðat sɔːt əv θiŋ—'plɛznt 'fɛlouz
'ðiːz—'wɛl bi'heivd 'tuː—'vɛri.'

From *The Pickwick Papers*, by CHARLES DICKENS

7.

'waitbeit

ai wəz 'riːsntli 'tɔːkiŋ in ə vɛri 'tʌtʃiŋ ən pou'ɛtikl 'strein
əbaut ði ə'bʌv 'dɛlikit 'fiʃ tə mai frɛnd *'fuːzl ənd səm 'ʌðəz
ət ðə 'klʌb, ənd iks'peiʃietiŋ əpən ði 'ɛksələns əv ðə 'dinə witʃ
auə 'litl 'frɛnd *'gʌtlbəri əd 'givn ʌs, wɛn 'fuːzl, 'lukiŋ 'raund
ə'baut him wið ən ˌɛər əv 'traiəmf ənd i'mɛns 'wizdəm, 'sɛd,—

'ai l 'tɛl juː 'wɔt, *ˌwagstɑːf, 'ai m ə 'plein 'man, ən dis'paiz
ɔːl jɔː 'gɔːməndaiziŋ ən 'kikʃɔːz. ai 'dount nou ðə 'difrəns
bitwiːn 'wʌn əv jɔːr əb'səːd 'meid ˌdiʃiz ənd ə'nʌðə; 'giv miː
ə 'plein 'kʌt əv 'mʌtn ɔː 'biːf. ai m ə 'plein 'iŋgliʃmən, 'ai
am, ən 'nou 'glʌtn.'

'fuːzl, ai ˌsei, 'θɔːt 'ðis 'spiːtʃ ə 'tɛrəbl 'sɛt'daun ˌfɔː mi;
and in'diːd 'aktid ʌp tu iz 'prinsəplz. juː mei 'siː im 'ɛni dei
ət 'siks 'sitiŋ 'daun bifɔːr ə 'greit 'riːkiŋ 'dʒɔint əv 'miːt, hiz
'aiz 'kwivəriŋ, hiz 'feis 'rɛd, ənd 'hiː 'kʌtiŋ 'greit 'smoukiŋ
'rɛd 'kɔləps aut əv ðə 'biːf bi'fɔːr im, witʃ iː di'vauəz wið
kɔris'pɔndiŋ 'kwɔntitiz əv 'kabidʒ ən pə'teitouz, ən ði 'ʌðə
'greitis 'lʌkʃəriz əv ðə 'klʌb 'teibl.

'wɔt ai kəm'plein ɔv 'iz, 'nɔt ðət ðə man ʃud in'dʒɔi hiz
'greit 'miːl əv 'stiːmiŋ 'biːf—'lɛt im bi 'hapi ouvə 'ðat, əz 'mʌtʃ
əz ðə 'biːf hiː z di'vauəriŋ wəz in 'laif 'hapi ouvər 'ɔil-keiks ɔː
'maŋgl'wəːzl—bət ai 'heit ðə ˌfɛlouz 'bruːtl 'sɛlfkəm'pleisnsi,
ənd hiz 'skɔːn fər 'ʌðə 'piːpl huː hav 'difrənt 'teists frəm 'hiz.
ə 'man huː 'bragz riˌgɑːdiŋ imˌsɛlf, ðət wɔt'ɛvə hiː 'swɔlouz iz
ðə 'seim tə him, ənd ðət hiz 'kɔːs 'palit ˌrɛkəgnaiziz 'nou
'difrəns bitwiːn 'vɛnzn ən 'təːtl, 'pudiŋ, ɔː 'mʌtn'brɔθ, az hiz
in'difrənt 'dʒɔːz 'klouz 'ouvə ðəm, 'bragz əbaut ə 'pəːsnl
di'fɛkt—ðə ˌrɛtʃ—ən 'nɔt əbaut ə 'vəːtjuː. it s laik ə 'man
'boustiŋ ðət iː haz 'nou 'iə fə 'mjuːzik, ɔː 'nou 'ai fə 'kʌlə, ɔː
ðət iz 'nouz 'kɑːnt 'sɛnt ðə 'difrəns biˌtwiːn ə 'rouz nd ə
'kabidʒ. ai 'sei, əz ə 'dʒɛnrəl 'ruːl, 'sɛt ðat man 'daun əz ə
kən'siːtid ˌfɛlou huː 'swagəz əbaut 'nɔt 'kɛəriŋ fər iz 'dinə.

'wai 'ʃudnt wiː ˌkɛər əˌbaut it? wəz 'iːtiŋ 'nɔt 'meid tə biː
ə 'plɛʒə tu əs? 'jɛs, ai ˌsei, ə 'deili ˌplɛʒə—ə 'plɛʒə fə'miljə jɛt
'ɛvə 'njuː; ðə 'seim ənd 'jɛt hau 'difrənt! it s 'wʌn əv ðə
ˌkɔːziz əv doumɛs'tisiti. ðə 'niːt 'dinə meiks ðə 'hʌzbənd 'pliːzd,
ðə 'hauswaif 'hapi; ðə 'tʃildrən ˌkɔnsikwəntli ɑː 'wɛl brɔːt
'ʌp, ənd 'lʌv ðɛə pə'pɑː; ən mə'mɑː. ə 'gud 'dinə iz ðə 'sɛntər
əv ðə 'səːkl əv ðə 'souʃl 'simpəθiz. it 'wɔːmz ə'kweintənʃʃip
intə 'frɛnʃip; it mɛn'teinz ðat 'frɛnʃip 'kʌmfətəbli 'ʌnim'pɛəd;
'ɛnimiz 'miːt ouvər it ənd ə 'rɛkənsaild. 'hau ˌmɛni əv 'juː,
diə ˌfrɛndz, həz ðat 'leit 'bɔtl əv 'klarət 'wɔːmd intu ə'fɛkʃnit
fə'givnis, 'tɛndə rɛkə'lɛkʃnz əv 'ould 'taimz, ənd 'ɑːdnt 'glouiŋ
antisi'peiʃnz əv 'njuː? ðə 'brein iz ə tri'mɛndəs 'siːkrit. ai
bi'liːv sʌm 'kɛmist wil ə'raiz ə'nɔn huː l 'nou hau tə 'dɔktə

ðə 'brein az ðei ˌduː ðə 'bɔdi 'nau, az *'liːbig¹ 'dɔktəz ðə
'graund. ðei l ə'plai səːtn 'mɛdsinz, ən prə'djuːs 'krɔps əv
'səːtn 'kwɔlitiz ðət ə 'laiiŋ 'dɔːmənt 'nau fə 'wɔnt əv inti'lɛk-
tjuəl 'gwaːnou. bət 'ðis iz ə 'sʌbdʒikt fə 'fjuːtʃə spɛkju'leiʃn—
ə pə'rɛnθəsis ˌgrouiŋ aut əv ə'nʌðə pəˌrɛnθəsis. 'wɔt ai wud
'əːdʒ is'pɛʃəli 'hiə iz ə 'pɔint witʃ 'mʌs bi fə'miljə wið 'ɛvri
'pəːsn ə'kʌstəmd tu 'iːt 'gud 'dinəz—ˌneimli ðə 'noubl ən
'frɛndli 'kwɔlitiz ðət ðei i'lisit. 'hau 'iz it wiː 'kʌt sʌtʃ 'dʒouks
ouvə ðəm? 'hau 'iz it wiː bi'kʌm sou ri'maːkəbli 'frɛndli?
'hau 'iz it ðət 'sʌm əv ʌs, in'spaiəd bai ə 'gud 'dinə, hav 'sʌdn
'gʌsts əv 'dʒiːnjəs ʌn'noun in ðə 'kwaiət ʌn'fɛstiv 'steit?
'sʌm mɛn meik 'spiːtʃiz; 'sʌm 'ʃeik ðɛə 'neibə bai ðə 'hand,
ənd in'vait him, ɔː ðəm'sɛlvz, tə 'dain; 'sʌm 'siŋ prə'didʒəsli;
mai ˌfrɛnd *'salədin, fər ˌinstəns, 'gouz 'houm, hiː ˌsɛz, wið ðə
moust 'bjuːtəfl 'haːməniz 'riŋiŋ in iz 'iəz; ənd 'ai, fə 'mai paːt,
wil teik 'ɛni 'givn 'tjuːn, ən 'meik vɛəri'eiʃnz əpɔn it fər 'ɛni
'givn 'piərĭəd əv 'auəz, 'greitli, nou ˌdaut, tə ðə di'lait əv 'ɔːl
'hiərəz. 'ðiːz ər 'ounli 'tɛmprəri inspəˌreiʃnz 'givn ʌs bai ðə
'dʒɔli 'dʒiːnjəs, bət 'aː ðei tə bi dis'paizd ɔn 'ðat əkaunt?
'nou. 'gud 'dinəz həv biːn ðə 'greitist 'viːiklz əv bi'nɛvələns
sins 'man bi'gan tu 'iːt.

ə 'teist fə 'gud 'liviŋ, ðɛn, iz 'preizˌwəːði in mɔdə'reiʃn—
laik 'ɔːl ði 'ʌðə 'kwɔlitiz ənd in'daumənts əv 'man. 'if ə man
wə tə ni'glɛkt hiz 'famili ɔːr iz 'biznis ɔn ə'kaunt əv iz 'lʌv fə
ðə 'fidl ɔː ðə 'fain 'aːts, hiː d kə'mit 'dʒʌst ðə 'kraim ðət ðə
'dinə ˌsɛnʃuəlist iz 'gilti ɔv. bət tu in'dʒɔi 'waizli iz ə 'maksim
əv witʃ 'nou man niːd bi ə'ʃeimd. bət 'if juː 'kaːnt 'iːt ə 'dinər
əv 'həːbz əz 'wɛl əz ə 'stɔːld 'ɔks, 'ðɛn juər ən ʌn'fɔːtʃnit 'man;
jɔː 'lʌv fə 'gud 'dinəz həz 'paːst ðə 'houlsəm 'baundəri, ən
di'dʒɛnəreitid intə 'glʌtn̩i.

From the *Essay on Whitebait*, by W. M. THACKERAY

---

¹ German pronunciation 'liːbiç (for ç see Part I, § 376).

8.

A Specimen of RP showing Intonation

ət 'ðis 'moumənt   ə 'ʃril 'vɔis 'kɔːld *'doudou frəm ðə 'drɔiŋrum.

''doudou, 'doudou,' it ˌkraid,

'ðə 'man 'brɔːt miː 'tuː 'tɛpid 'poutʃt 'ɛgz!

'duː sɛn mi ˌsʌmθiŋ 'ɛls.   'iz ðə sʌtʃ ə θiŋ əz ə 'grild 'boun?'

'ðiːz ri'maːks wə 'spiːdili ˌfɔloud 'ʌp

bai ði ə'piərəns əv 'mis *'steinz   ət ðə 'dainiŋrum 'dɔː.

in 'wʌn 'hand   ʃiː 'hɛld ðə dis'paizd 'ɛgz,

in ði 'ʌðə   ə 'kwaiər əv 'mjuːzik ˌpeipə.

bi'haind həː ˌfɔloud ə 'futmən   wið əː 'brɛkfəs trei,

in iks'kju:zəbl 'ignərəns   əz tu wɔt wəz ri'kwaiəd ɔv him.

''diə 'doudou,' ʃi wɛnt ˌɔn,

' ju: 'nou wɛn ai m kəm'pouziŋ ə 'simfəni

ai 'wɔnt ˌsʌmθiŋ 'mɔːr ik'saitiŋ ðən 'tu: 'poutʃt 'ɛgz.

mistə *'brɔkstn ai 'nou ḷ ˌteik mai ˌsaid.

ju: 'kudnt iːt 'poutʃt 'ɛgz ət ə 'bɔːl,   'kud juː?

ðei mait 'du: vɛri 'wɛl fər ə 'fjuːnrəl 'maːtʃ   ɔːr ə 'nɔktəːn,

bət ðei 'wount du: fr ə 'simfəni,   is'peʃli fə ðə 'skɛətsou.

ə 'brandi ən 'soudə ənd ə 'grild 'boun

iz wɔt wʌn 'riəli ˌwɔnts fr ə ˌskɛətsou,

ounli 'ðat əd bi 'kwait aut əv ðə 'kwɛstʃn.'

*'i:diθ 'steinz ˌtɔ:kt in ə 'laud di'tə:mind 'vɔis,

ənd 'ɛmfəsaizd həː 'pɔints

wið litl 'daʃiz n 'flʌriʃiz   əv ðə 'diʃ əv 'poutʃt 'ɛgz.

ət 'ðis 'moumənt 'wʌn əv ðəm 'flu: ɔn tə ðə 'flɔː ənd iks'ploudid.

bət it s ən 'il 'wind ðət blouz 'noubədi ɛni ˌgud,

ənd ət 'ɛni reit 'ðis ri'li:vd ðə 'futmən

frəm iz 'steit əv indi'siʒn.

hiz i'mi:djət 'dju:ti wəz 'kliəli tə ri'mu:v it.

'doudou 'θru: əːˌsɛlf 'bak in əː 'tʃɛə   wið ə 'pi:l əv 'lɑːftə.

''gou 'ɔn, 'gou 'ɔn,' ʃi ˌkrɑid,   juə 'tu: 'splɛndid.

'tɛl əs wɔt juː ˌrɑit ðə 'prɛstou ɔn.'

PHONETIC TEXTS

'ai 'kɑːnt 'weist ə'nʌðə 'moumənt,' sɛd ˌiːdiθ;

ai m in ðə 'midl əv ə moust in'trɑːnsiŋ mouˈtiːf,

witʃ iz 'wəːkiŋ 'aut 'bjuːtəfli.

'djuː main mai 'smoukiŋ in ðə 'drɔiŋrum?

ai m 'ɔːfli 'sɔri,　bət it meiks 'ɔːl ðə 'difrəns tə mai 'wəːk.

'bəːn ə litl 'insɛns ðɛər 'ɑːftəwədz.

'duː sɛn mi ə 'boun, ˌdoudou.

'kʌm ənd 'hiə miː 'plei ðə 'skɛətsou 'leitər 'ɔn.

it s ðə 'bɛst 'θiŋ ai v 'ɛvə 'dʌn.　'ou,　'bai ðə 'wei

ai 'tɛligrɑːft tə hɛə*'trufən tə 'kʌm tə'mɔrou—

hiː z mai kən'dʌktə, juː ˌnou.　juː kən 'put im 'ʌp in ðə 'vilidʒ

193

ɔː ðə 'koulhoul if ju ˌlaik.   hiː z 'kwait 'hapi

if iː ˌgɛts inʌf 'biə.   hiː z mai 'dʒəːmən kən'dʌktə, juː ˌnou.

ai 'meid him in'taiəli.

ai 'tuk im tə ðə prin'sɛs ði ʌðə 'dei   wɛn ai wəz ət *'eiks,

ənd wiː 'ɔːl had 'biə təˌgɛðə   in ðə və'randə əv ðə *'bou 'siːt.

juː l bi ə'mjuːzd wið him.'

''ou, 'raːðə,' sɛd ˌdoudou;   ''ðat l bi 'ɔːl 'rait.

hiː kn ˌsliːp in ðə 'haus.   'wil iː kʌm 'əːli təˌmorou?

'lɛt s 'siː—   tə'morou z 'sʌndi.   'iːdiθ,   ai v 'gɔt n̩ ai'diə.

wiː l hav ə 'diə litl 'səːvis in ðə 'haus—

wiː 'kaːnt gou tə 'tʃəːtʃ if it 'snouz—   ənd 'juː ʃl 'plei jɔː 'mas,

194

. . • . . . . ✓

ənd hɛə 'wɔtsizneim ʃl kən'dʌkt,

. . • . . . ✓ . • . . . ⌃

ən *'bəːti ən *'grɑːnti ənd 'juː ənd 'ai l̩ 'siŋ. 'wount it bi 'lʌvli?

. . ✓ . . • . . . .

'juː ənd 'ai l̩ 'sɛtl 'ɔːl 'ðat ðis ɑːftə'nuːn.

. • . . . . ✓

zi 'tɛligrɑːf tə 'trʌflə ɔː wɔt'ɛvər iz ˌneim 'iz

. . . . . • . . ⌃ . ✓

tə 'kʌm bai ði 'eit 'twɛnti. ðɛn hiː l bi 'hiə bai 'twɛlv,

. • . . . . • . . .

ənd wiː l hav ðə 'səːvis ət ə 'kwɔːtə 'pɑːst.'

⌃ . . ⌃ . . • . • ✓

''doudou, ðat l bi 'grand,' sɛd 'iːdiθ.   'ai 'kɑːnt 'weit 'nau.

. • ✓ . . . . •

'gud'bai.   'hʌri 'ʌp mai 'brɛkfəst—

. ⌃ . ✓ . • . . • . .

ai m 'ɔːfli 'ʃɑːp 'sɛt.'   'iːdiθ wɛnt 'bak tə ðə 'drɔiŋrum

• ✓ . . . . • .

'wisliŋ in ə pə'tikjələli 'ʃril 'manə.

From *Dodo*, by E. F. BENSON

195

9.

kən'tɛntmənt

'frɛnd, ðɛə bi 'ðei ɔn huːm 'mishap
ɔː 'nɛvə ɔː sou 'rɛəli 'kʌmz,
ðat 'wɛn ðei 'θiŋk ðɛərˌɒv ðei 'snap
di'raisiv 'θʌmz;

ənd ðɛə bi 'ðei huː 'laitli 'luːz
ðɛər 'ɔːl, jɛt 'fiːl 'nou 'eikiŋ 'vɔid;
ʃud 'ɔːt ə'nɔi ðəm, ðei ri'fjuːz
tə biː ə'nɔid;

ənd 'fein wud 'ai biː 'iːn əz 'ðiːz!
'laif iz wið 'sʌtʃ 'ɔːl 'biər ən 'skitlz;
ðei 'aː nɔt 'difikəlt tə 'pliːz
əbaut ðɛə 'vitlz;

ðə 'traut, ðə 'graus, ði 'əːli 'piː
bai 'sʌtʃ, if 'ðɛə, aː 'friːli 'teikən;
'if 'nɔt ðei 'mʌnʃ, wið 'iːkwəl 'gliː,
ðɛə ˌbit əv 'beikən.

ənd 'wɛn ðei 'waks ə litl 'gei
ən 'tʃaːf ðə 'pʌblik aːftə 'lʌnʃn,
'if ðeiə kən'frʌntid wið ə 'strei
pə'liːsmənz 'trʌnʃn,

ðei 'geiz ðɛərˌat wið 'autstrɛtʃt 'nɛks
ənd 'laːftə witʃ 'nou 'θrɛts kən 'smʌðə,
ən 'tɛl ðə 'hɔrə-strikn 'ɛks
ðət ''hiː z ə'nʌðə'.

in 'snou-taim if ðei 'krɔs ə 'spɔt
wɛər 'ʌn-səsˈpɛktid 'bɔiz həv 'slid,
ðei 'fɔːl nɔt 'daun—ˌðou ðei wud 'nɔt
'maind if ðei 'did.

'wɛn ðə 'spriŋ 'rouzbʌd witʃ ðei 'wɛə
  'breiks 'ʃɔːt ən 'tʌmblz frəm its 'stɛm,
'nou 'θɔːt əv biːiŋ 'aŋgri 'ɛə
  'dɔːnz əpən ˌðɛm;

'ðou twəz *'dʒiˈmaiməz 'hand ðət 'pleist,
  (əz 'wɛl juː 'wiːn) ət 'iːvniŋz 'ɑuə,
'in ðə ˌlʌvd 'bʌtnhoul ðat 'tʃeist
  ən 'tʃɛriʃt 'flɑuə.

ənd 'wɛn ðei 'travl, 'if ðei 'fɑind
  ðət ðei əv 'lɛft ðɛə 'pɔkit 'kʌmpəs
ɔː *'mʌri ɔː 'θik 'buːts biˌhɑind,
  ðei 'reiz nou 'rʌmpəs.

bət 'plɔd siˈriːnli 'ɔn wiˈðuet;
  'nouiŋ it s 'bɛtə tu inˈdjuə
ðiː 'iːvil witʃ biˈjɔnd 'ɔːl 'dɑut
  juː 'kanɔt 'kjuə.

'wɛn fə ðat 'əːli 'trein ðeiə 'leit,
  ðei 'duː nɔt 'meik ðɛə 'wouz ðə 'tɛkst
əv 'səːmənz in ðə *'tɑimz, bət 'weit
  'ɔn fə ðə 'nɛkst;

ən 'dʒʌmp inˈsɑid, ənd 'ounli 'grin
  'ʃud it əˈpiə ðət 'ðat 'drɑi 'wag,
ðə 'gɑːd, ouˈmitid tə 'put 'in
  ðɛə 'kɑːpitˌbag.

From Fly Leaves, by C. S. CALVERLEY
(after the manner of Horace)

10.

ðə 'blakbəːd

hiː 'kʌmz ɔn 'tʃouzən 'iːv(ə)niŋz,
mɑi 'blakbəːd 'bɑuntiful, ənd 'siŋz

'ouvə ðə 'gɑːdnz əv ðə 'taun
'dʒʌst ət ði 'auə ðə 'sʌn gouz 'daun.
hiz 'flait əˌkrɔs ðə 'tʃimniz 'θik,
bai sʌm di'vain ə'riθmətik,
'kʌmz tu hiz 'kʌstəməri 'stak,
ənd 'kautʃiz ðɛə hiz 'pluːmidʒ 'blak,
ənd 'ðɛə hiː 'lifts hiz 'jɛlou 'bil,
'kindld əˌgenst ðə 'sʌnsɛt, til
ðiːz 'sʌbəːbz ɑː laik *'dimək 'wudz
wɛə 'mjuːzik haz həː 'sɔlitjuːdz,
ənd 'wail hiː 'mɔks ðə 'wintəz 'rɔŋ
'rapt ɔn hiz 'pinəkl əv 'sɔŋ,
'figəd əˌbʌv auə 'gɑːdn 'plɔts
'ðouz ɑː si'lɛstjəl 'tʃimnipɔts.

                                   JOHN DRINKWATER

11.

ðə 'tʃɛri triː

'lʌvljist əv 'triːz, ðə 'tʃɛri 'nau
iz 'hʌŋ wið 'bluːm əˌlɔŋ ðə 'bau,
ənd 'standz əˌbaut ðə 'wudlənd 'raid
'wɛəriŋ 'wait fər 'iːstətaid.

'nau, əv mai 'θriːskɔː 'jəːz ənd 'tɛn
'twɛnti wil nɔt 'kʌm ə'gɛn,
ənd 'teik frəm 'sɛvnti ˌspriŋz ə 'skɔː,
it 'ounli 'liːvz miː 'fifti 'mɔː.

ənd 'sins tu 'luk ət 'θiŋz in 'bluːm
'fifti 'spriŋz ɑː 'litl 'rum,
ə'baut ðə 'wudləndz ai wil 'gou
tu 'siː ðə 'tʃɛri 'hʌŋ wið ˌsnou.

                From *A Shropshire Lad*, by A. E. HOUSMAN

12.

'ou, ðət ðə 'dɛzət wəː mai 'dwɛliŋ͵pleis,
wið 'wʌn 'fɛə 'spirit fə mai 'ministə,
ðət ai mait 'ɔːl fə'gɛt ðə 'hjuːmən 'reis,
and, 'heitiŋ 'nou wʌn, 'lʌv bʌt 'ounli 'həː!
jiː 'ɛlimənts!—in huːz i'noubliŋ 'stəː
ai 'fiːl mai͵sɛlf ig'zɔːltid—'kan jiː nɒt
ə'kɔːd miː sʌtʃ ə 'biːiŋ? 'duː ai 'əː
in 'diːmiŋ 'sʌtʃ in'habit 'mɛni ə 'spɒt?
ðou 'wið ðɛm tu kən'vəːs kən 'rɛəli biː auə 'lɒt.

ðɛər iz ə 'plɛʒə in ðə 'paːθlis 'wudz,
ðɛər iz ə 'raptʃə ɒn ðə 'lounli 'ʃɔː,
ðɛər iz sə'saiəti wɛə 'nʌn in'truːdz,
bai ðə 'diːp 'siː, ənd 'mjuːzik in its 'rɔː;
ai 'lʌv nɒt 'man ðə 'lɛs, bət 'neitʃə 'mɔː,
frəm 'ðiːz auər 'intəvjuːz, in 'witʃ ai 'stiːl
frəm 'ɔːl ai 'mei biː, ɔː 'hav 'biːn bi'fɔː,
tu 'miŋgl wið ðə 'juːnivəːs, ənd 'fiːl
wɒt ai kən 'nɛər iks'prɛs, jɛt 'kanɒt 'ɔːl kən'siːl.

'roul 'ɒn ðau 'diːp ənd 'daːk 'bluː 'ouʃn—'roul!
'tɛn 'θauzənd 'fliːts 'swiːp ouvə ðiː in 'vein;
'man 'maːks ði 'əːθ wið 'ruin—hiz kən'troul
'stɒps wið ðə 'ʃɔː;—əpɒn ðə 'wɔːtri 'plein
ðə 'rɛks aːr ɔːl 'ðai 'diːd, 'nɔː dʌθ ri'mein
ə 'ʃadou əv 'manz 'ravidʒ, seiv hiz 'oun,
'wɛn, fər ə 'moumənt, laik ə 'drɒp əv 'rein,
hiː 'siŋks intu ðai 'dɛpθs wið 'bʌbliŋ 'groun,
wi'ðaut ə 'ɡreiv, ʌn'nɛld, ʌn'kɒfind, ənd ʌn'noun.

From *Childe Harold* (Canto IV, st. 177–9),
by LORD BYRON

13.

'antəni. 'frɛndz, 'roumənz, 'kʌntrimən, 'lɛnd miː jɔːr 'iəz;
ai 'kʌm tu 'bɛri *'siːzə, 'nɔt tu 'preiz him.
ði 'iːvil ðət mɛn 'duː 'livz 'aːftə ðɛm;
ðə 'gud iz 'ɔft in'təːrid wið ðɛə 'bounz;
'sou lɛt it ˌbiː wið 'siːzə. ðə 'noubl *'bruːtəs
haθ 'tould juː 'siːzə wɔz am'biʃəs;
if it 'wəː sou, it wəz ə 'griːvəs 'fɔːlt,
and 'griːvəsli haθ 'siːzər 'aːnsəd it.
'hiə, ʌndə 'liːv əv 'bruːtəs ənd ðə 'rɛst—
fɔː 'bruːtəs iz ən 'ɔnərəbl man;
'sou aː ðei 'ɔːl, 'ɔːl 'ɔnərəbl mɛn—
'kʌm 'ai tu 'spiːk in 'siːzəz 'fjuːnərəl.
hiː wəz mai 'frɛnd, 'feiθful ənd 'dʒʌst tu miː;
bʌt 'bruːtəs 'sɛz hiː wɔz am'biʃəs,
and 'bruːtəs iz ən 'ɔnərəbl man.
hiː haθ brɔːt 'mɛni 'kaptivz 'houm tu *'roum,
huːz 'ransəmz did ðə 'dʒɛnərəl 'kɔfəz 'fil;
'did 'ðis in 'siːzə 'siːm am'biʃəs?
'wɛn ðət ðə 'puə həv 'kraid, 'siːzə haθ 'wɛpt;
am'biʃən ʃud bi 'meid əv 'stəːnə stʌf;
jɛt 'bruːtəs 'sɛz hiː wɔz am'biʃəs,
and 'bruːtəs iz ən 'ɔnərəbl man.
juː 'ɔːl did 'siː ðət ɔn ðə *'luːpəːkal
ai 'θrais pri'zɛntid him ə 'kiŋli 'kraun,
witʃ ˌhiː did 'θrais ri'fjuːz. 'wɔz 'ðis am'biʃən?
jɛt 'bruːtəs 'sɛz hiː wɔz am'biʃəs,
and 'ʃuə hiː iz ən 'ɔnərəbl man.
ai 'spiːk 'nɔt tu 'dis'pruːv wɔt 'bruːtəs 'spouk,
bʌt 'hiər ai 'am, tu 'spiːk wɔt ai duː 'nou.
juː 'ɔːl did 'lʌv him 'wʌns, 'nɔt wiðaut 'kɔːz;
'wɔt 'kɔːz wiθ'houldz juː ðɛn tu 'mɔːn fə him?
'ou 'dʒʌdʒmənt ! ðau aːt 'flɛd tu 'bruːtiʃ 'biːsts,

and 'mɛn həv 'lɔst ðɛə 'riːzn. 'bɛə wið miː;
mai 'haːt iz in ðə 'kɔfin 'ðɛə wið 'siːzə,
and ai mʌst 'pɔːz til it kʌm 'bak tu miː.

From *Julius Caesar* (Act III, Sc. 2), by SHAKESPEARE
(Compare text No. 20.)

14.

ət ə 'sɔləm 'mjuːzik

'blɛst 'pɛər əv 'saiərənz, 'plɛdʒiz əv 'hɛvnz 'dʒɔi,
'sfiəbɔːn haː'mounjəs 'sistəz, 'vɔis ənd 'vəːs,
'wɛd jɔː di'vain 'saundz, ənd 'mikst 'pauər im'plɔi,
'dɛd θiŋz wið 'inbriːðd 'sɛns 'eibl tu 'piəs;
and tu auə 'haireizd 'fantəsi pri'zɛnt
ðat 'ʌndis'təːbid 'sɔŋ əv 'pjuə kɔn'sɛnt,
'ei 'sʌŋ bifɔː ðə 'safaiə‚kʌləd 'θroun
tu 'him ðət 'sits ðɛə‚rɔn,
wið 'seintli 'ʃaut ənd 'sɔləm 'dʒuːbiliː;
wɛə ðə 'brait 'sɛrəfim in 'bəːniŋ 'rou
ðɛə 'laud ʌp'liftid 'eindʒəl'trʌmpits 'blou,
and ðə tʃɛ'ruːbik 'houst in 'θauzənd 'kwaiəz
'tʌtʃ ðɛər i'mɔːtl 'haːps əv 'gouldən 'waiəz,
wið 'ðouz 'dʒʌst 'spirits ðət 'wɛə vik'tɔːriəs 'paːmz,
'himz di'vaut ənd 'houli 'saːmz
'siŋiŋ ɛvə'laːstiŋli;
ðət 'wiː ɔn 'əːθ wið 'ʌndis'kɔːdiŋ 'vɔis,
mei 'raitli 'aːnsə ðat mi'loudjəs 'nɔiz;
az 'wʌns wiː 'did, til 'disprə'pɔːʃənd 'sin
'dʒaːd əgɛnst 'neitʃəz 'tʃaim, ənd wið 'haːʃ 'din
'brouk ðə 'fɛə 'mjuːzik ðət 'ɔːl 'kriːtʃəz 'meid
tu 'ðɛə 'greit 'lɔːd, huːz 'lʌv ðɛə 'mouʃn 'sweid
in 'pəːfikt daiə'peisn, 'wailst ðei 'stud
in 'fəːst ou'biːdjəns ənd ðɛə 'steit əv 'gud.

'ou mei wiː 'suːn ə'gein ri'njuː ðat 'sɔŋ,
ənd 'kiːp in 'tjuːn wið 'hɛvn, til 'gɔd ɛə 'lɒŋ
tu hiz si'lɛstjəl 'kɔnsɔːt ʌs juː'nait,
tu 'liv wið 'him, ənd 'siŋ in 'ɛndlis 'mɔːn əv 'lait!

JOHN MILTON

15.

[A specimen of Southern English in a form of transcription
which allows for the pronunciation of those who lengthen the
traditionally short vowels. The symbols ι, ᴅ and ꙩ have to be
introduced to denote the qualities of the vowels in such words
as *in*, *top*, *wood*. See Part I, §§ 429, 430. ː is used to show
where lengthenings would be likely to take place; lengthenings
would also be possible in some syllables not marked with ː.]

ðι ə'pιərəns əv ðι 'ailənd wɛn ai 'keim ᴅn 'dɛːk nɛkst
'mɔːnιŋ wəz 'ɔltəgɛðə 'tʃeindʒd. ɔl'ðꙩꙩ ðə 'briːz həd 'naꙩ
'ʌtəlι 'feild, wi əd meid ə 'greit dil əv 'wei djꙩəriŋ ðə 'nait,
ənd wə 'naꙩ laιιŋ bι'kaːmd əbaꙩt 'haf ə 'mail tə ðə 'saꙩθ
'ist əv ðə 'loꙩ 'istən 'koꙩst. 'greι ˌkʌləd 'wɔːdz kʌvəd ə 'laːdʒ
'paːt əv ðə 'səːfιs. 'ðιs 'iːvn 'tιnt 'wᴅːz ιndiːd 'broꙩkn 'ʌp bai
'striks əv 'jɛloꙩ 'sandbreιk ιn ðə 'loꙩə laːndz, ənd bai 'mɛnι
'tɔːl 'triːz əv ðə 'pain ˌfamιlι 'aꙩt'tɒpιŋ ðι 'ʌðəz—'sʌm 'sιŋglι,
'sʌm ιn 'klʌmps; bət ðə 'dʒɛnrəl 'kʌlərιŋ wəz 'junιfɔːm ənd
'saːd. ðə 'hιlz 'ran 'ʌp 'klιə əbʌv ðə vɛdʒi'teιʃn ιn 'spaιəz əv
'neιkιd 'rᴅːk. 'ɔːl wə 'streindʒlι 'ʃeιpt, ənd ðə *'spaι-glaːs,
wιtʃ wəz bai 'θriː ɔ 'fɔː hʌndrəd 'fit ðə 'tɔːlιst ᴅn ðι 'ailənd,
wəz 'laιkwaιz ðə 'streindʒιst ιn kənfιgjꙩ'reιʃn, 'rʌnιŋ 'ʌp 'ʃιə
frəm ˌɔlmoꙩst 'ɛvrι 'said, ənd 'ðɛːn 'sʌdnlι 'kʌt 'ᴅf ət ðə 'tɒːp
laιk ə 'pɛdιstl tə pꙩt ə 'statju ᴅːn.

From *Treasure Island*, by R. L. STEVENSON

16.

A Specimen of English spoken with a
South-Western accent

[*Notes.* *r*'s are sounded (as ɹ) finally and before consonants.
When the letter ɹ follows a vowel symbol, it is either pronounced as a separate ɹ, or the vowel symbol and ɹ form a
digraph denoting an r-coloured vowel. Thus 'hɔɹs is pronounced
by some with ɔ+ɹ and by others with an r-coloured ɔ (ɒ, see
§§ 355, 356). ɹ following a consonant, as in fɹːst, 'leitɹ, has the
value of r-coloured ə.
A rather front aː replaces RP ɑː.
The diphthong ai begins with a rather front a (as with many
RP speakers). The diphthong aü also begins with a front or
raised front a, and it ends with a somewhat fronted u (ü),
except when ɹ follows.
Final unstressed short i, as in 'twɛnti, 'rapidli, tends to be
rather close, i.e. to have the same quality as the long iː.
ʌ is not distinguished from ə.
The remaining sounds are as in RP.]

ðə 'prɛznt van iz 'taimd tə 'liːv ðə 'taün ət 'foːɹ in ði
aːftɹ'nun priː'saisli, ənd it iz 'naü 'haːf paːst 'θriː bai ðə 'klɔk
in ðə 'tərət ət ðə 'tɔp əv ðə 'striːt. in ə 'fjuː 'sɛkəndz 'ɛrən(d)bɔiz
frəm ðə 'ʃɔps bə,gin tu ə'raiv wið 'pakədʒəz, witʃ ðei 'fliŋ intə
ðə ˌviːəkl, ən 'tɹːn ə'wei 'wisliŋ, ən 'kɛɹ fɹ ðə 'pakədʒəz nou
'moːɹ. ət 'twɛnti 'minəts tə 'foːɹ ən 'ɛldɹli 'wumən 'pleisəz hɹ
'baːskət əpən ðə 'ʃaːfts, 'slouli 'maünts, 'teiks əp ə 'siːt in'said,
ənd 'fouldz ɹ 'handz ənd hɹ 'lips. ʃiː həz sə'kjuːrd hɹ 'kɔɹnɹ fɹ
ðə 'dʒɹːni, ðou ðɛːɹ 'iz əʒ jɛt 'nou 'sain əv ə 'hɔɹs biːiŋ put ˌin,
nɔɹ əv ə 'kariɹ. ət ðə 'θriːkwɔɹtɹz, 'tuː 'əðɹ ˌwimən əˌraiv, in
huːm ðə 'fɹːst 'rɛkəgnaizəz ðə 'poustˌmistrəs əv 'əpɹ *'lɔŋˌpədl
ən ðə 'rɛdʒistraːɹz 'waif, 'ðei 'rɛkəgnaiziŋ 'hɹː əz ði 'eidʒəd
'grousərəs əv ðə 'seim 'vilədʒ. ət 'faiv 'minəts tə ði 'auɹ ðɛːɹ
ə'proutʃ mistɹ *'prɔfit, ðə 'skuːlˌmaːstɹ, in ə 'sɔft 'fɛlt 'hat, ən
*'kristəfɹ *'twiŋk, ðə 'maːstɹ'θatʃɹ; and əz ði 'auɹ 'straiks, ðɛːɹ

'rapidli 'drɔp 'in ðə 'pariʃ 'klaːɹk ənd iz 'waif, ðə 'siːdzmən ənd
iz 'eidʒəd 'faːðɹ, ðə rɛdʒis'traːɹ; 'ɔːlsou mistɹ *'dei, ðə
'wɹːld-igˌnoːɹd 'loukəl 'lanskeipˌpeintɹ, ən 'ɛldɹili 'man huː
ri'zaidz in hiz 'neitiv 'pleis, ənd həz 'nɛvɹ 'sould ə 'piktʃɹ
aüt'said it. . . .

  *'bɹːðn, ðə 'kariɹ, iz bai 'ðis taim 'siːn 'bəsliŋ raünd ðə
'viːəkl; ðə 'hɔːrsəz ɹ put 'in, ðə prə'praiətɹ ə'reindʒəz ðə 'reinz
ən 'spriŋz 'əp intu iz 'siːt əz if iː wɹ 'juːst tu it—witʃ iː 'iz.

  'iz 'ɛvribɔdi 'hiːɹ?' hiː 'aːsks prə'parətrili ouvɹ iz 'ʃouldɹ tə
ðə 'pasəndʒɹz wi'ðin.

  az 'ðouz huː wɹ 'nɔt ðɛːɹ 'did nɔt riː'plai in ðə 'nɛgətiv, ðə
'məstɹ wəz ə'suːmd tə bi kəm'pliːt, ənd ˌaːftɹ ə 'fjuː 'hitʃəz ənd
'hindrənsəz ðə 'van wið its 'hjuːmən 'freit wəz 'gɔt ˌəndɹ 'wei.

From *A Few Crusted Characters* in *Life's Little Ironies*
by THOMAS HARDY

17.

A Specimen of one type of Scottish Pronunciation

[*Notes.* The traditionally long i is pronounced quite short
except finally and when followed by inflexional endings such as
-d or -z. Hence it is necessary to employ the special symbol ʋ
to denote the quality of the traditionally short i. See also § 75.

  e and o have about cardinal values.

  No distinction is made corresponding to that existing in
Southern English between a and ɑː. Both are replaced by a
short a slightly retracted from cardinal value.

  No distinctions are made corresponding to those existing in
Southern English between ɔː and ɔ, and uː and u. The sound
used in the first case is an ɔ of about cardinal value, and in
the second case a rather advanced u (which is here written u,
but which might be written ü). Both vowels are short except
finally or when followed by inflexional endings.

  In this text the length-mark is only employed to show the
lengthening of vowels by inflexional -d or -z.

  For the unstressed vowels see § 153.

  t is often dental before r, as in triːz; otherwise it is alveolar.

PHONETIC TEXTS

r beginning a syllable is a tongue-tip flap or roll (generally not more than two taps). **r** terminating a syllable or followed by a consonant is generally a single flap, but may be fricative.

hw may be interpreted either as **h+w** or as **ʍ** (§ 380).

All **l**'s are 'dark' (§§ 293, 301).]

'ivnɪŋ 'loːrd ʌrʌund *'mortn ʌz hi ʌd'vanst ʌp ði 'naro 'dɛl hwɪtʃ mʌst ʌv 'wʌns bin ʌ 'wud, bʌt wʌz 'nʌu ʌ rʌ'vin dɪ'vɛstɪd ʌv 'triːz, ʌn'lɛs hwer ʌ 'fju frʌm ðɪr ɪnʌk'sɛsɪbl sɪtju'eʃn ɔn ði 'ɛdʒ ʌv prɪ'sɪpɪtʌs 'baŋks, ɔr 'klɪŋɪŋ ʌmʌŋ 'rɔks ʌnd 'hjudʒ 'stonz, dɪ'faed ði ɪn've̟ʒn ʌv 'mɛn ʌnd ʌv 'katl, lʌik ði 'skatɪrd 'trʌibz ʌv ʌ 'kɔŋkɪrd 'kʌntre, 'drɪvn tu tek 'rɛfjudʒ ɪn ði 'barn 'strɛŋθ ʌv ɪts 'mʌuntɪnz. 'ðiz 'tu, 'westɪd ʌn dɪ'keːd, simd 'raðɪr tu ɪg'zɪst ðʌn tu 'flʌrɪʃ, ʌnd 'onle 'sɛrvd tu 'ɪndɪkel hwɔt ði 'lanskep mʌst 'wʌns hʌv 'bin. bʌt ði 'strim 'brɔld 'dʌun ʌ'mʌŋ ðɪm ɪn 'ɔl ɪts 'frɛʃnɪs ʌnd vɪ'vasɪte, gɪvɪŋ ði 'lʌif ʌnd anɪ'meʃn hwɪtʃ ʌ 'mʌuntɪn 'rɪvjulɪt ʌ'lon kʌn kʌn'fɛr ɔn ði 'berɪst ʌnd most 'savɪdʒ 'sinz, ʌnd hwɪtʃ ði ɪn'habɪtɪnts ʌv sʌtʃ ʌ 'kʌntre 'mɪs hwɛn 'gezɪŋ ivn ʌpɔn ði 'traŋkwɪl 'wʌindɪŋ ʌv ʌ mʌ'dʒɛstɪk 'strim θru 'plenz ʌv fɛr'tɪlɪte, ʌnd bɪsʌid 'palɪsɪz ʌv 'splendɪr. ði 'trak ʌv ði 'rod 'fɔloːd ði 'kors ʌv ði 'bruk, hwɪtʃ wʌz 'nʌu 'vɪzɪbl, ʌn 'nʌu 'onle tu bi dɪs'tɪŋgwɪʃt bae ɪts 'brɔlɪŋ 'hɛrd ʌmʌŋ ði 'stonz, ɔr ɪn ði 'klɛfts ʌv ði 'rɔks, ðʌt ʌ'keʒnʌle ɪntɪ'rʌptɪd ɪts 'kors.

''mʌrmɪrɪr ðʌt ðʌu 'art,' sɛd ˌmortn, ɪn ði ɛn'θuzeazm ʌv hɪz 'rɛvɪre, ''hwae 'tʃef wɪθ ði 'rɔks ðʌt 'stɔp ðae 'kors fʌr ʌ 'momɪnt? ðɪr z ʌ 'si tu rɪ'siv ði ɪn ɪts 'buzɪm; ʌnd ðɪr z ʌn ɪ'tɛrnɪte fʌr 'man hwɛn hɪz 'frɛtful ʌnd 'heste 'kors θru ði 'vel ʌv 'tʌim ʃl bɪ 'sist ʌnd 'ovɪr. 'hwɔt 'ðae 'pɛte 'fjumɪŋ ɪz tu ði 'dip ʌnd 'vast 'bɪloːz ʌv ʌ 'ʃorlɪs 'oʃn, ar 'ʌur 'kerz, 'hops, 'firz, 'dʒɔez ʌnd 'sɔroːz tu ði 'ɔbdʒɪkts hwɪtʃ mʌst 'ɔkjupae ʌs θru ði 'ɔfl ʌnd 'bʌundlɪs sʌk'sɛʃn ʌv 'edʒɪz.'

From *Old Mortality*, by SIR WALTER SCOTT

18.

A Specimen of one type of American Pronunciation

[*Notes.* In characteristic American English there are no consistent relationships between the lengths and qualities of vowels, as there are in Southern British in the case of iː and i, ɔː and ɔ, etc. Consequently all the vowel qualities of American English have to be represented in phonetic transcription by separate letters. The vowel letters needed are i, ɪ, e, ɛ, a, ɑ, ɔ, o, ɵ, u and ə. i, ɪ, a, ɑ and u have about the same qualities as the Southern British iː, i, a, ɑː and uː respectively. e and o are a little lower than cardinal, and are often slightly diphthongal (i.e. they tend towards eɪ, oɵ). ɛ is a rather open variety. ɔ is a very open variety, and is generally long; it differs considerably from the Southern British long ɔː. ɵ has very little lip-rounding. The diphthongs here written ɑɪ, ɑɵ are similar to the Southern British ɑi, ɑu.

The short ɔ of British English is represented in some words by a and in others by ɔ.

ɛɪ, ɑɹ, ɔɹ, oɹ stand for 'r-coloured vowels' (§§355, 356). ɹ used syllabically stands for an r-coloured close variety of ə. It may occur initially, but no instance occurs in this passage; an example would be 'ɹɪŋ (*erring*).

Vowels are noticeably nasalized when adjoining nasal consonants.

All l's are 'dark'. The 'darkness' is particularly noticeable in words like *lift, silly*.

The symbol ţ denotes a voiced flap resembling ɾ (§232). Some Americans substitute d for it; this pronunciation is admitted by the *New (Third) Webster International Dictionary*.

'ɑɪ 'θɪŋk ɑɪ 'had 'tu mətʃ 'dɪnɹ 'last 'ivnɪŋ. ju 'ɔtnt tə 'sɹv ðoz 'hɛvi bə'nanə 'frɪţɹz.'

'bətʃu 'askt mi tə ˌhav ˌsəm.'

'ɑɪ 'no, bət—ɑɪ 'tɛl ju, hwɛn ə 'fɛlə gɛts 'past 'fɔɹţi, hi 'haz tə lʊk 'aftɹ ɪz dɑɪ'dʒɛstʃən. ðɹ z ə 'laţ ə fɛloz ðət 'dont tek 'prɑpɹ 'kɛɹ əv ðəmsɛlvz. ɑɪ 'tɛl ju, ət 'fɔɹţi ə man z ə 'ful ɔɹ ɪz 'dɑktɹ— ɑɪ 'min, hɪz 'on ˌdɑktɹ. 'foks 'dont 'gɪv ə'nəf ə'tɛnʃən tə 'ðɪs 'maţɹ əv 'dɑɪəţɪŋ. naɵ 'ɑɪ 'θɪŋk—'koɹs ə man 'ɔt tə hav ə

'gɒd 'mil 'aftɹ ðə 'dez 'wɹk, bət ɪt əd bi ə 'gɒd 'θɪŋ fɹ 'boθ əv əs
ɪf wi tɒk 'laɪtɹ 'ləntʃəz.'

'bət, 'dʒɔɹdʒi, 'hɹ ət 'hom ɑɪ 'ɔlwəz 'du hav ə 'laɪt 'ləntʃ.'

''min tɒ ɪm'plaɪ ɑɪ mek ə 'hag əv mə,sɛlf, 'ɪtɪŋ 'daɒn'taɒn?
'jɛs, 'ʃɔɹ! 'ju d hav ə 'swɛl 'taɪm ɪf ju 'had tə 'it ðə 'trɛk ðat
'nu 'stuɹd 'handz 'aɒt tə əs ət ðə aθ'lɛtɪk 'kləb! bət ɑɪ 'sɹtnli
'du fil 'aɒt əv 'sɔɹts ðɪs ˌmɔɹnɪŋ. 'fəni, gɑt ə 'pen daɒn 'hɹ ɑn
ðə 'lɛft 'saɪd—bət 'no, 'ðat 'wɒdn bi əpɛndə'saɪtɪs, 'wɒd ɪt? 'las
'naɪt, hwɛn ɑɪ wəz 'draɪvɪŋ ovɹ tə *'vɹdʒ *'gəntʃəz, ɑɪ 'fɛlt ə
'pen ɪn maɪ 'stəmək 'tu. 'raɪt 'hɹ ɪt waz—kaɪnd əv ə 'ʃɑɹp
'ʃutɪŋ pen. 'hwaɪ dontʃu 'sɪv 'moɹ 'prunz ət 'brɛkfəst? əv 'koɹs
ɑɪ ɪt ən 'apl 'ɛvri 'ivnɪŋ—ən 'apl ə 'de kips ðə 'daktɹ ə,we—bət
'stɪl, ju 'ɔt tə hav 'moɹ 'prunz, ən 'nɑt ɔl ðiz 'fansi 'dudadz.'

'ðə 'las taɪm ɑɪ had 'prunz ju 'dɪdn 'it ðəm.'

''wɛl, ɑɪ 'dɪdnt 'fil laɪk 'ɪtɪŋ əm, ɑɪ spoz. 'matɹ ə 'fakt,
ɑɪ 'θɪŋk ɑɪ 'dɪd it 'səm əv əm. 'ɛniwe—ɑɪ 'tɛl ju ɪt s 'maɪti
ɪm'pɔɹtnt tɒ—ɑɪ wəz 'seɪŋ tə 'vɹdʒ 'gəntʃ, 'dʒəst 'last 'ivnɪŋ,
'mos pipl 'dont tek sə'fɪʃnt 'kɛɹ əv ðɛɹ daɪ'dʒɛstʃənz.'

From *Babbitt*, by SINCLAIR LEWIS

19.

A Specimen of London Dialectal Speech
(See note on p. 179)

[The italicized words are to be read in RP. In the dialect
transcript the following conventions are to be observed. ɑ: is
a back variety (about cardinal). ɛ (representing RP a) appears
to be pronounced with some accompanying pharyngeal contraction. a (representing RP ʌ) is about cardinal. ɑi begins
with cardinal ɑ. əi and əu begin with a high variety of ə.
ɫ is a particularly dark variety, with an ɔ-like resonance; the
dark l of RP (§ 296) is sometimes replaced by a vowel, here
written o.]

''ɑi v 'fɛən əm!', sɛd iz 'lanleidi igˈzaltəntli, əz i: 'stambld
intə ðə 'narou, 'dimli ˌlaitid 'pasidʒ. ''ɑi v 'fɛən əm, mistə
*ˌmeriweðə, n 'glɛd naf ɑi 'ɛm tə ə 'bəin ə sam 'səːvis tˢəu jə.'

ʃiː wəz ə vi'veiʃəs ould 'leidi in ə 'biːdid 'kap wið ə 'laivli 'nɔlidʒ
əv ði ə'fɛəz əv 'aðə 'piːpl, ən 'dʒʌst 'nau 'kiːnli 'intristid in ðə
'njuː 'ɔkjupənt əv hɜː 'bɛd'sitiŋrum. 'ndʒə 'masn 'θɛ̃ʔ məi, kɔz
ai m 'aunli 'tˢəu 'pləizd tə briŋ 'frenz n 'rɛɫtivz tə'geðə.'

''nɛu wotʃə 'kɛʔlin əbɛəʔ, məm?', hiː ˌaːskt pəˌlaitli.

''aː,' riplaid ði ˌould ˌleidi ˌtʃiəfəli, ''joːɫ 'səun 'nau. wi
'ʃaːmp bi 'lɔŋ 'nɛu. iʔ o bi əz 'gud əz ə 'plai tə 'səi 'jəu 'tˢəu
'məiʔ.' ʃi 'wɛpt ənd 'rʌbd hɜːr 'aiz. 'ˌpəiʔo mə 'sai wɔʔ ðə
'laiʔ, bəʔ ðɛəz 'nafiŋk in 'oːɫ ðis 'waid 'wəːɫd tə bi kəm'peːəd
tə 'tˢəu 'lavin 'aːts.'

''leʔ mi ɛv mai 'sapə,' hiː ˌsɛd ˌpeiʃntli, 'n 'ðen 'ləiv mi 'bəi.
ai 'wɔn ə ɛv ə 'smauʔ n ə 'θiŋʔ.'

''jəu 'waun 'dʒəu matʃ 'θĩʔʔin,' riˌmaːkt ðə ˌlanleidi ˌnouiŋli,
'wen jə 'iːə ðə 'niuz 'ai gɔʔ ˌfoː jə. jə 'sedʒə 'naim wəz
'meriweðə, 'dʒidntʃə?'

'ai 'dʒaun di'nai iʔ.'

'ndʒə 'sedʒə gɔʔ 'frenz niːər 'iːə—jə d fə'gɔʔ ði ə'dres.'

'ai 'maiʔ ə leʔ 'foːɫ ə 'kɛʒ̊ɫ rəi'maːk,' sɛd *'bɛl 'kɛəfəli, əz
iː 'hɛld ðə 'handl əv iz 'dɔː, 'oːə 'staiʔmənʔ tə 'ðɛʔ i'feʔ.
wɔʔ'evər ai 'sed ai ɫ 'stiʔ tˢəu.'

''ai 'niu 'ðɛʔ,' riplaid ði ˌould ˌlanleidi, 'ai 'aup ai kn 'tˢɛɫ
ə 'dʒɛ̃ʔomən frəm ə 'miːə 'kɔmən ˌpəːsn. 'sam ˌpəiʔo luʔ 'dʒəun
ɔn 'sailəz ən 'satʃ laiʔ, bəʔ 'ai m 'nɔʔ 'wan ə 'ðɛʔ 'soːʔ. ɛz 'ai
'oːfn 'sai, 'weːə d auɫd 'hiŋlənd bəi wi'ðɛəʔ əm?'

''ari 'ap wi ðɛʔ 'sapə,' sɛd ˌmistə 'bɛl.

'ʃl ai 'lai fə 'tˢəu, mistə ˌmeriweðə?', aːskt ði ˌould ˌleidi.

''koːs nɔʔ! ai m 'aunli 'wan.'

'bəʔ ðə 'laidəiʔ?'

''wɔʔ ˌlaidəi?'

''wai,' ʃi ˌsɛd, 'joːə 'waif!' 'mistə 'bɛl 'puld ðə 'handl frəm
ðə 'dɔː ən 'stud 'lukiŋ at hɜː 'blaŋkli. ðə 'lanleidi geiv ə
'dʒɛstʃər əv 'sɛlf-ri'pruːvl. ''ðɛʔ s 'məi 'oːɫ 'auvə. ai fə'geʔ
wɔʔ ai 'ɛv sed n ai fə'geʔ wɔʔ ai 'ɛvnʔ sed. wɔʔ ai 'oːʔ tə ə
tˢəuɫdʒə bi'foːə 'bləːʔn iʔ 'ɛuʔ laiʔ 'ðɛʔ wɔz ðəʔ ai v dis'kavədʒə

'wɑif, 'misiz 'meriweðə, in *'grɑndəi strəiʔ; ðəʔ ʃəi z ˌsimpli
auvə'dʒɔid tə 'iːər ɔv jə, n ɑi v 'ɑːst ə tə 'kam 'iːə ðis 'əivnin.'

''ðen,' sɛd mistə 'bɛl 'sɔləmli, ən 'ʃeikiŋ ðə 'wait 'dɔːhandl
in ði 'ould 'leidiz 'feis, ''jəu 'dʒes 'lisn tə 'məi. 'jəu v 'ɑːst ə
tə 'kam 'iːə; jə kn 'dʒes 'dʒɔli 'wɛɫ 'ɑːst ə tə 'gau ə'wai əgain.
ɑi n 'nɔʔ gain ə 'səi ə.'

''weɫ, 'weɫ, ''weɫ,' sɛd ði ə'meizd 'lanleidi, ''iːə z ə priti
ɛədʒə'dᶻəu ! n ʃi 'tˢoːʔ sau 'feʔʃnʔ əˌbɛətʃə 'tˢəu, n ʃi sez ''' 'au,''
ʃi sez, '' ɑi 'dᶻəu sau 'lɔŋ tə 'luk ɔn mi 'swəiʔ wanz 'fais əgain.''
ɑi ɛd ðə 'ləis drɔʔ ə 'spirits wið ə, n wi 'drɛ̃ʔ 'jɔːə 'gud 'ɛɫθ.'

''veri 'kɑind ɔv jə,' sɛd mistə 'bɛl 'dɔgidli, 'bəʔ 'ðɛʔ 'dᶻaũʔ
ə'feʔ 'mɑi pə'ziʃn. 'wen ʃi 'kamz, 'jəu geʔ 'rid əv ə, n in
'fiutʃə 'dᶻauŋ gau 'pɔʔrin ə'bɛəʔ n 'miʔsn jəsɛtf 'ap in 'mɑi
əfeːəz, kɔz ɑi 'waũʔ 'ɛv iʔ. 'səiʔ ɑi gɔʔ 'pleni tə 'wari əbɛəʔ,'
adid mistə 'bɛl 'fiəsli—'moːə ðn 'jəu 'θiŋʔ foːə; n ɑi 'dᶻaũʔ
wɔnʔ 'nau hintə'fiːrin ɔuɫ 'kɛʔ—.'

''wen jə 'kwɑiʔ dᶻan 'jəuzin 'lɛŋgwidʒ,' intə'rʌptid ði 'ould
'leidi, 'braidliŋ, ''prɛps 'joːɫ 'kɑinli 'puʔ 'bɛʔ 'ðɛʔ ðeːə 'dᶻoːərəndl
weː jə 'fɛən iʔ. 'leʔn jəu mɑi 'grɛun'floːə 'franʔ fr ə 'poːɫtri
'foːərənsiʔs ə 'wəiʔ 'dᶻaunʔ n'tˢɑiʔo jə tə 'woːʔ ə'bɛəʔ wið 'biʔs
əv iʔ in jər 'ɛnz. sə 'ðeːə nɛu !' ʃiː 'wɛnt təwɔːdz ðə 'dɔː,
sə'liləkwaiziŋ. ''hintə'fiːrin ɔuɫ 'kɛʔ ndᶻəid. 'ɑi ɫ 'ləːn im !'

From *London Only*, by w. PETT RIDGE

20.

A Specimen of reconstructed Elizabethan Pronunciation

(See note on p. 179)

[ɤ denotes a sound intermediate between RP u and ʌ. Long
aː may be taken to be about cardinal No. 4; but there were
probably considerable variations of quality according to
phonetic context. Short a was probably near to the present-
day sound. For ɛː in *they, their, faithful* and oː in *told, withhold,
know* see the Preface to this (4th) edition. *Ambitious, ambition*
and *sure* are rendered here with sj or si on the ground that this
pronunciation, though perhaps somewhat old-fashioned, was

still in existence and likely to have been preferred to the forms
with ʃ in reciting serious verse; see § 401 (iii) and footnote.

It is perhaps impossible to ascertain the extent to which
weak forms of words like *that, have, was, of* were used in
Elizabethan times. But in the absence of evidence to the
contrary it seems fairly safe to assume that such words were
treated much as they are to-day. In this text the following
conjectural principles have been adopted: strong forms are
written in the following weak positions, (1) at the beginnings of
lines, (2) wherever the words, though unstressed, might have
had some degree of metrical accent.]

'antəni. 'frɛndz, 'roːmənz, 'kʌntrimɛn, 'lɛnd mi: juːɹ 'iːɹz;
əi 'kʌm tu 'bɛri 'seːzəɹ, 'nɔt tu 'preːz him.
ði 'iːvil ðat mɛn 'duː 'livz 'aftəɹ ðɛm;
ðə 'guːd iz 'ɔft in'taːrid wið ðɛːɹ 'boːnz;
'soː lɛt it 'biː wið 'seːzəɹ. ðə 'noːbl *'brjuːtəs
haθ 'toːld juː 'seːɹɛɹ waz am'bisiəs;
if it 'wɛːɹ soː, it waz ə 'griːvəs 'fɔːlt,
and 'griːvəsli həθ 'seːɹɛɹ 'ansəɹd it.
'hiːɹ, ʌndəɹ 'leːv əv 'brjuːtəs and ðə 'rɛst—
fɔɹ 'brjuːtəs iz ən 'ɔnərəbl man;
'soː aːɹ ðɛːɹ 'ɔːl, 'ɔːl 'ɔnərəbl mɛn—
'kʌm 'əi tu 'speːk in 'seːɹəɹz 'fjuːnərəl.
hiː waz məi 'frɛnd, 'fɛːθfəl ənd 'dʒʌst tu miː;
bʌt 'brjuːtəs 'sɛz hiː waz am'bisiəs,
and 'brjuːtəs iz ən 'ɔnərəbl man.
hiː haθ brɔːt 'mɛni 'kaptivz 'hoːm tu *'ruːm,
huːz 'ransəmz did ðə 'dʒɛnərəl 'kɔfəɹz 'fil;
did 'ðis in 'seːɹəɹ siːm am'bisiəs?
'hwɛn ðat ðə 'puːɹ həv 'krəid 'seːɹəɹ həθ 'wɛpt;
am'bisjən ʃuːd biː 'mɛːd ɔv 'staːɹnəɹ stʌf;
jit 'brjuːtəs 'sɛz hiː waz am'bisiəs,
and 'brjuːtəs iz ən 'ɔnərəbl man.
juː 'ɔːl did 'siː ðət ɔn ðə *'ljuːpəɹkal
əi 'θrəis pri'zɛntid him ə 'kiŋli 'krəun,

hwitʃ 'hiː did 'θrəis ri'fjuːz. waz 'ðis am'bisjən?
jit 'brjuːtəs sɛz hiː waz am'bisiəs,
and 'sjuːɹ hiː iz ən 'ɔnərəbl man.

əi 'speːk 'nɔt tu 'dis'pruːv hwat 'brjuːtəs 'spoːk,
bʏt 'hiːɹ əi 'am, tu 'speːk hwat əi duː 'noː,
juː 'ɔːl did 'lʏv him 'wʏns, 'nɔt wiðəut 'kɔːz;
'hwat 'kɔːz wiθ'hoːldz juː ðɛn tu 'moːɹn fər him?
'oː 'dʒʏdʒmənt ! ðəu aːɹt 'flɛd tu 'brjuːtiʃ 'beːsts,
and 'mɛn həv 'lɔst ðɛːɹ 'reːzn. 'bɛːɹ wið miː;
məi 'haːɹt iz in ðə 'kɔfin 'ðɛːɹ wið 'seːzəɹ,
and əi mʏst 'pɔːz til it 'kʏm 'bak tu miː.

From *Julius Caesar* (Act III, Sc. 2), by SHAKESPEARE

(Compare text No. 13.)

21.

A Specimen of Reconstructed fourteenth-century Pronunciation

[The long eː, ɛː, aː, ɑː, ɔː and oː may be taken to be the cardinal sounds (§§ 46 ff.). The short ɛ, a and ɔ probably had values near to those of present-day English. The short ɑ was probably about cardinal. iː, i, uː, u should be read as the modern RP vowels in *see, sit, food, good*. ə is to be interpreted as a rather close variety of central vowel, not far removed from i; it was undoubtedly a very different sound from the modern ə of *sofa*.

The s and z sounds are treated on the assumption that they had become separate phonemes by the fourteenth century, but that some traces of their previous use still remained.[1] So the words *as* and *is* are shown with z when a following word begins with a voiced sound; otherwise they are shown with s. Written

---

[1] In Old English the s and z sounds undoubtedly belonged to a single phoneme, the allophone z being used when single, and between two voiced sounds, and the allophone s in all other situations, namely (1) initially, (2) finally, (3) when double, (4) when next to a voiceless consonant.

ss is rendered as a single **s**, since when **s** became a phoneme separate from **z**, there would no longer have been any reason to double the sound in medial position. The second *s* in *suffise* is rendered with **z** on account of the final **ə** which is elided in this instance.

The pairs **θ ð** and **f v** are treated on similar assumptions. Accordingly *th* is rendered as **θ** in all initial positions (i.e. in *this*, *that*, etc., as well as in *thing*) but as **ð** in the words *the* and *this* when preceded by a voiced sound. *Of* is shown with **v** when the following word begins with a voiced sound, but otherwise with **f**. The same would apply to *with*, which however does not happen to occur in this passage with a voiced sound following it.

The pronunciation recorded here may be slightly archaic for the period. Some authorities think that by the fourteenth century a beginning had been made with the 'Great Vowel Shift'.[1] There is also a possibility that the modern pronunciation of *the*, *this*, *that*, etc., with **ð** in all situations was beginning to establish itself.]

'fleː froː ðə 'prɛːs, and 'dwɛl wiθ 'soːθfast'nɛsə;
su'fiːz θiːn 'ounə 'θiŋg, 'θɔux hit beː 'smɑl.
for 'hoːɹd haθ 'haːt, and 'kliːmbiŋg 'tikəl'nɛsə,

---

[1] The 'Great Vowel Shift' is the name given to the set of changes by which during the last 700 years or so

aː	became	ei (via ɛː)	in words like		*make*
ɛː	„	eː (with an eventual replacement by iː)	„	„	*sea*
eː	„	iː	„	„	*see*
iː	„	ai or ɑi (via əi)	„	„	*time*
ɑ(ː)	„	ɔː	„	„	*wall*
ɔː	„	ou (via varieties of oː)	„	„	*bone*
oː	„	uː	„	„	*food*
uː	„	ɑu or au (via əu)	„	„	*town*
u	„	ʌ (via ɤ)	„	„	*up*

See the Chart of the Great Vowel Shift by D. Jones and C. L. Wrenn (obtainable from the Secretary of the I.P.A., Dept. of Phonetics, University College, London, W.C. 1).

'prɛːs haθ ɛn'viː and 'weːl 'blɛnt ɔːɹəɪ 'ɑl.
saː'vuːɹ 'nɔː 'moːɹ θan 'θeː bə'hoːvə 'ʃal;
'riul 'wɛl θiː'sɛlf θat 'oːðəɪ 'fɔlk kanst 'rɛːdə;
and 'truːðə ʃal də'livɹ, it iz 'nɔː 'drɛːdə.

tɛm'pɛst θeː 'nɔuxt 'ɑl 'kroːkəd toː rə'drɛsə,
in 'trust ɔf 'hiɹ θat 'tuɹnəθ az a 'bɑl;
'grɛːt 'rɛstə 'stant in 'litl bɛzi'nɛsə.
beː 'waɪr θɛːɹ'foːɹ toː 'spuɹn agɛin an 'ɑl;
'striːv 'nɔuxt az doːθ θə 'krɔkkə wiθ θə 'wɑl;
'daɪntə ðiː'sɛlf θat 'daɪntəst 'oːðɪəs 'deːdə;
and 'truːðə ʃal də'livɹ, it iz 'nɔː 'drɛːdə.

'θat θeː is 'sɛnt rə'sɛiv in 'buksum'nɛsə;
θə 'wrastliŋg fɔɹ ðis 'wuɹld 'aksɛθ a 'fɑl;
'heːɹ niz 'nɔːn 'hɔːm, 'heːɹ niz but 'wildəɪ'nɛsə.
'foːɹθ, ˌpilgrim, 'foːɹθ! 'foːɹθ, 'bɛːst, uːt ɔf θiː 'stɑl!
'knɔu ðiː kun'treː! 'loːk 'up! 'θaŋk 'gɔd ɔv 'ɑl!
'hould ðə 'hiː 'wɛi, and 'lat θiː 'gɔːst θeː 'lɛːdə,
and 'truːðə ʃal də'livɹ, it iz 'nɔː 'drɛːdə.

CHAUCER

213

APPENDIX 1

Key to the Texts

(I) DIFFICULT WORDS IN TEXTS I—18

Most of the words in these Texts are easy of identification. In cases of doubt reference may be made to the author's *English Pronouncing Dictionary* (Dent).

Below is given a list of words in the Texts which are not included in that dictionary, together with the most noteworthy other words which beginners might have difficulty in identifying immediately.

The abbreviation (T. 15) means that the word occurs in Text No. 15 illustrating a special type of Southern English pronunciation; the abbreviations (S.W.), (Sc.) and (Am.) mean that the words occur in Texts Nos. 16, 17 and 18 illustrating South-Western, Scottish and American pronunciation respectively.

The alphabetical order of phonetic symbols adopted here is:
ɑ a ʌ b d dʒ ð e ei ɛ ə: ə f g h iː i ɩ j k l m n ŋ oː o ou ɔː ɔ ɒ p r ɹ s ʃ t tʃ θ uː u ɷ v w z ʒ.

ɑː *are, ah*	'berɩst *barest* (Sc.)
ai *I, eye*	'bɛri *bury*
aiv *I have*	'bəːti *Bertie*
ɑn *on* (Am.)	bə *by*
'antəni *Antony*	'bəsliŋ *bustling* (S.W.)
auɹ *hour* (S.W.)	bikɔz *because*
ʌ *a* (Sc.)	bin *been*
ʌ'keʒnʌle *occasionally* (Sc.)	'bleizou *Blazo*
ʌ'mʌŋ *among* (Sc.)	'bou 'siːt *Beau Site*
ʌnd *and* (Sc.)	'brɔkstn *Broxton*
'ʌn'nɛld *unknelled*	brɔld *brawled* (Sc.)
ʌur *our* (Sc.)	'bɹːðn *Burthen* (S.W.)
ʌv *of* (Sc.)	buru'ʃaski *Burushaski*
bae *by* (Sc.)	d *would, had*

'dɑktɹ *doctor* (Am.)

dei *day, Day*

'deivis *Davis*

dɛl *dell, Dell*

dɛːk *deck* (T. 15)

'dimək *Dymock*

'diŋli *Dingley*

'dudadz *doodads* (Am.)

dʒɑːd *jarred*

dʒʌs *just*

dʒi'maiməz *Jemima's*

'dʒiŋgl *Jingle*

dʒɔez *joys* (Sc.)

ðʌu *thou* (Sc.)

ðʌt *that* (Sc.)

ðɛːn *then* (T. 15)

ðɛːɹ *there* (S.W.)

ðɛə(r) *there, their*

ðə *the, there*

ei *aye*

'ei 'ɛm *a.m.*

eiks *Aix*

ɛə *air, e'er*

əː *err, her*

əːdʒ *urge*

'əːnist *earnest*

əːr *her*

əːˌsɛlf *herself*

əːθ *earth*

ə *a, are*

əd *had, would*

'əðɹ *other* (S.W.)

ə'gɛn *again*

ə'gɛnst *against*

ə'kɔːd *accord*

əl *will*

əm *them*

ən *an, and*

ənd *and*

ˌəndɹ *under* (S.W.)

əp *up* (S.W.)

'əpɹ *Upper* (S.W.)

əs *us*

ət *at*

əv *have, of*

əz *as*

əʒ *as*

'fəni *funny* (Am.)

firz *fears* (Sc.)

'flɔrəns *Florence*

foks *folks* (Am.)

foːɹ *four* (S.W.)

fr *for*

fɹ *for* (S.W., Am.)

fɹːst *first* (S.W.)

'fuːzl *Foozle*

gɑt *got* (Am.)

'gəntʃəz *Gunch's* (Am.)

grɑːnt *Grant*

'grɑːnti *Grantie*

'gʌtlbəri *Guttlebury*

glɛg *Glegg*

hɑg *hog* (Am.)

'hɑireizd *high-raised*

'heste *hasty* (Sc.)

hɛə *hair, Herr*

hɛrd *heard* (Sc.)

həv *have*

hiːɹ *here* (S.W.)

hʌɹ *here* (Am.)

hops *hopes* (Sc.)

hɔɹs *horse* (S.W.)

hɹ *her* (S.W.)

hɹː *her* (S.W.)

huː *who*

iː *he*

iːn *e'en* (= *even*)

iə *ear*

iəz *ears*

ig'zaktli *exactly*

ig'zɔːltid *exalted*

iks'plein *explain*

im *him*
im‚sɛlf *himself*
i'nublin *ennobling*
in'tɜːrid *interred*
is'pɛʃli *especially*
it‚sɛtrə *etc.*
iz *is, his*
iʒ *is*
jəːz *years*
jɔːk *York*
jɔːz *yours*
ju *you*
juə(r) *you are*
juː *you*
'juːklid *Euclid*
juːst *used (to)*
'juːʒəl *usual*
'kariɹ *carrier* (S.W.)
kʌn *can* (Sc.)
'kʌndʒərə *conjuror*
kʌn'fɛr *confer* (Sc.)
kɛɹ *care* (Am.)
kɛːɹ *care* (S.W.)
kəd *could*
'kidiz *kiddies*
kn *can*
kors *course* (Sc.)
koɹs *course* (Am.)
kɔn'sɛnt *concent*
'kɔnsɔːt *consort*
'kristəfɹ *Christopher* (S.W.)
'kwaŋkou *Quanko*
'kwaiə(r) *quire*
'kwaiəz *choirs*
l, | *will*
las *last* (Am.)
lʌik *like* (Sc.)
ləntʃ *lunch* (Am.)
'lisn *listen*
'liːbig *Liebig*
'loɹd *lowered* (Sc.)

'lɔŋ‚pədl *Longpuddle*
'luːpəːkal *Lupercal*
m *am*
'magi *Maggie* [S.W.]
'maːstɹ'θatʃɹ *master-thatcher*
'mʌri *Murray (guide-book)*
'mʌrmɪrɪr *murmurer* (Sc.)
mʌs *must*
mek *make* (Am.)
məs *must*
'məstɹ *muster* (S.W.)
'mjuːzikhɔːl *music-hall*
moːɹ *more* (S.W.)
moɹ *more* (Am.)
mos *most* (Am.)
mɔː(r) *more*
n *and*
ṇ *an*
nɑt *not* (Am.)
'naʃnḷ *National (Gallery)*
nd *and*
nɛə(r) *ne'er*
nɔɹ *nor* (S.W.)
nu *new* (Am.)
ɔːf *off*
'ɔːfn *often*
ɔɹ *or* (Am.)
ɒf *off* (T. 15)
ɒn *on* (T. 15)
pen *pain* (Am.)
pɛ'kaːviː *peccavi*
'pɛte *petty* (Sc.)
'pɔːtrit *portrait*
priː'saisli *precisely* (S.W.)
'prɔfit *Profitt*
rʌ'vin *ravine* (Sc.)
rɛks *wrecks*
'rɛvɪre *reverie* (Sc.)
riː'zaidz *resides* (S.W.)
rod *road* (Sc.)
roum *Rome*

rɔː *roar*
rɒːk *rock* (T. 15)
ɹ *her* (S.W.), *are* (S.W.)
s *is, us*
'sɑːdʒənt *Sargent*
'safaiəˌkʌləd *sapphire-coloured*
'salədin *Saladin*
'sambə *Samba*
sɛn *send*
'səːdʒən *surgeon*
sə'ʃɛvərəl *Sacheverell*
'sfiəbɔːn *sphere-born*
si'flœːr *siffleur*
si'riːnli *serenely*
'siːzə(r) *Caesar*
sɔː *sore*
'spaɪ-glɑːs *Spyglass* (T. 15)
sɹv *serve* (Am.)
steinz *Staines*
'stɛliŋ *Stelling*
'stuɹd *steward* (Am.)
ʃd *should*
ʃl *shall*
'ʃɔrlɪs *shoreless* (Sc.)
ʃɔː *shore*
ʃɔɹ *sure* (Am.)
taimz *Times*
tek *take* (Am.)
tə *to*
'tərət *turret* (S.W.)
'tɔməs *Thomas*

tɒːp *top* (T. 15)
'trʌflə *Truffler*
trək *truck* (Am.)
'trufən *Truffen*
tɹːn *turn* (S.W.)
twəz *'twas*
twiŋk *Twink*
tʃef *chafe* (Sc.)
v *have*
vel *vale* (Sc.)
'viːəkl *vehicle*
vɹdʒ *Verg.* (short for *Vergil*)
'waiəz *wires*
'waitkʌft *white-cuffed*
'wagstɑːf *Wagstaffe*
'wakiŋ *whacking*
'waksnfeist *waxen-faced*
wɛə(r) *where*
wəz *was*
'wisliŋ *whistling*
'wispəd *whispered*
witʃ *which*
'wɔːtri *watery*
wɒt *what*
'wɒtsizneim *what's-his-name*
wɒːz *was* (T. 15)
wɹ *were* (S.W.)
wɹk *work* (Am.)
'wɹːld-igˌnɔːɹd *world-ignored* (S.W.)
wɔːdz *woods* (T. 15)
z *is*

(2) ORTHOGRAPHIC VERSION OF TEXT NO. 19

'I've found 'em!' said his landlady exultantly, as he stumbled into the dimly lighted passage. 'I've found 'em, Mr Merryweather, and glad enough I am to 'ave been of some service to you.' She was a vivacious old lady in a beaded cap with a lively knowledge of the affairs of other people, and just now keenly interested in the new occupant of her bed-sitting-room. 'And you mustn't thank me, because I'm only too pleased to bring friends and rel'tives together.'

'*Now* what are you cacklin' about, ma'am?' he asked politely.

'Ah,' replied the old lady cheerfully, 'you'll soon know. We shan't be long now. It'll be as good as a play to see you two meet.' She wept and rubbed her eyes. 'People may say what they like, but there's nothing in all this wide world to be compared to two lovin' 'earts.'

'Let me 'ave my supper,' he said patiently, 'and then leave me be. I want to 'ave a smoke and a think.'

'*You* won't do much thinking,' remarked the landlady knowingly, 'when you 'ear the news I've got for you. You said your name was Merryweather, didn't you?'

'I don't deny it.'

'And you said you'd got friends near 'ere—you'd forgot the address.'

'I might have let fall a casual remark,' said Bell carefully, as he held the handle of his door, 'or statement to that effect. Whatever I said I'll stick to.'

'I knew that,' replied the old landlady, 'I 'ope I can tell a gentleman from a mere common person. Some people look down on sailors and such-like, but I'm not one of that sort. As I often say, where would Old England be without 'em?'

''Urry up with that supper,' said Mr Bell.

'Shall I lay for two, Mr Merryweather?' asked the old lady.

'Course not! I'm only one.'

'But the lady?'

'What lady?'

'Why,' she said, 'your wife!' Mr Bell pulled the handle from the door and stood looking at her blankly. The landlady gave a gesture of self-reproval. 'That's me all over. I forget what I 'ave said and I forget what I 'aven't said. What I ought to 'ave told you before blurtin' it out like that was that I've discovered your wife, Mrs Merryweather, in Grundy Street; that she's simply overjoyed to 'ear of you, and I've asked her to come 'ere this evening.'

'Then,' said Mr Bell solemnly, and shaking the white door-handle in the old lady's face, 'you jest listen to me. You've asked her to come 'ere; you can jest jolly well ask her to go away again. I'm not going to see her.'

'Well, well, *well*,' said the amazed landlady, ''ere's a pretty how-d'ye-do! And she talked so affectionate about you, too, and she says, "Oh!" she says, "I do so long to look on my sweet one's face again." I had the least drop of spirits with her, and we drank your good 'ealth.'

'Very kind of you,' said Mr Bell doggedly, 'but that don't affect my position. When she comes, you get rid of her, and, in future, don't go potterin' about and mixing yourself up in my affairs, because I won't have it. See? I got plenty to worry about,' added Mr Bell fiercely—'more than you think for; and I don't want no interferin' old cat—'

'When you've quite done using language,' interrupted the old lady, bridling, 'p'raps you'll kindly put back that there door-'andle where you found it. Letting you my ground-floor front for a paltry four-and-six a-week don't entitle you to walk about with bits of it in your 'ands. So there, now!' She went towards the kitchen, soliloquising. 'Interferin' old cat indeed! *I'll* learn him!'

(3) ORTHOGRAPHIC VERSION OF THE POEM
BY CHAUCER (TEXT NO. 21)

Flee fro the prees, and dwelle with sothfastnesse,
Suffise thine owene thynge though hit be smal;
For hord hath hate and clymbyng tikelnesse,
Prees hath envye, and wele blent overal.
Savour no more than thee bihove shal;
Reul wel thyself, that other folk canst rede,
And trouthe shal delivere, it is no drede.

Tempest thee noght al croked to redresse
In trust of hir that turneth as a bal;
Greet reste stant in litel besynesse;
Be war therfor to sporne ageyn an al;
Stryve noght as doth the crokke with the wal.
Daunte thyself, that dauntest otheres dede,
And trouthe shal delivere, it is no drede.

That thee is sent receyve in buxumnesse,
The wrastling for this worlde axeth a fal;
Her nis non hoom, her nis but wildernesse.
Forth, pilgrim, forth! Forth, beste, out of thy stal!
Know thy contree, look up, thank God of al!
Hold the hye wey, and lat thy gost thee lede,
And trouthe shal delivere, it is no drede.

APPENDIX 2

Books for further Study

In the books marked † the pronunciation transcribed is substantially the same as that described in this book.

In the books marked with asterisks the pronunciation is represented by the alphabet of the International Phonetic Association: * simplified transcription of RP; ** the somewhat 'narrower' EPD transcription[1] or a notation very near to this; *** 'narrow' transcription.

(I) PHONETIC THEORY

D. JONES, *An Outline of English Phonetics*, new edition (Heffer, Cambridge).†**

—— *The Phoneme, its Nature and Use* (Heffer, Cambridge).†*

P. A. D. MACCARTHY, *English Pronunciation* (Heffer, Cambridge).†*

H. SWEET, *Primer of Spoken English* (Oxford).†

—— *The Sounds of English* (Oxford).†

A. C. GIMSON, *An Introduction to the Pronunciation of English* (Edward Arnold, 1962).†***

J. D. O'CONNOR, *Better English Pronunciation* (Cambridge University Press, 1967).†**

I. C. WARD, *The Phonetics of English* (Heffer, Cambridge).†***

—— *Speech Defects, their nature and cure* (Dent).

J. T. PRING, *Colloquial English Pronunciation* (Longmans).†**

R. KINGDON, *The Groundwork of English Stress* (Longmans).

---

[1] I.e. the form of transcription used in the author's *English Pronouncing Dictionary*. This differs from the transcription used in the present book in the following respects:

	EPD	Present book
vowel in *red*	e	ε
„ *cat*	æ	a
diphthong in *high*	ai	ɑi
„ *how*	au	ɑu

G. F. ARNOLD, *Stress in English Words* (North-Holland Publishing Co., Amsterdam).

W. RIPMAN, *English Phonetics* (Dent, London).†**

J. S. KENYON, *American Pronunciation* (George Wahr, Ann Arbor, Michigan).*

C. K. THOMAS, *The Phonetics of American English* (Ronald Press, New York).*

C. M. WISE, *Applied Phonetics* (Prentice-Hall, Inc., Englewood Cliffs, N.J.).*

CARRELL and TIFFANY, *Phonetics: Theory and Application to Speech Improvement* (McGraw-Hill Book Company).*

Also the works on *Intonation* quoted in footnote 1 to § 474.

(2) PHONETIC READERS

D. JONES, *Phonetic Readings in English,* new edition (Winter, Heidelberg, 1956).†**

J. D. O'CONNOR, *New Phonetic Readings* (Franke, Bern).†**

N. C. SCOTT, *English Conversations in Simplified Phonetic Transcription* (Heffer, Cambridge).†*

E. L. TIBBITTS, *A Phonetic Reader for Foreign Learners of English* (Heffer, Cambridge).†*

E. L. TIBBITS, *Practice Material for the English Sounds* (Heffer, Cambridge).†**

L. E. ARMSTRONG, *An English Phonetic Reader* University of London Press).†***

P. A. D. MACCARTHY, *English Conversation Reader* (Longmans, Green & Co., London).†*

(3) PRONOUNCING DICTIONARIES

D. JONES, *An English Pronouncing Dictionary,* new edition, 1956 (Dent, London).†**

P. A. D. MACCARTHY, *An English Pronouncing Vocabulary* (Heffer, Cambridge).†*

KENYON and KNOTT, *Pronouncing Dictionary of American English* (Merriam, Springfield, Mass.).*

HORNBY and PARNWELL, *An English Reader's Dictionary* (Oxford University Press).†*

OTHER WORKS BY THE SAME AUTHOR

The Phoneme, its Nature and Use (Heffer, Cambridge).

An Outline of English Phonetics, 8th edition, revised, enlarged and re-set, 1956 (Heffer, Cambridge).

An English Pronouncing Dictionary, 12th (1964) and subsequent editions (Dent, London).

Phonetic Readings in English, new improved edition, 1956 (Winter Heidelberg).

Cardinal Vowels. Double-sided gramophone records of the primary and secondary cardinal vowels, with explanatory booklet (Linguaphone Institute, London).

Colloquial French for the English, by E. M. Stéphan and D. Jones. Complete Course (586 pp.) with 15 double-sided gramophone records, together with Key-book and Pupils' Book (H.M.V. Gramophone Co., London).

Intonation Curves (Teubner, Leipzig).*

Shakespeare in the Original Pronunciation. Texts in phonetic tran-scription with notes, on pp. 36–45 of *English Pronunciation through the Centuries* (Linguaphone Institute, London). Accompanies a double-sided Linguaphone record of passages from Shakespeare in the original pronunciation spoken by D. Jones and E. M. Evans.

Dhe Fonetik Aspekt ov Speling Reform (Pitman, London, for the Simpli-fied Spelling Society).

Concrete and Abstract Sounds (off-print from the *Proceedings of the Third International Congress of Phonetic Sciences*, Ghent, 1938).†

The Great English Vowel Shift (chart), by D. Jones and C. L. Wrenn.†

The Problem of a National Script for India (Pioneer Press, Lucknow).†

A Colloquial Sinhalese Reader, by D. Jones and H. S. Perera (Manchester University Press).

A Sechuana Reader, by D. Jones and S. T. Plaatje (University of London Press).

A Cantonese Phonetic Reader, by D. Jones and Kwing Tong Woo (University of London Press).

The Tones of Sechuana Nouns (International African Institute, 10 Fetter Lane, London, E.C. 4).

---

* Out of print.
† Obtainable from the Department of Phonetics, University College, London, W.C. 1.